# LENIN

# LENIN

by

M. C. MORGAN

OHIO UNIVERSITY PRESS 1971

© M. C. Morgan 1971

First published 1971 by
Edward Arnold (Publishers) Ltd.
41 Maddox Street, London W1R 0AN

ISBN: 8214-0094-0

LC: 74-158177

# *Contents*

Grau, teurer Freund, ist alle Theorie,
Und grün des Lebens goldener Baum.

(All theory is grey, my dear friend, but
the golden tree of life is green.)

> (Goethe, *Faust*, quoted with
> emphatic approval by Lenin)

The point is not to understand the
world, but to change it.

> (Marx)

Either—Or.    (Kierkegaard)

The meaning of the Liberal Party for the individual Liberal
will be dealt with later; for the nation, the party was an
answer to the most important question of modern domestic
politics in all countries. That question is, what group should,
or rather can, rule when the landowners have ceased to be
able to do so by themselves, as an aristocracy?

> (John Vincent)

# *Preface*

After the old and middle generations, whose branded, perhaps dis
figured faces are too obviously history books, the young are a cheering
spectacle. Uniformity is here replaced by a wide variety of clothes
and looks and habits. Faces and attitudes have not been bludgeoned,
eyes not become vacant and lack-lustre. Circumstances beyond our
experience have not cut them off by a great emotional barrier.
The young have grown up in conditions of relative normalcy and
this is expressed on their faces. The division between those who rise
and those who fall, those who assert themselves and those who
collapse, is not so evident here. With the young we leave Dostoevsky-
land for a saner, healthier, better world.[1]

Exactly. This was Lenin's aim in a nutshell: to create a saner,
healthier, better world. More accurately and extendedly, to act as
midwife to the revolution that would liquidate the old, capitalist
environment and create the conditions in which man could
live a saner, healthier, better life. To this task Lenin brought
an uncommon, ruthless and maybe perverting tenacity that made
him a great revolutionary leader. I have tried to portray him not
as a mythical combination of hero and monster, but as a man: a
man who, had he lived in a less rotten society, would have risen
to the top in the law or politics or business: essentially a constructive, not a destructive personality.

I should like to thank Mrs Valerie Jensen, Mr Boris Elkin and
Mr B. Lubetkin for their help. I am especially grateful to Professor
C. M. MacInnes, Dr H. R. Stevens and my wife, all of whom
have read the book in manuscript and much improved it by their
criticisms and suggestions, and to Mrs Mary Denniston, who read
the proofs. I hope the reader will feel they have not laboured in
vain.

M. C. Morgan

[1] John Gooding, *The Catkin and the Icicle* (1965), 22.

*Dates*
Events in Russia before 25 October/7 November 1917 are dated according to the Julian Calendar used at that time, which was twelve days behind the Western Calendar in the nineteenth century and thirteen in the twentieth. Events between 25 October/ 7 November and 1/14 February 1918, when Russia adopted the Western Calendar, are dated in both styles; events after 1/14 February 1918 according to the Western Calendar.

*Names*
In the first World War the Russian capital St Petersburg was renamed with its Russian equivalent, Petrograd; on Lenin's death it was renamed Leningrad. Here for simplicity it is called St Petersburg throughout.

# Acknowledgements

The Publishers' thanks are due to the following for permission to use copyright material:

Transatlantic Book Service, London for an extract from Angelica Balabanoff's *Impressions of Lenin*; Macmillan & Co. Ltd. for an extract from W. H. Chamberlain's *The Russian Revolution* and 21 lines of poetry from Dorothy Wellesley's *Lenin*; Oxford University Press for extracts from C. R. Crutwell's *A History of the Great War 1914–1918*, Isaac Deutscher's *Stalin* and N. N. Sukhanov's *The Russian Revolution*, trans. J. Carmichael; Faber & Faber Ltd. for an extract from D. Footman's *Civil War In Russia*; Lawrence & Wishart Ltd. for extracts from Gorky's *Days with Lenin* and N. K. Krupskaya's *Memories of Lenin*; Cassell & Co. Ltd. for an extract from *The Kerensky Memoirs*; Penguin Books Ltd. for an extract from A. Lunacharsky's *Revolutionary Silhouettes*; W. Reeves Ltd., London for extracts from Marx and Engel's *The Communist Manifesto*; The Harvill Press Ltd. for an extract from K. Paustovsky's *In That Dawn*; Estaben Volkov for an extract from Trotsky's *History of the Russian Revolution*; J. M. Dent & Co. Ltd. for an extract from I. Turgenev's *Fathers and Sons* and Abraham Yarmolinsky for an extract from *Count Witte's Memoirs*.

To W. H. Bruford

# Prologue

When Lenin was sixteen his brother Alexander, four years older, was arrested for his part in a conspiracy to assassinate Tsar Alexander III. None of the family knew anything of Alexander's revolutionary activities and the news of his arrest came as a great shock to them. His mother travelled at once to St Petersburg to see her son and plead for his life. She was unsuccessful, for neither Alexander nor the authorities were willing to listen to her. In talk with his mother and in court Alexander explained that he must fight for Russia's freedom and that the only way to bring this about was to assassinate the tsar. His bearing in court compelled the admiration of the public prosecutor and he faced death with complete calm. He was hanged on 8 May 1887.

According to the family governess when Lenin heard the news he said: 'Well it seems that Alexander could not have done otherwise.' According to another report he exclaimed: 'I'll make them pay for this! I swear it!' Both remarks may well be true. They are perfectly natural remarks in the circumstances and they are quite in character. Young Lenin greatly admired Alexander and did his best to imitate him and keep up with him. He was also notably pugnacious. Nevertheless the remarks will not bear the weight that has sometimes been put on them. There is no evidence that Lenin as a grown man was a warped or embittered or neurotic character, and there is a great deal of evidence to the contrary. Nor did he ever show any personal animus against the tsar or his family; he looked on them as inevitable victims of the revolution.

Lenin did however in later life tell his wife how disgusted he was at the cowardly behaviour of their acquaintances in Simbirsk. When his mother was planning to travel to St Petersburg no-one was willing to go with her because her son was under arrest. As an adult Lenin hated and despised bourgeois liberals and he might very well have read these emotions back into his sixteen year old self. On the other hand he was so reticent in talking about his childhood and youth that it seems likely that when he did he was recalling a real incident and the emotion associated with it. So it is probable that this incident was at the root of Lenin's adult feeling. But if it was at the root, it was not the ground of his feeling or his thought. This was the state of Russia at the end of the nineteenth century.

# I  Revolutionary soil

## I  Disenchantment and reaction

In 1855, in the middle of the Crimean War, Tsar Nicholas I, the 'Iron Autocrat', died broken-hearted. The war had shown up the autocracy and cast grave doubts on whether the regime could survive in its existing form. Very many Russians shared the tsar's disillusion. Under the impact of military defeat and on the wave of this disillusion the new tsar Alexander II embarked on a series of fundamental reforms that earned him the title, the 'Tsar Liberator'. They were designed to transform feudal Russia into a more or less contemporary society.

The most fundamental reform was the emancipation of the serfs in 1861. Serfs made up two-thirds of the population of Russia: 40 out of 60 millions. Serfdom, in the words of Nicholas I himself, was 'the indubitable evil of Russian life'.[1] But he saw no way of abolishing it without undermining the power and authority of the nobles on whom his autocratic regime depended. Alexander II faced this dilemma and produced a scheme of emancipation designed to meet it. By this the peasant became personally free and could buy, sell and own land. But he did not get all the land and he had to buy what he did get. From the point of view of the tsar and the nobleman this was perfectly fair: the land belonged to the landowner and he was entitled to compensation for the land he had to give up. But this was not how it appeared to the peasant. For him 'the land was God's and the right of using it belonged to him who tilled it'.[2] Having to buy the land was seen as a fundamental wrong that no amount of explanation or argument or rhetoric could put right.

Furthermore the details of the scheme favoured the nobleman and added to the peasant's resentment. The landlord kept his demesne land which the peasant of course had to work. But as well as this he kept part of the land previously held by the peasants.

---

[1] Quoted in B. H. Sumner, *Survey of Russian History* (1944), 148
[2] E. Lampert, *Sons against Fathers* (1965), 25

This varied in amount from a fifth to two-fifths and the peasant's attitude to the matter can be seen in the nickname that came to be given to this land—the 'cut-offs'. The landlord also often kept the woodland and meadows and deprived the peasant of his immemorial rights to cordage and pasture and to water. Possibly more unfair and vexatious were the redemption payments. The peasant could not pay for his land all at once, so the emancipation decree laid down that he should pay the landlord only a fifth and the government would advance the other four-fifths. The peasant would repay this to the government in instalments. But it has been calculated that the value of these redemption payments exceeded the real value of the land by as much as 50 to 70 per cent, and this saddled the peasants with arrears of debt that had eventually to be cancelled.

The government also wanted to avoid creating either landless labourers or smallholders, so it decided not to deal with the peasant as an individual but with the village community (*mir*) as a whole.[3] The land did not pass to the individual peasant in outright ownership but to the *mir* with the right and duty of redistributing it periodically to take account of the changes in the village population. The *mir* was also made responsible for the collection of the redemption payments and the poll tax, and for the issue of the passports necessary for travel in Russia. It can be seen that the *mir* had a strong interest in preventing peasants leaving the village and going off to try their luck in Siberia or in town.

Logically connected with the emancipation of the serfs was the reform of justice. As long as the landowner owned the serfs he was their lord too. Custom and he ordered their lives. He controlled their work, imposed dues on them, punished their offences, hired them out as labourers to other landlords, sold them with the estate to which they belonged or, sometimes, gambled them away and, most dreaded of all, packed them off to military service. Now he was no longer their lord there was need of some kind of body to

[3] The Russian word *mir* means, in the first place, 'peace' and 'world'. In its narrower meaning of 'village community' it therefore carries 'religious or mystical associations, which almost justify the translation of the word *Mir* by *Congregation*, and suggest an echo of the saying that the voice of the people is the voice of God' (John Maynard, *The Russian Peasant* (1942), 30). The *mir* embraces the whole village population, male and female. It conducts its affairs by a village meeting in which the village elder, chosen as a kind of agent by the village as a whole, has as much influence as his reputation warrants, but no more. The best description of the *mir* is in D. Mackenzie Wallace, *Russia* (1877).

administer local justice, and opportunity to undertake a thorough tidying-up of the judicial muddle that existed.

At the bottom in a village or group of small villages (*volost*) came into being *volost* courts which dealt only with cases between peasants and had peasant judges. They did not know the written law or attempt to apply it. They were, in the words of Mackenzie Wallace, 'guided merely by traditional custom and plain common sense'.[4] Above them were the normal courts: for the district (*uezd*), courts conducted by justices of the peace; for the province, regional courts, and above them ten chambers of justice for the whole of Russia, in which criminal cases were tried by jury: both these manned by paid, professional judges. At the top were two courts of appeal, one civil, one criminal, entitled courts of cassation of the Senate, their name and their function copied from French law. This system led to the rapid development of the law as a profession, and to a high standard of professional competence and honour.

Several features of the system are of great interest. The justices of the peace copied from England had jurisdiction over minor civil and criminal offences as in England, but contrary to English custom they were not appointed by the crown. Instead they were elected by the district *zemstvos*, which meant that they were chosen by people of all classes. They were amateurs, usually local bigwigs, mostly quite ignorant of law. This and the exaggerated expectations of the peasants led to all kinds of irregular, bizarre and comic happenings. But the courts were full of promise. Like the *volost* courts they were down to earth and applied a strong dose of common sense to their cases. The work of the justice of the peace, especially perhaps the work of the justices sitting collectively as a bench in monthly session, was an admirable training in social responsibility. Their election by the *zemstvos* provided not only a link between local justice and local administration, which might be criticized as dangerously blurring the edges of the two areas, but a mechanism of self-government.

So too did the *zemstvos* themselves. Before the reforms the provincial governors had been advised by provincial and district assemblies (*zemstvos*) composed exclusively of noblemen. By the act of 1864 these were to be elected in future: the district *zemstvos* in three separate colleges for the nobility, the townsmen and the

[4] *Op. cit.*

peasants, the peasants' college by a process of indirect election; and the provincial *zemstvos* by the district *zemstvos*. Both chose an executive committee to conduct their business when they were not in session. The president of the *zemstvo* at each level was the local marshal of the nobility. Their powers were never precisely defined and they were always very carefully watched by the provincial governors, but they had a pretty free hand over roads, hygiene and education, and were authorized to levy a local rate to cover their expenditure. The rates rose fast enough to occasion much local criticism, and the countryside was not immediately transformed by a network of roads, hospitals and schools, as is clear from Chekhov's stories. There was much apathy, sloth and graft. But the *zemstvos* began to do good work. More important were the possibilities inherent in them. They were a means of getting things done. They were a counter to the routine-bound, corrupt bureaucracy which had up till then constituted Russian government. They gave an opportunity to energetic men of public spirit as well as to cranks, busybodies and self-important people, who felt they must cut a figure locally. They gave a measure of responsibility for local affairs to local men, who could use it to develop a sense of responsibility as citizens in themselves and in those who had chosen them as their representatives. They were organs of representative government and from them could have developed representative and responsible government on a national scale.

In line with these reforms were others affecting the press and education. During the reign of Nicholas I the censorship of the press had been severe and preventive: all articles in the newspapers or journals had to be submitted to one or other of the censorship boards before publication. This was now relaxed. Editors could take the risk of publishing what they wanted and facing action in the courts or from the censors. This was a great improvement on the previous situation both in theory and in practice.

The reforming spirit also touched education at all levels. The government laid down the important principle that both primary and secondary schools should be open to all children without distinction of religion or class. In primary schools the teaching was 'to strengthen religious and moral notions and to spread basic useful knowledge'.[5] The secondary schools were of two types:

[5] Quoted in Hugh Seton-Watson, *The Russian Empire* (1967), 359

classical and modern. In the classical schools the curriculum was based on Latin and Greek and on modern European languages; in the modern schools on science and drawing. The government also introduced a measure of autonomy into education. It set up school councils at provincial and district level in which there were to be two members from the appropriate *zemstvo*, though they were in a clear minority to the official members. The Councils were responsible for opening and closing schools and for engaging and dismissing teachers. The new university statute of 1863 largely gave responsibility for a university to the university itself. The professors were to constitute the governing body of the university, and were to elect the rector and appoint new professors as occasion offered. The ministry of education retained the formal right to confirm appointments, but for the time being it refrained from exercising it.

These were great reforms. But the reforming wave exhausted itself and sank back into a sea of lethargy and scepticism and, after the Polish Rebellion of 1863, of fear. The reforms were not withdrawn but they were not steadily pursued; administrative action restricted and cancelled reforming initiative in almost every field.

Meanwhile the reforms had excited the imagination and stimulated revolutionary feeling and action. As early as 1861, immediately after the emancipation, the peasants of Bezdna took revolutionary action. Led by a peasant called Anton Petrov they proclaimed themselves entirely free and divided up the local estate among themselves. Five thousand of them prevented Petrov's arrest when the authorities attempted it. A month later troops arrived to do the job. Their commanding officer, General Apraksin, ordered the peasants to hand over Petrov. When they refused the troops opened fire. They killed perhaps 500 people (57 with 77 wounded according to official figures). Petrov was tried by a military tribunal on the spot and shot in front of his fellow villagers. A few days later the students of Kazan University held a requiem for him at which the historian Shchapov gave an address. The tsar ordered him to be arrested, the monks who had celebrated mass to be sent to monastic imprisonment and sixteen students to be expelled from the university.

It was characteristic, and prophetic of the future, that the students and a professor showed their solidarity with the peasants in this way. Students in nineteenth-century Europe had strong revolutionary tendencies and had played a conspicuous part in the 1848 revolutions in France, Germany, Austria and Italy. But much of their revolutionary feeling was national rather than social, and, after the creation of the new national states of Germany and Italy and of Hungarian autonomy within the Habsburg Empire, very many of the students found their way into the government and the professions, and as adults took a full share in the life and work of the regime. Not so in Russia. Here the students and ex-students to a great extent formed a class apart, for which a new word was coined: the *intelligentsia*. The intelligentsia was essentially rootless and theoretical. It was not peasant, tilling the soil; it was not bourgeois, engaging in business and trade; it was not aristocratic, serving at court and in the army; it was not even bureaucratic, manning the civil service. It was a body of men and women devoted to the pursuit of abstract ideas. It engaged in much talk and writing, but few of its members had the opportunity to translate their ideas into practice: the nearest that most of them came to a practical job was the editing of a left-wing news-paper or journal. This meant that their ideas were in no way anchored to the ground of facts and experience but took flight on the wings of the Russian language and soared into the critical and imaginative empyrean. They were philosophical, meta-physical, revolutionary.

Behind the intelligentsia was a tradition of revolution and violence, derived from the Decembrist plotters against Nicholas I on his accession and flowering as anarchism and nihilism. Reaction against an autocratic regime and a stuffy provincial society drove the young idealists towards an imagined society based on individual freedom and human fellowship. Anger, impatience, a horror of cruelty, revengefulness, a romantic feeling for violence and a despairing (nihilist) feeling that only out of the ashes of destruction could the burnished phoenix of a new life arise drove them towards the means of realizing it: assassination. As early as 1866 an ex-student of Kazan University, D. V. Karakozov, tried to assassinate the tsar, and in the seventies there were many secret societies and propagandists of violence and assassination plotting the same end. Their efforts bore fruit in 1878 when Vera Zasulich attempted to shoot the police chief of St Petersburg, General Theodore Trepov, and culminated, after a number of murders, in the successful assassination of Alexander II by bomb-throwing on 1 March 1881.

The new tsar, Alexander III, was a straightforward, honest, likeable man, but he was a reactionary. His policy was, in a brilliant phrase of Olga Kireyev's, to 'Re-Russianize Russia'—to recreate the paternal society in which the tsar was the 'little father' of his people and the noblemen were miniature 'little fathers' whose task was to protect and control his children. Alexander could not restore serfdom, but short of this he did all he could to restore authority and power to the nobility. In 1885, on the centenary of Catherine the Great's charter to the nobility, he issued a manifesto extolling the nobility and proclaiming its right to the first place in the government of Russia. He followed this up by a series of measures embodying this policy in a practical form. He abolished the justices of the peace and replaced them by 'land captains'. These officials, who had to be members of the hereditary nobility, were appointed by the governor of the province and approved by the ministry of the interior. They had wide administrative and judicial powers and became, with the police, the peasants' rulers on the spot: 'nurses to the peasantry' or in a peasant's words 'commanding officers'.

In 1890 another law put more power into the hands of the nobility and officials by curtailing peasant representation in the *zemstvos* and giving the minister of the interior and the provincial governors more power over them and their professional employees. (It is fair to add that this did not prevent the growth during these years of a new body of professional men—doctors, teachers, engineers, statisticians: a body of great value to Russia, but from its situation much inclined to revolutionary ideas.)

The same policy applied to the towns. The town justices of the peace were abolished at the same time as the country ones, and their functions were transferred to judges appointed by the minister of justice. In 1892 a law drastically reduced the number of municipal voters—in St Petersburg, for example, from 21,176 to 7,152.

This restrictiveness applied also to the press and to education. There was a new press law in 1882. It partially restored preventive censorship by laying down that any newspaper that had been 'warned' three times had in future to submit each issue to pre-censorship. It introduced new special regulations for the control of public libraries and reading-rooms. It set up a special committee consisting of the ministers of justice, education and the interior, and the procurator of the holy synod, with power to suppress any periodical and to forbid the publishers and editors to publish or edit any other periodical in future.

The inclusion of the procurator of the holy synod in this committee is typical of the government's attitude. One of the most influential men in the government, Alexander III's old tutor Pobedonostsev, was himself procurator and fanatically devoted to the Orthodox church: for its own sake, for its pure 'Russianness' and for its power as social cement. This attitude is revealed in all its ugliness in education and in Russification.

Primary schooling had already a moral and religious bias, but this now became more marked. The curriculum consisted of the three Rs (with agricultural and artisan techniques in some schools) together with scripture, church Slavonic and church singing.

In secondary education this attitude affected not only the curriculum but the intake of pupils. In the curriculum heavy emphasis was placed on Latin and Greek, even to the extent of having to import noticeably large numbers of Czechs to teach them owing to the shortage of competent Russian teachers. So much time was devoted to the classics that it adversely affected the study of history and modern languages, for which there was not time enough. Science was actively discouraged. The reasons for this emphasis were political as well as intellectual. The case for the classics was argued not only on the orthodox lines of training the young mind but on the narrower ground that they produced sound judgement and fortified it against wildcat revolutionary ideas. But the authorities' trust in this argument seems to be contradicted by their simultaneous elimination of the poorer pupils. In 1887 school fees were raised, and at the same time a circular went out to the provinces instructing the school boards to admit only pupils from suitable backgrounds and to get rid of the 'children of coachmen, servants, cooks, washerwomen, small shopkeepers' etc.[6]

University fees were raised in the same year. Three years before, in 1884, a new university statute replacing that of 1863 restored control to the officials. The minister of the interior was

[6] Quoted in Seton-Watson, *op. cit.*, 476

to appoint the rectors and professors instead of the professors themselves, and the inspectors gained additional powers.

This policy of restricting the numbers of poor children entering the secondary schools and universities was not simply nonsensical, for experience suggests that training large numbers of intellectuals, who then cannot find employment, may produce little but unease and restlessness in their minds and in society at large. But what the policy overlooked was the need for trained minds in industry, which was growing fast in this period. The policy was grounded in blindness and fear.

So was the policy of Russification—only more so. Russification was the dark side of re-Russianizing. Glorifying, even idealizing, Russia and the Russian people meant glorifying everything Russian: Russian (Orthodox) religion, the Russian language, Russian culture, Russian *mores*. The complement of this attitude was despising and denigrating non-Russians and everything non-Russian, and, one stage further, feeling that they ought as far as possible to become Russian. Arrogance and fear drove the government to try and realize this feeling. It persecuted not only its old enemies like the Poles but its old friends like the Finns, the Baltic Germans and the Armenians. It persecuted the non-Orthodox: Orthodox sectaries, Roman Catholics and Moslems alike. Above all it persecuted the Jews. Here government and popular hatred and fear combined to produce the pogrom, the organized massacre and plunder of the Jews.

Re-Russianizing was in fact an illusion, based not on the facts of life but on nostalgia for the past and hostility to the winds of change.

The peasantry was indeed a passive support for the regime, but no more. Resentment at the land settlement lay in the peasant's unconscious and inhibited whole-hearted co-operation with the tsar. Nor is there any doubt that the *mir*, whatever its merits, acted as a brake on the development of a class of individual peasant landowners with an interest in farming their property as well as possible and in supporting the regime that had given them the property. The *mir*, saddled with the responsibility for the redemption payments and unsupported by technical aid of any sort, acted as a strongly conservative force. This was a period of agricultural stagnation.

The nobility was no longer dominant. Since the emancipation

it had as a class run more and more into debt. Many landowners
were absentees ordering their estates through stewards and living
as well as they could off the rentroll. A good many had sold out to
bourgeois capitalists of the stamp of Lopakhin in *The Cherry
Orchard*, and many more had mortgaged their land to the Nobles
Land Bank founded in 1885. Contrariwise they had not maintained their economic and social grip by going into business and
directing the new industrial and financial concerns. As there had
never been in Russia a respect for aristocracy as such, the erosion
of its economic base was steadily eroding the nobles' influence as
well as their power.

The autocracy itself was out of date. It was no longer necessary
to have a tribal leader who could lead his warriors in battle,
repel invaders and weld his people together: the military leadership of Alexander I against Napoleon had been no more than a
fiction. It was no longer necessary to drag Russia into Europe.
Russia was one of the recognized Great Powers of Europe and
the tsar one of its sovereigns. There was no call to 'civilize'
Russia. Whatever the respective merits of western and Slav
culture, the conflict between the westernizers and the slavophils
is witness to the extent to which western culture had already
permeated Russia. The tasks confronting Russia were of a
different order: to develop agriculture and industry; to allow the
emergence of a prosperous and contented farming community; to
prove Marx wrong in his dogma of the inevitability of the class
war; to educate its people; and to integrate the non-Russian
peoples into Russian society. Russia could perform these tasks
without the tsar. Indeed it could hope to perform them better,
for his will and his sole, ultimate responsibility prevented the
ideas and institutions that Russia most needed from emerging.

In Russia there was no parliament or national assembly. On
the day of his death Alexander II had been on the point of
signing a decree setting up an advisory assembly, but he had no
intention of its developing into a fully representative and responsible parliament; after twenty four hours' consideration Alexander
III decided not to sign the decree.

Nor was there a responsible ministry. Each minister was
appointed by the tsar and was individually responsible to him.
There were no cabinet meetings and no prime minister.

There was no free press. There was pre-censorship in the

provinces and partial pre-censorship in St Petersburg and Moscow. Further, there were separate censorships concerned with military and ecclesiastical matters as well as the normal political censorship.

There was no free education. Primary schools were in the hands of the church, in Russia not much more than a branch of the state. Secondary schools were state schools. The universities were effectively under state control. The pursuit of truth was tainted at its source.

Justice was not inviolate. There was far too much corruption: 'veut-on être compris d'un tchinovnik [official], il faut, dit le proverbe, parler rouble.'[7] This was traditional and deep-rooted, but perhaps slightly less common owing to the glimmerings of public opinion on the subject and the beginnings of professional standards in the law. What was worse was the arbitrariness of justice. 'L'exception est redevenue la règle,' as Leroy-Beaulieu remarks, 'et l'arbitraire a remplacé la loi.'[8] Officials were not under the jurisdiction of the ordinary courts, but were tried in special administrative courts. Special tribunals were set up for political offences. Above all life was permeated by suspicion and surveillance. Every *dvornik* (gatekeeper of a tenement block in a Russian town) was a police agent and spy. Side by side with the ordinary police was the secret police. Alexander II had abolished the Third Section of the Imperial Chancery responsible to the tsar personally and transferred responsibility for state security to the minister of the interior. This change cost the secret police its independence and something of its sinister prestige, but it did nothing to end its existence or curtail its activities. It still had the power to arrest, imprison, intern and deport anyone without trial and without any possibility of redress through the normal channels of the law; the only hope was to appeal to the clemency of the tsar personally. Siberia and the Peter and Paul Fortress were still words of evil repute.

The peaceful process of change was blocked at every turn. The *zemstvos* continued to exist and did good work in their field, but not even the *zemstvo* of St Petersburg could function as a national assembly. It was impossible to found a political party, to conduct a political campaign or carry a programme of reform

[7] A. Leroy-Beaulieu, *L'Empire des Tsars*, Tome II (1893), 104
[8] *Ibid.*, 416

based on the support of the country. There was no forum for the public debate of great issues, no theatre for developing the arts of the politician let alone the gifts of the statesman. Nor was it possible to bring the written word to bear on the situation instead of the spoken. It was impossible to sustain a press campaign against the government or the administration. It was impossible to discuss serious public issues in an open, critical spirit (though the opposition papers became extremely skilful at discussing them allusively for their quick-witted public). It was next to impossible to create and educate public opinion. It was impossible to train a generation of boys and girls in the disinterested pursuit of truth, and particularly in the principles of the natural sciences. Most fundamental of all, it was impossible to embark on any activity in the certainty of being able to pursue it unhindered, provided it did not interfere with the lives of one's neighbours or outrage their deepest feelings. Without *habeas corpus* the foundation was lacking for a free, creative society.

In 1863 Chernyshevsky had published a novel with the title *What is to be done?* in which the hero Rakhmetov spends his life trying to educate the peasants. The nihilist Pisarev regarded Rakhmetov as the prototype of 'the thinking realist [whose] love of others was in direct proportion to the depth of his egotism'.[9] But for him the ideal nihilist was Bazarov, the hero of Turgenev's novel *Fathers and Sons* published in 1862, for he combined the knowledge and the will needed for the work of revolution. In the novel Bazarov goes to stay at his friend's house in the country. As soon as he arrives he goes off with two young serfs to catch frogs.

'For what do you want frogs, *barin*?' asked one of the lads.
'To make them useful,' replied Bazarov . . . 'You see, I like to open them, and then to observe what their insides are doing. You and I are frogs too, except that we walk upon our hind legs. Thus the operation helps me to understand what is taking place in ourselves.'
'And what good will that do you?'
'This. That if you should fall sick, and I should have to treat you, I might avoid some mistakes.'
'Then you are a doctor?'
'I am.'[10]

[9] Lampert, *op. cit.*, 322
[10] Turgenev, *Fathers and Sons* (Everyman edn. 1921), 23–4

Bazarov's study of frogs, however, helped him not only to cure human beings but also to understand human society. Fundamentally human beings are all alike, like plants or animals. Some are better developed specimens than others but this is due to conditions: change the conditions and you change the specimen.

> 'Then you think ... that, once the social body has been rectified, stupid and evil people will cease to exist?'
> 'At all events, once the social body is properly organized, the fact that a man be wise or stupid, good or bad, will cease to be of importance.'
> 'Ah! I understand! That is because we all possess an identical spleen?'
> 'Precisely so, madam.'[11]

How to rectify the social body? That was the problem. By revolution and science was the nihilist answer. In Russia as it was, revolution was the only method of altering the condition of the social body and creating the possibility of organizing it properly. Science would bring knowledge and mastery of nature and provide man with the means for fully understanding the social body and organizing it properly in the light of this knowledge.

[11] *Ibid.*, 115

The revolutionary

## 2   *Lenin and Marxism*

Lenin was born Vladimir Ilyich Ulyanov on 10 April 1870 in the provincial capital of Simbirsk on the Volga.[1] He was the third child and second son of Ilya Nikolayevich Ulyanov and Maria Aleksandrovna Blank. His father was a teacher who rose to be a school inspector and eventually director of primary education for the province. His mother was the daughter of a doctor and small landowner who had married into a Volga German family, and she may have been brought up a Protestant. The family was middle-class, comfortably off and happy; the family atmosphere was calm but bracing.

Ulyanov was a good man: loyal, conscientious, reliable and sensible, with a quick temper and a sense of fun. His wife was more intelligent and better educated. She knew English, French and German, was a great reader, and brought up her children to read and think. She had great strength of character and gave her family security and drive. She outlived her husband by forty years and died aged 81 in 1916. She kept up a regular correspondence with Lenin all her life and twice visited him in exile, the last time in 1913.

Lenin developed rather slowly—for example he learned to walk late—but was otherwise a thoroughly normal boy: healthy, vigorous, boisterous, fond of games and outdoor activities, given to teasing his sisters. His only abnormal trait was his power of concentration and hard work. He showed this even before he went to school, in learning to read at five and in playing chess which his father taught him. At school he worked very hard and won the gold medal for the most deserving pupil in ability, progress and conduct. He was well liked though rather aloof, with no close friends.

In the autumn of 1887 Lenin went to Kazan University to

[1] Lenin was one of a number of pen names used by Vladimir Ilyich, which he eventually adopted as his regular party name.

study law. But he had not been there a term when he was rustic-
ated for being a member of a deputation of protest to the university
authorities against the university inspector. He was ordered to
Kukushkino in Kazan province where he helped to farm his
grandfather's estate of 225 acres. His first experience of practical
affairs was not altogether a success. As he later told his wife: 'It
would not work: my relations with the *muzhiks* [peasants] got to be
abnormal'; which probably meant that he did not behave like the
normal landowner and treat his peasants like the serfs they had
been until a generation before, but tried to establish equal relations with them on a friendly footing: there was never anything of
the *seigneur* or of the *de haut en bas* about Lenin.

He also read widely in his uncle's miscellaneous collection of
books as well as studying law hard. After a suitable lapse of time
he applied to be re-admitted to the university but his request was
refused. He then applied to go abroad. This too was refused.

In 1889 he moved to Alakayevka outside Samara on the Middle
Volga where his mother had bought a small farm. He was never
allowed to return to Kazan University, but finally in 1891 his
mother got permission for him to take the final examination of St
Petersburg University as an external student. He passed the
examination with honours, coming out first.

During these years he studied Marxism as well. He learned
German in order to read *Capital* and other works in the original;
his method of learning, which he often recommended to other
people, was to copy out and learn so many words a day. He got
through the two volumes of *Capital* then published, and read
Plekhanov's Marxist analysis of the social and economic development of Russia, *Our Differences* (1884), which in the words of
Theodore Dan 'for the first time laid a firm scientific foundation
underneath Russian Marxism'.

By the time he was allowed to go to St Petersburg in 1893 he was
already a convert to Marxism. Here he met the girl who was to
become his wife, Nadezhda Konstantinova Krupskaya, and was
introduced by her to the workers she and her friends were secretly
educating. He laughed at their so-called 'Committee of Literacy',
which he thought amateurish, but this did not stop him from
helping them to hectograph and distribute the Little Yellow
Books.

In 1895 Lenin was allowed by the authorities to go abroad after a severe bout of pneumonia. He went to Paris, and then to Switzerland where he met the leaders of the Liberation of Labour Group, whose personalities and history summarized the Russian Marxist movement. The oldest of them, at forty-five, was P. B. Akselrod, a Jew from Southern Russia who had been converted to Marxism by his experiences working as a carpenter in Russia and, after his flight in 1874, in Germany. He had a deep faith in the proletariat, and this more than his intellect was the mainspring of his socialism. G. V. Plekhanov and Vera Zasulich both came from the gentry and had been associated with the anarchist movement in their twenties. Vera Zasulich was a living legend: the woman who as a young girl had shot General Trepov out of disinterested rage at his cruelty and, acquitted by the jury, had been in exile since 1879. Plekhanov was the dominant member of the group, a cultivated intellectual who had come to think that anarchism was sterile and that the only hope for Russia lay in an organized Marxist party. In exile since 1880, he had been close to Engels and was without question the leading Russian Marxist theorist. Lenin felt a deep respect for Plekhanov, and Plekhanov in turn at once recognized Lenin's abilities and thought they had found in him what the group so badly needed—a first-rate organizer.

In the autumn Lenin returned to Russia after arranging for illegal literature to be smuggled in. In St Petersburg he at once got into touch with the workers: he explained factory law to them, encouraged them to strike and was preparing to bring out an illegal newspaper, when he and the other members of their group (The Union of Struggle for the Liberation of the Working Class) were arrested.

After 14 months in prison Lenin was exiled for three years to Siberia. In prison he communicated in simple code with Krupskaya, who had not been arrested. In 1898, a year after Lenin had arrived in Siberia, she was allowed to join him on condition they were legally married. There was some 'red tape' delay over this but they were eventually married on 10 July. They were together until Lenin's death in 1924, except for a year from 1900 to 1901 when Krupskaya was still in Siberia and his term of exile had ended. Their marriage was a genuine partnership. Krupskaya was an educated woman with a highly developed social conscience, whose intelligence enabled her to cope with Lenin on the intel-

lectual plane. More important, she was a woman of calm strength
of character. She sustained and fortified Lenin during the long
years of exile and the few, killing years of the revolution.

Their life in Siberia was healthy and regular: 'Lenin sang a
great deal and with great gusto,' Krupskaya writes in her *Memories*,[2] He walked about the countryside for the good of his health
at all times of the year, and whenever he could he went out
shooting, for which he had a passion. One day he was out after
foxes, when a fox ran straight towards him. They stopped and
stared at each other. Then the fox bolted. 'Why on earth didn't
you fire?' 'Well, he was so beautiful, you know.'[3] He played
chess until he found it was interfering with his work and gave it
up; as he had given up skating as a boy when he found it made
him so sleepy that he could not work. For above all he worked.
He read much economic literature for the book that he had
started writing in prison and finished in Siberia: *The Development
of Capitalism in Russia*. He worked at German and learnt English as
Krupskaya and he were translating Sidney and Beatrice Webb's
*History of Trade Unionism* into Russian. He read philosophy:
Helvetius, Holbach, Kant and Hegel. For relaxation he read
Pushkin, Lermontov and Nekrasov. He wrote to his mother that
he was toying with the idea of subscribing to the weekly illustrated *Niva*: 'it would be very jolly for Prominsky's youngsters
to see it, while I would get the complete works of Turgenev
promised by the *Niva* in twelve volumes as a free gift. And all this
for seven roubles, including postage. Very tempting!'[4] Lenin
was soaked in the Russian classics and loved them. (Once in a
Swiss train he was shocked at a German's ignorance of Dürer.)
He especially valued Nekrasov, Chekhov, Turgenev and Tolstoy.
'What a Colossus, eh?' he once remarked to Gorky of Tolstoy,
'What a marvellously developed brain! ... And do you know
something still more amazing? You couldn't find a genuine
*muzhik* in literature until this Count came on the scene.'[5]

Towards the end of his exile he received a copy of Eduard
Bernstein's *Die Voraussetzungen des Sozialismus und die Aufgaben der
Sozialdemokratie*. Krupskaya and he read it at once. It astounded

[2] N. K. Krupskaya, *Memories of Lenin*, Vol. 1, (N.Y. n.d.), 26
[3] *Ibid.*, 33
[4] *Letters of Lenin*, ed. Hill and Mudie (1937), 57
[5] M. Gorky, *Days with Lenin* (N.Y. 1932), 51

and shocked them, and Bernstein's statement that many Russians supported him 'absolutely infuriated' them. Lenin characterized it as 'indifferent opportunism ... and cowardly opportunism at that, for Bernstein simply does not want to get anywhere near a programme'.[6]

This was in fact true. The whole point of Bernstein's 'revision' of Marxism was to abandon Marx's *programme* as outdated by events and to restate the Marxist faith in a form that would allow its original insights to shine forth purged of the elements that time had falsified.

Marx and Engels drafted the *Communist Manifesto* for the Communist League in the winter of 1847 and published its German text in London in February 1848, a few weeks before the outbreak of the revolution in Paris.

In a note to the German edition of 1890 Engels wrote: 'This proposition [i.e. the basic idea of the manifesto] which, in my opinion, is destined to do for history what Darwin's theory has done for biology, we, both of us, had been gradually approaching for some years before 1845. How far I had independently progressed towards it is best shown by my *Condition of the Working Class in England* [published in Germany in 1845]. But when I again met Marx at Brussels, in spring, 1845, he had it ready worked out, and put it before me, in terms almost as clear as those in which I have stated it here.' Marx published his *Critique of Political Economy* in 1859 and the first volume of *Capital* in 1867. The basic idea arose as a reaction to the philosophy of Hegel who had died in 1831 and to the state of the economy, especially the British economy, as it was before 1848, at a time when capitalism had transformed large numbers of agricultural workers into factory hands and before it had to any great extent benefited them by raising their standard of living. When the *Communist Manifesto* proclaimed: 'The proletarians have nothing to lose but their chains', it was proclaiming what was not far from the truth. Furthermore the spectre of the French Revolution had not been

[6] *Letters of Lenin*, 95

laid, but made frequent appearances in Europe in the years after Waterloo and Napoleon's exile to St Helena. The French Revolution of 1848 was the most formidable since 1789 and in one way was even more alarming to the ruling class, for in it the working class of Paris played an unmistakable and independent role for the first time. It might well have seemed that a Communistic revolution lay in 'the logic of history'.

For Marx 'the logic of history' was no mere phrase, but a metaphor which gave a real insight into reality. He fully accepted Hegel's view of the universe as through and through dynamic not static, and of its process as radically dialectic, a process that reaches the absolute by an almost infinite series of confrontations, each of which produces a higher synthesis until the ultimate synthesis, the absolute, is reached. But whereas Hegel saw the universe as essentially spiritual and the absolute therefore as absolute spirit, i.e. God, Marx saw it as essentially material. Where for Hegel the confrontations were mental events, steps in a cosmic argument initiated and conducted by absolute spirit and reaching its logical conclusion in absolute spirit, for Marx they were material events, stages in a natural, evolutionary process, whose conclusion would be here on earth. For Hegel 'the logic of history' was a strictly accurate description of the process of the universe, for Marx it was only a pregnant metaphor.

Marx was a thorough-going materialist. He regarded the history of the universe as the history of the development of matter. Human history was a mere extension of natural history. The mechanism of development was the same in each: the instinct of self-preservation and the preservation of the species. This involved a struggle for existence, in natural history between different species and in human history between different classes, i.e. groups of people who had come together to ensure their further existence. Since the Reformation this had simplified itself into a struggle between capital and labour, or between capitalists and proletarians—workers whose only possession was their labour power, who had nothing to lose but their chains. This struggle was approaching its climax, which would not be long delayed. The workers would overthrow the capitalists and capitalism, and inaugurate a socialist regime whose task it would be to guide the transition to communism.

This struggle lay not only in 'the logic of history' but also in that of economics. Marx, basing his analysis of capitalism on the work of Adam Smith and Ricardo, carried the argument to its logical conclusion. The mainspring of capitalism was the pursuit of private profit. The capitalist's aim was to maximize profits: an aim tersely expressed in the motto—buy in the cheapest, sell in the dearest market. This motto applied as much to labour as to goods; and labour was in fact the key to success. For it was labour, and labour alone, that created surplus value and so the capitalist's profit. The value of a commodity was determined by the quantity of socially necessary labour that had gone into its manufacture. But the capitalist did not pay the worker the full value of his labour in wages. He naturally bought his labour as cheap as he could. And even if he was kindly and wanted to pay his worker more than the minimum he could not, for he was bound, so the economists thought, by 'the iron law of wages'. 'The worker's wages are limited to what is necessary to keep body and soul together' (Turgot). 'The natural price of labour is that price which is necessary to enable the labourers, one with another, to subsist and to perpetuate their race, without either increase or diminution' (Ricardo). If an employer pays his worker a little more than 'natural' or 'subsistence' wages, all that happens is that the worker breeds more freely, the population increases, there are redundant workers and wages fall again to their natural level. Labour therefore creates surplus value which the capitalist pockets. He may spend or save this. What he saves is his capital. With this he expands his business and employs more workers, whose hours of work he may also lengthen. He increases his profits and ploughs back a part of them into his business, and so expands again, and so on and so on. Alternatively he may install a machine in his factory instead of employing more workers. If so he further increases his profits, for the machine does more work than a hand; it too creates surplus value, for its value is determined by the amount of labour that has gone into its manufacture, the labour of mere 'hands'. Then the machine throws workers out of work and creates a pool of surplus labour. Thus the gap between the capitalist and his workers continually widens. The worker's wage is more or less fixed, fluctuating only with the price of necessities. The capitalist's profits increase: he is getting richer both absolutely and relatively.

But the competition between capitalists is fierce. Each is trying

B

to maximize his profits and expand his business. Some go bankrupt
and their businesses are taken over by their rivals; some sell out in
time; some do a deal with their rivals and amalgamate their
businesses. In any event the tendency is towards concentration and
ultimately to monopoly. There are fewer and fewer capitalists who
get richer and richer, and more and more workers who get
relatively poorer and poorer. But the workers will not endure this
for ever. Sooner or later they will revolt. There will be a revolution which will destroy capitalism and bury the capitalists in its
ruins. Capitalism will be its own gravedigger.

The revolution is inevitable. Both history and economics lead
to this conclusion. The revolution will be successful. But to bring
about the revolution, to direct it and to ensure its success, the
workers will need leadership. This will be supplied by the workers'
representatives, the members of the Communist Party. Marx
always claimed that Marxist socialism was scientific: that it was
based on a scientific diagnosis of the facts of life, and not, like all
other brands of socialism, on notions derived from a study of the
gospels or on sentimental sympathy with the workers. Correct
diagnosis was vital, and just as the Christian doctors had been of
great importance to the church in the early centuries of its
history, so were Marx and his fellow 'doctors' to the workers'
international. Given that their general diagnosis of the situation
was correct, there was one moment of crucial importance
for them. Just as the medical doctor must recognize the crisis of an
illness and shape his course of treatment in relation to it, so the
Marxist doctor must recognize the critical moment of history, and
time the party's action to coincide with it; Marx was absolutely
opposed to engineering revolutions here, there and everywhere
with the object of shaking the foundations of capitalism; he
thought this as futile in its own way as contesting parliamentary
elections and entering into the game of party politics. The party's
job was to clarify its doctrine and to build up its disciplined
strength for the decisive moment, when it would give the workers
the leadership they needed to bring off the revolution.

But 1898 was not 1848. The expected revolution had not occurred. The tide of history was running much more slowly than
Marx had thought, was even perhaps going out and not coming
in. In Western Europe there were not fewer capitalists but more.
Despite the development of trusts and cartels there were hundreds

and hundreds of small and medium-sized businesses. Moreover, the development of the joint stock company with limited liability in the second half of the century had greatly increased the number of shareholders, small-scale capitalists, a property-owning middle class. Nor were the workers living in ever increasing misery. Their standard of living was rising and their working lives were increasingly protected by industrial reforms. To a great extent they had the parliamentary vote. In a word democracy was developing. And with it the critical moment of history was vanishing away, to be replaced by an infinite series of moments demanding decisive, but not revolutionary, action. Times had changed and the party's job had changed too. It was now, in Bernstein's view, 'to organize the working classes politically and develop them as a democracy, and to fight for all reforms in the State which are adapted to raise the working classes and transform the State in the direction of democracy'.[7]

All this was anathema to Lenin. He accepted Marx's diagnosis without qualification. This was by no means a sign of stupidity, of blind adherence to authority, or of an inability or unwillingness to consider evidence, for he had good reasons for sticking to Marx. The first and fundamental reason was that like Marx he was a Hegelian. He was convinced that the universe and history were dialectical in character. History proceeded towards its goal by a series of clashes of opposites. From each clash arose a synthesis of the opposites until the final synthesis was reached. Both intellectually and materially this synthesis was communism. This attitude of mind is incompatible with the empirical, scientific attitude dominant in Western Europe.

The second reason for Lenin's conviction was the backwardness of Russia, economically, socially and politically. Since 1861 there had indeed been a revolution in Russian industry in scale and in technique. By 1900 production of coal had gone up over 50 times to 16 million tons a year, of steel over 1500 times to $2\frac{1}{2}$ million tons a year, of oil almost 400 times to not far short of $10\frac{1}{2}$ million tons a year. There were about 30,000 miles of railway, a fifty-fold increase. Moscow was connected with all the main towns of European Russia, and the line to Samarkand was about to be extended to Tashkent, itself already connected to the Caspian Sea. The Trans-Siberian had been begun, and was finished in

[7] E. Bein, *Evolutionary Socialism* (N.Y. 1961), xxvii

1905. The population had increased from 64 to 94 millions, but the urban population had doubled, from six to twelve millions. There were fifteen towns of over 100,000, including Moscow and St Petersburg, each over a million. The workers were not only concentrated in towns but increasingly in large factories. Between 1879 and 1895 the number of factories employing over 100 workers had risen from a little over 1200 to a little under 1500, but the number employing over 500 had risen by a third to 332. Concentration was not only urban but geographical and financial. Coal was principally mined in the Donets basin, iron ore round Krivoy Rog. The oil industry centred on Baku in the Caucasus. Moscow and St Petersburg were the only very large industrial towns. In 1904 eighteen Donets mines set up a trust which controlled 60 per cent of the output of coal, while the engineering industry had already set up a cartel in 1902. More important and more characteristic of Russian industry was the very large part played by the state. It dominated the railways and the banks, the sugar and timber trades, and had a monopoly of the sale of vodka. Furthermore, foreign capital had to a very large extent financed the development of Russian industry, as there had not been the spare capital at home to finance it. These two things taken together had meant that there were many fewer capitalists, large and small, than in the west. There were no Wedgwoods or Fords, and there was no middle class comparable to that in Western Europe.

Russia had indeed experienced an industrial revolution, but it still lagged far behind the most advanced industrial nations in the volume of its production and trade, in its national income and in the standard of living of most of its people. Housing conditions in towns and conditions of work in factories were 'almost incredible' and hours of work excessive. Laws were passed in the eighties and nineties to limit hours, but they were almost wholly nullified by administrative action and by the ineffectiveness of the inspectors. Trade unions and strikes were illegal. When Lenin wrote *The Development of Capitalism in Russia* almost everything in the picture of industry seemed to confirm Marx's diagnosis.

But after all, Russia was still an overwhelmingly peasant country: only an eighth of the population lived in towns. As we have seen, the period after the emancipation of the serfs was a period of agricultural stagnation. The terms of the emancipation and the institution of the *mir* made for stability rather than change and were intended to do so. Nevertheless change did take place. As early as the sixties almost a quarter of a million acres of land changed hands annually, and by the nineties this had risen to very nearly two million acres. By 1905 about a third of the nobles' land had been sold and another third mortgaged to the Nobles Land Bank. Of this some was bought by bourgeois and some by peasants, but over the whole period from the emancipation to the 1905 revolution there was a marked tendency for peasant buyers to predominate. Before 1877 townsmen had bought twice as much as peasants, about 32 million acres compared with about 16 million. But in the eighties the current set the other way; and by 1905 the townsmen had increased their holding to only about 43 million acres, while the peasants held almost 65 million acres.

Another factor making for agricultural stagnation was the rather rapid increase in the rural population and the simultaneous discouragement of labour movement by the government and the *mir* alike. Despite this, as many as 300,000 souls migrated to Siberia in the first quarter of a century after the emancipation. Then at the very end of the eighties the government changed its policy and began actively to assist migration. The result was dramatic: in the ten years 1894–1903 the migrants to Siberia averaged about 115,000 a year.

These changes in land-holding and in village population began to be reflected in the wealth of different peasant households. By 1905 about five per cent of these households held under six acres a household, about a quarter held up to fifteen acres, while a minute fraction of them (one-fifth of one per cent) held over 250 acres. Perhaps of even greater practical importance was the horse, the normal plough-animal in the greater part of Russia. Here too there were already differences. By the end of the nineties about a third of the households owned no horse, about a third owned a single horse and another third owned two or more. A rich peasant was already called a *kulak* (fist).

Not all this was clear to contemporaries, nor were all the statistics then available. Nor was it clear beyond doubt which way Russian agriculture was going. Nor is it clear now. For the Stolypin reforms introduced after 1905 (see pp. 58–60) were based on quite different premises from those of the sixties, and cut sharply across the developments of the previous years. Nevertheless, it can be seen that there is a good deal of evidence of capitalist tendencies in Russian agriculture and peasant life, and it was by no means foolish in the nineties to suppose that economic forces in general would accelerate these tendencies and overcome the conservative emotions and habits of government and peasant alike. Lenin clearly believed this and showed in *The Development of Capitalism in Russia* that the agricultural evidence as much as the industrial and financial evidence confirmed Marx's diagnosis.

All Lenin's studies in philosophy, in history and in economics, therefore, combined to convert him to Marxism in the first place and then to fortify his Marxism.

These were the fundamental causes of his amazement and rage at Bernstein's book, but there were other, minor ones. In his book Bernstein quotes from Engels' preface to the 1895 edition of *Class Struggles in France* in support of his thesis that direct revolutionary attack was now out-of-date and that the parliamentary method was the correct one for Social-Democrats. In fact this preface was published in the German Social-Democrat paper *Vorwärts* in an expurgated version, which made it seem that Engels unreservedly condemned barricades, street fighting and revolution, and by implication approved the parliamentary methods of German Social-Democracy. Engels was very angry at this and wrote strong letters of protest to a number of his friends, including Marx's son-in-law, Paul Lafargue.[8] Lenin knew this,[9] probably from Lafargue whose acquaintance he made when he was in Paris in June 1895, and not unnaturally shared Engels's anger, especially as Bernstein was the London correspondent of *Vorwärts* as well as being Engels's friend and executor. It is hard to see how Bernstein could have quoted Engels in good faith, and Lenin almost certainly thought him guilty of deliberate misrepresentation.

Then there were the Russian revisionists known as 'Economists'. Bernstein had exaggerated their numbers and this was infuriating, but there was undoubtedly a group of them in St Petersburg and it was impossible to know in Siberia how large it was. What was clear was that two of the best-known professional Marxist economists, P. B. Struve and Tugan-Baranovsky, had abandoned orthodoxy and turned into 'legal' Marxists, who advocated legal

---

[8] *Engels-Lafargue Correspondence*, Vol. III (Moscow n.d.), 373
[9] Lenin, *Collected Works*, 4th edn., (Moscow, 1960–67), Vol. 5, 29. All references are to this edition

methods for attaining their goal. Furthermore, just before he received Bernstein's book Lenin had got a copy of an 'Economist' statement, subsequently known as *Credo*, which argued that tsarism was so strong as to make political attack impossible and therefore Russian Marxists should concentrate on backing the radical and liberal opposition, on economic activity and on educating the masses. This alarmed Lenin and other Social-Democrat exiles so much that they contrived to meet and to issue a protest drafted by Lenin, which was published in December 1899 as the *Protest of Seventeen*. This reaffirmed the correct line mapped out by Marx—revolutionary political action that avoided conspiracy on the one hand and reformist tinkering on the other— and asserted that the Russian Social-Democratic Party, like *Narodnaya Volya* small in numbers but great in effect, basing itself on the proletariat and on revolutionary theory, would 'be able to render itself invincible'.

All in all, Lenin had good cause to be concerned and to be anxious to get away from Siberia.

## 3   *The party split*

Lenin's and Krupskaya's exile came to an end in February 1900. They travelled together as far as Ufa. But Lenin had to leave his wife there, as he had not been able to get permission for her to come with him to Pskov where he was to live. There he was joined by two other exiles, Martov and Potresov, and they made their final plans to go abroad and bring out a newspaper with the Liberation of Labour Group. A special meeting in May attended by Struve and Tugan-Baranovsky endorsed this decision. As soon as he had received official permission to go abroad Lenin made his dispositions and went. With his mother and his sister, Anna, he went to Ufa to say goodbye to Krupskaya, and he then visited Moscow and St Petersburg to arrange secret communications with the local Social-Democrat groups. His visit to St Petersburg, to which he was forbidden to go, nearly landed him in disaster. He was arrested, put in prison for three weeks and then taken under police escort to Podolsk. Here the local chief of police confiscated his exit permit. Lenin saw Europe vanishing over the horizon, but he kept his head and bluffed the policeman into returning the permit by threatening to report him to headquarters in St Petersburg.

Lenin crossed the frontier safely into Germany. A little later Potresov joined him, and together they negotiated with the Liberation of Labour Group about their relations and about the paper.

Lenin had, as we know, met Plekhanov and Akselrod on his visit to Europe in 1895 and had met them as an unknown young man meeting the founding fathers of Russian Marxism. He had impressed them both with his grasp of theory and of the detail of organization, and appeared to them a future leader of the party.

Now, matured by practical experience of revolutionary work and by exile, he met them as an equal. He was not impressed by their age, their reputation or their gifts. He was determined that men like himself and Potresov, newly arrived from Russia, with up-to-date knowledge of the situation and with contacts they had worked hard to renew before they left, should not be mere members of the Liberation of Labour Group and obedient reporters for a newspaper edited by Plekhanov and published in Geneva where he lived. Lenin got his way. By the autumn it was agreed that the editorial board of the paper was to consist of Plekhanov, Akselrod, Vera Zasulich, Lenin, Martov and Potresov, with Plekhanov having two votes, but that it would be published and printed in Germany, not in Switzerland. Its policy was to be rigidly orthodox. It was to be called *Iskra* ('The Spark'), in allusion to the words used by the Decembrist exiles in reply to a letter of greeting from Pushkin: 'The spark will kindle a flame'. The first number came out in Munich on 24 December 1900.

But *Iskra* was not merely to make converts. It was to fortify the faithful. It was to bring news of events in Russia to all its readers wherever they might be, and to comment on them from a correct Marxist angle and so relieve the local party members' sense of isolation and combat their rather strong tendency towards parochialism. This it consistently did while Lenin was one of the editors. Perhaps even more important in the editors' view, it was to define and clarify Marxist doctrine and wage non-stop war on socialists who deviated from it—at this juncture the Economists and legal Marxists, later the Social-Revolutionaries (SRs), who played up the role of the peasants in the revolution and supported terrorism as a means of bringing down the autocracy.

Lenin wrote about the shooting at the Obukhov steelworks in May 1901, about the *zemstvos* and their treatment by the government, about the penal servitude regulations, about famine and the government's ultra-bureaucratic plans for coping with it: he tellingly relates the innumerable steps that have to be taken before anyone is actually fed and in a paragraph conveys the atmosphere of the bureaucracy to his readers.

[The circular on food policy] is a mass circumlocution of ... in the grand style of the chancelleries, with periods 36 lines long, in a 'jargon' that makes the heart bleed for our native Russian language. As you read deeply into this effusion, you feel as though you were in a Russian police-station with its musty walls and its all-pervading specific stench, in which the officials personify in their appearance and bearing the most casehardened bureaucracy, while in the courtyard ... gloomy buildings loom reminiscent of the torture chamber.[1]

Lenin wrote on the protest of the Finnish people against the government's arbitrary alteration of their constitution, about the annual budget, about the draft of a new strike law in 1902, about the trade union movement sponsored by the police, about the policy of the *Bund*, the Jewish organization affiliated to the Russian Social-Democratic Labour Party and claiming to be the sole representative of the Jewish workers, and against the Social-Revolutionaries, whom he compares to the German followers of Bernstein in an article headed *Les Beaux Esprits Se Rencontrent* (*which may be interpreted roughly as: Birds of a Feather Flock Together*). This article is typical of Lenin's sharpness as a controversialist. Superficially the SRs and the Bernsteinites were poles apart, the SRs recommending terror as a weapon of revolution and the Bernsteinites the ballot box as an instrument for transforming the state and society. But Lenin spotted that they both wanted a society in which the ownership of property was not socialized but very widely diffused, what he calls a petty-bourgeois society, and he mercilessly hammers this comparison home. This is one-sided, and to that extent unfair. But it is good journalism. Furthermore it is fundamentally just. The Bernsteinites still thought and called themselves Social-Democrats and the SRs were unflinching left-wing revolutionaries, but neither were genuine Marxists. So it was a duty as well as a pleasure to point this out for anyone convinced that Marxism and a proper Marxist party alone could educate and lead the proletariat to victory in the revolution, and alone could guide the transformation of society through the dictatorship of the proletariat.

Lenin was deeply convinced of this. From the first he had envisaged *Iskra* as something not merely providing information but also control. The editorial board would not only edit the paper but control the local branches of the party that would get it. This was essential if the party was not to disintegrate. For it had to contend with formidable difficulties. The numbers in any one branch were small and they were liable all the time to be made smaller by arrests and deportations. The members were in their very nature independent and argumentative, and their independence was liable to turn into anarchic individualism, and their

[1] *Iskra*, No. 9, October 1901, in *Collected Works*, Vol. 5, 231–2

arguments into irreconcilable quarrels. The distances made communication between branches very difficult. Daily life in the town and the country was very different, and there was not much imaginative sympathy between the factory worker and the peasant. The intellectuals were rootless and undisciplined, and especially prone to fall into apathy or to fly off the handle.

During 1902 Lenin developed his idea of the party's role in relation to the working class in *What is to be Done?*; with Plekhanov and the other editors of *Iskra* he drafted a party programme and prepared for a party congress that would adopt it. Lenin, who had soon realized that the 'elders', as Plekhanov, Akselrod and Vera Zasulich came to be nicknamed, were incapable of organizing anything and who had himself a decided taste for organization, made this his own special business. He had grasped what all good administrators know: the success of a conference depends on efficient preparatory work. So he worked hard to ensure that enough of the right delegates turned up to back the *Iskra* line, to produce a clear, comprehensive and practical programme and a working agenda, and to get the editorial board to agree on this and stick to it.

The draft programme begins by setting out the basic economic situation of Russia. Capitalist production is increasing and so is technical progress. Both are worsening the condition of the workers, as are the periodic and inevitable industrial crises. This will promote the solidarity of the proletariat. The proletariat must free itself. To do this it 'must win political power, which will make it master of the situation and enable it to remove all the obstacles along the road to its goal. In this sense the dictatorship of the proletariat is an essential political condition of the social revolution.' It is the task of Russian Social-Democracy to explain the inevitable struggle to the workers and to 'organize a revolutionary class party capable of directing the struggle'.

The programme then goes on to outline what is immediately necessary in the peculiar Russian conditions. This is to overthrow the autocracy and to set up a democratic republic which would ensure the basic democratic reforms: popular sovereignty with a legislative assembly representative of the people; universal, equal, direct suffrage and the secret ballot; the inviolability of the person and the home; freedom of conscience, speech and the press, and freedom of assembly; the right to strike and to organize

trade unions; freedom of movement and occupation; the abolition of social castes and equality for all citizens irrespective of
sex, religion or race; the right to national self-determination
within Russia; the right to prosecute an official; the general
arming of the people; the separation of church and state and of
church and school; universal, free and compulsory education up
to the age of sixteen. The republic would also enact the necessary
reforms of working conditions, including compensation for
industrial accidents, pensions and factory courts. It would replace
the existing indirect taxes by a progressive income tax. It would
end the remnants of serfdom and establish peasant committees
to supervise this process and the return to the peasants of the
'cut-offs', the land cut off from the peasants when serfdom was
abolished and assigned to the landlords.

The programme ends by affirming that the party backs all
'oppositional and revolutionary movements [against the regime
but] emphatically rejects' all kinds of reformism. All this can be
achieved only by 'overthrowing the autocracy and convoking a
Constituent Assembly, freely elected by the whole people'.

The congress met from 30 July to 23 August 1903, first in
Brussels and then, after it had been turned out by the police, in
London. There were 43 delegates with 51 votes between them. They
represented five émigré organizations and 21 organizations in
Russia. The majority were supporters of *Iskra* but there were five
votes for the *Bund*, two for the Union of Russian Social-Democrats, the émigré group from which Lenin and his friends had
split off, and one for a St Petersburg group hostile to *Iskra*. There
were also two votes for a small group called *Yuzhnyy Rabochiy*
(Southern Worker) which in general followed the *Iskra* line but
was somewhat independent.

The first question on the agenda was the status of the *Bund*.
This organization wished to retain the autonomy granted to it
by the first party congress in matters 'especially concerning the
Jewish proletariat' and to be recognized as the sole agent of the
party to the Jewish proletariat. It also asked the congress to
concede 'cultural autonomy' to the Jews: by this it meant freedom
to run their own cultural affairs and, most important, to run their
own schools in their own language (Yiddish). These demands
involved two important and interconnected principles: the nature
of Marxism and the nature of the party.

Marxism was a diagnosis of capitalism and of the inevitable crisis of the capitalist economy, and its conclusions applied to all capitalists and all proletarians, Christian, Jewish, Moslem or atheist. The party had recognized the realities of the Russian situation by including national self-determination in its programme. But to yield to the claims of the *Bund* would be to deny the universal validity of Marxism and to admit that the Jewish proletariat was not just a part of the proletariat like, say, the St Petersburg or Moscow proletariat, but something peculiar that the party was not competent to manage and needed its own special agent, the *Bund*. This would mean that the party here and now was a federation and not a centralized body, and would make it much more difficult to exercise effective control over the branches. Moreover it would open the way to similar claims by other groups and so possibly weaken the party irretrievably. Beyond this in the mists of time lay the new socialist society. What would be its shape if from the very beginning there were citizens who were not simply ex-proletarians like the mass of their fellow-citizens but present Jews consciously inheriting the Jewish tradition in all its distinctness? The delegates, including all the Jewish delega es like Akselrod, Martov and Trotsky, were united on this question and voted against the *Bund*.

The next question was the nature of the party and its relation to the proletariat. The basic difficulty here rose from the facts of life and from Marxist analysis of them. The economy of Europe was capitalist and was developing on capitalist lines. This development was approaching its inevitable crisis, resulting in the revolutionary seizure of power by the proletariat which would then inaugurate the transition to the socialist society. The Social-Democrat party was to hasten this development and to act as the agent of the proletariat in the revolution. It could not therefore be a straightforward political party playing the party game according to the European rules. Its avowed object was to disrupt the game as soon as it could. Any European government that took it seriously must regard it as a conspiratorial group, and Bismarck's action in outlawing the party in Germany was quite logical. In such a party there was a need for secrecy that did not exist in an ordinary democratic party, and this was bound to affect its organization and its propaganda.

This basic difficulty was accentuated for the Russian Social-

Democratic Labour Party by the facts of Russian life. The party was illegal, all its leading members were in exile and it had to smuggle its literature into Russia and to distribute it there clandestinely; its agents and its members were tracked by the police and were frequently arrested; there were pitifully few members of the party in relation to the total population of Russia; the masses, proletarian and peasant, were still ignorant and indifferent; trade unions in which workers could fight for their rights and gain experience of political action were still subject to the criminal law, and there was no parliament to which they could be elected and in which their leaders could become democratic statesmen.

In these circumstances the leaders were almost bound to be intellectuals, for the proletariat had not yet had time to throw up a proletarian leader who had earned his living as a factory worker and received his political training in the factory and the trade union; and they were almost bound to be exiles, for they could not act as leaders inside Russia and hope to escape arrest indefinitely. This meant that they were doubly divorced from their followers: they were divorced by distance and by class. The problem was how to overcome this divorce.

There was much earnest and passionate debate on this which concentrated at first on the meaning of the phrase 'dictatorship of the proletariat'. The delegates who were democrats fighting the autocracy for basic democratic reforms were uneasy at the idea of dictatorship, and wondered how it could be reconciled with these. On the other hand they knew that Marx himself had envisaged the dictatorship of the proletariat and that it would hardly be possible to ensure the success of the revolution without at least threatening to curtail the freedom of its opponents. Trotsky put forward the ingenious argument that the dictatorship of the proletariat would not be the dictatorship of a minority but the dictatorship of the vast majority over itself. This theory would have been cold comfort to the bourgeois feeling the rough edge of the dictatorship, but it suffered from a more serious defect: it left unanswered the question who would actually exercise the dictatorship. Here Trotsky was at one with Lenin. It could only be the party. And the party must not be afraid of the responsibility or of the charge that it was acting dictatorially. The party statutes, said Trotsky in a striking phrase, should express 'the leadership's organized distrust' of the members. This view was most sharply contested by Akimov who said: 'The concepts Party and Proletariat are set in opposition to each other, the first as an active, causative, collective being, the second as a passive medium on which the Party operates.'

Lenin certainly thought this. The workers left to themselves could see the hardships and injustices they suffered and could organize themselves locally to fight against them. They could even combine on a national scale to secure improvements in their conditions and perhaps elementary political rights. What they could not do was to develop political consciousness and bring it to bear on the social and political situation. In the course of the debate Lenin remarked of an amendment that it 'would give the idea that the development of consciousness is a spontaneous thing [...] Aside from the influence of the Social-Democracy there is no *conscious* activity of the workers.'[2]

The debate was long, deeply-felt, dramatic and exhausting. At times it was hectic and uncontrolled, as when Rozanov hissed Plekhanov who seemed to him to be subordinating democracy to revolution. The delegates got tired. They were living in dingy and often squalid lodgings. They were shut up indoors for far too long each day. The London August days 'increased in heat until they became torrid ... ragged urchins hailed the appearance of watercarts with whoops of joy ... the pitiless sun gave every street the appearance of a hard, hot snapshot; and, as the heat got on people's nerves, the cries of children at play become intolerably strident.'[3]

There was much backroom discussion and manoeuvring of which Lenin was the centre. This naturally bred suspicion among those left out, and this suspicion in turn generated more suspicion and contempt which expressed itself in bitter, wounding speech. Lenin himself became conscious of this and wrote to Potresov shortly after the congress: 'I am reviewing all the events and impressions of the congress, I am aware that often I acted and behaved in terrible irritation, "madly", and I am willing to admit this my guilt to anybody—if one can call guilt something that was naturally caused by the atmosphere, the reactions, the retorts, the struggle, etc.'[4]

---

[2] Quoted in Bertram D. Wolfe, *Three Who Made a Revolution* (1956), 239
[3] Oliver Onions, *In Accordance with the Evidence*, 2nd edn. (1968), 203
[4] Quoted in Deutscher, *The Prophet Armed* (1954), 80, n.2

The climax came over the draft rules of the party. Lenin's draft of Rule 1 read: 'A Party member is one who accepts the Party's programme and supports the Party both financially and by personal participation in one of its organizations.' To this Martov moved an amendment to substitute for the words after 'financially' '... and who gives the party his regular personal co-operation under the direction of one of the party organizations'. This trifling difference of wording concealed the real and vital difference over the nature of the party. Lenin wanted a small, tight band of professional revolutionaries, Martov a looser and larger group of professionals and active amateur helpers. Lenin wanted to hasten the revolution by making the party as disciplined and responsive to the initiative of the leaders as possible, Martov by bringing into the party as many genuine workers for the cause as possible. In the party slang of the day Lenin was 'hard' and Martov 'soft'. Their respective supporters were called 'hards' and 'softs'. The voting on this amendment was close, but Martov, with the support of the *Bund* and the Economist votes, carried the day by 28 votes to 23.

Behind this lay a question that went very deep: the relation of the intellectual to the proletariat. It was common ground to all Marxists that the intensification of the class struggle would eventually produce the revolution, and that the class interest of the proletariat would make it the agent of the revolution. The task of the party was to make the proletariat conscious of its role by propaganda and agitation. It could form groups of workers and instruct them by word of mouth; it could write simple leaflets and pamphlets and give them to the workers who could read; in suitable circumstances it could encourage strikes, not merely to make material gains for the workers, but, more important, to strengthen their working-class solidarity and develop their proletarian consciousness. Clearly the intellectuals must initiate most of this work, and very likely take the lead on the spot. But once the movement was under way they were much less necessary: any intelligent and forceful worker could see the point of trade union activity and direct it, much better than a bourgeois intellectual. If that were the end of the story it would also be the end of the intellectual.

But it was not. There were two further facets of life and revolution which made the intellectual still indispensable: Russia and its government; and the socialist content of revolution. Russia was a very large country. Its government still regarded trade union activity as criminal, and its police, though incompetent, were always on the look out for working-class agitators and for the agents of subversive political parties. In these circumstances it was clearly impossible for workers inside Russia to organize a national trade union movement, still less a workers' political party. Furthermore the revolution was to be a socialist revolution. It would not only overthrow capitalism and free the proletariat from its chains, but it would inaugurate the transition to a socialist society. Of this revolution the proletariat was the agent. But it was not a sufficient agent in itself. Its self-interest was by itself enough to make it fight the capitalists for its livelihood and welfare, even for effective power in the factory and in the state, but it would not make it fight for socialism. The proletariat would not of itself, spontaneously and intuitively, know socialism and formulate it in a programme of action and in a set of institutions capable of sustaining the socialist society. Here was the continuing role of the intellectuals: to permeate the entire proletariat with Marxist socialist knowledge; to draft the party programme; and to control and direct the party in action.

But this involved a certain tension between the intellectual and the proletariat. Lenin understood this very well. In *One Step Forward, Two Steps Back* he quoted with approval a passage from Kautsky on this theme:

> The problem ... that interests us so keenly today is the *antagonism between the intelligentsia* and the proletariat. ... This antagonism is a social one, it relates to classes, not to individuals. The individual intellectual, like the individual capitalist, may identify himself with the proletariat in its class struggle. When he does, he changes his character too. It is not *this type* of intellectual, who is still an exception among his class, that we shall mainly speak of in what follows. Unless otherwise stated, *I shall use the word intellectual to mean only the common run of intellectual who takes the stand of bourgeois society*, and who is characteristic of the intelligentsia as a *class*. This *class* stands in a certain *antagonism* to the proletariat.
>
> This antagonism differs, however, from the antagonism between labour and capital. The intellectual is not a capitalist. True, his standard of life is bourgeois, and he must maintain it if he is not to become a pauper; but at the same time he is compelled to sell the product of his labour, and often his labour-power, and is himself often enough exploited and humiliated by the capitalist. Hence

the intellectual does not stand in any economic antagonism to the proletariat. But his status of life and his conditions of labour are not proletarian, and this gives rise to a certain antagonism in sentiments and ideas.

As an isolated individual, the proletarian is nothing. His whole strength, his whole progress, all his hopes and expectations are derived from *organisation*, from systematic action in conjunction with his fellows. He feels big and strong when he forms part of a big and strong organism. This organism is the main thing for him; the individual in comparison means very little. The proletarian fights with the utmost devotion as part of the anonymous mass, without prospect of personal advantage or personal glory, doing his duty in any post he is assigned to with a voluntary discipline which pervades all his feelings and thoughts.

Quite different is the case of the intellectual. He does not fight by means of power, but by argument. His weapons are his personal knowledge, his personal ability, his personal convictions. He can attain to any position at all only through his personal qualities. Hence the freest play for his individuality seems to him the prime condition for successful activity. It is only with difficulty that he submits to being a part subordinate to the whole, and then only from necessity, not from inclination. He recognises the need for discipline only for the mass, not for the elect minds. And of course he counts himself among the latter. . . .

Kautsky concludes his argument by contrasting Stockmann in Ibsen's *An Enemy of the People*, 'the type of the intellectual [who] regards a "compact majority" as a monster that must be overthrown', with Karl Liebknecht, who 'marched cheerfully with the rank and file, worked in any post he was assigned to, subordinated himself whole-heartedly to our great cause, and despised the feeble whining about the suppression of his individuality which the intellectual . . . is prone to indulge in when he happens to be in the minority'. . . .[5]

Lenin applies this analysis to Martov and the other Menshevik leaders and rubs it in in the preface to *One Step Forward, Two Steps Back*:

As a matter of fact, the entire position of the opportunists in organisational questions already began to be revealed in the controversy over Paragraph 1: their advocacy of a diffuse, not strongly welded, Party organization; their hostility to the idea (the 'bureaucratic' idea) of building the Party from the top downwards, starting from the Party Congress and the bodies set up by it; their tendency to proceed from the bottom upwards, allowing every professor,

[5] *Collected Works*, Vol. 7, 324–6

every high-school student and 'every striker' to declare himself a member of the Party; their hostility to the 'formalism' which demands that a Party member should belong to one of the organisations recognised by the Party; their leaning towards the mentality of the bourgeois intellectual, who is only prepared to 'accept organisational relations platonically'; their penchant for opportunist profundity and for anarchistic phrases; their tendency towards autonomism as against centralism—in a word, all that is now blossoming so luxuriantly in the new *Iskra*, and is helping more and more to reveal fully and graphically the initial error.[6]

Lenin had lost control of the congress and all his plans for the organization of the party might have come to nothing but for an unexpected stroke of luck. The *Bund* and Economist delegates walked out: the *Bund* because the congress had rejected its claims; the Economists because they accepted the congress's vote that the League of Russian Revolutionary Social-Democrats was the sole representative abroad of the party, and drew the conclusion that the organization that they represented no longer existed. By this walk-out the position was reversed at a blow. Martov and his supporters were now in a minority and Lenin had the whip-hand.

He used it to make absolutely sure of what he called 'organizational consolidation'. It had been agreed already by the congress that the central direction of the party should consist of three bodies: the Central Committee in Russia, the Central Organ (*Iskra*) published abroad, and the Central Council abroad. The Central Council was to consist of five members: two elected by the Central Committee, two by the Central Organ, and one by the congress itself. The Council could do its work on the basis of majority decisions, for there would always be at least a 3:2 majority. But it was highly desirable for its members to be usually and genuinely in agreement to give unity and drive to the party. Lenin had already experienced much frustration on the editorial board of *Iskra* because it consisted of six members who frequently divided evenly, and before the congress the board had decided to invite a definite seventh person to join it should it be necessary to make a formal statement to the congress. But Lenin had also been busy formulating a plan to get rid of this frustration, a plan which he had circulated to other members of the board and of the party, which he called the plan for 'two trios'. These were a trio constituting the Central Committee and a trio constituting the

Central Organ. There was no difficulty about the committee trio, but there was about the other, for it involved not only party policy but old loyalties and affections. For the editors who would almost certainly be dropped were Akselrod, Vera Zasulich and Potresov; they were the least energetic and efficient, and the first two the least in sympathy with Lenin's policy, but they were nevertheless two of 'the founding fathers'. Many members thought this plan a too ruthless act of impiety.

But Lenin persisted in it. Not only was he determined to use his majority in the congress created by the walk-out, but he even implicated Martov in the plan. In the course of his speech on the election of the editorial board of *Iskra* he produced a draft of the plan, 'with Martov's corrections in red ink', which he alleged proved Martov's approval of the plan of the two trios. Martov denied this 'with almost hysterical vehemence'[7] and never forgave Lenin what he regarded as a piece of sharp practice. It is not quite clear from the draft what Martov had agreed. What is quite clear is that Lenin not only accepted Martov's main point against the plan but gloried in it. As he put it:

> ... I have no intention of denying Martov's assertion of the 'political significance' of the step we took in not endorsing the old editorial board. On the contrary, I fully and unreservedly agree with Comrade Martov that this step is of great political significance —only not the significance which Martov ascribes to it. He said that it was an act in a struggle for influence on the Central Committee in Russia. I go further than Martov. The whole activity of *Iskra* as a separate group has hitherto been a *struggle* for influence; but now it is a matter of something more, namely, the *organizational consolidation* of this influence, and not only a struggle for it. How profoundly Comrade Martov and I differ *politically* on this point is shown by the fact that he *blames* me for this wish to influence the Central Committee, whereas I count it *to my credit* that I strove and still strive to consolidate this influence by organizational means ... What would be the point of all our work, of all our efforts, if they ended in the same old struggle for influence, and not in its complete acquisition and consolidation? Yes, Comrade Martov is absolutely right: the step we have taken is undoubtedly *a major political step* showing that one of the trends now to be observed has been chosen for the future work of our Party. And I am not at all frightened by the dreadful words [used by Martov in his speech] a 'state of siege in the Party', 'emergency laws against particular individuals and groups', etc. We not only can but we must create a 'state of siege' in relation

[7] Schapiro, *The Communist Party of the Soviet Union* (1963), 51

to unstable and vacillating elements, and all our Party Rules, the whole system of centralism now endorsed by the Congress are nothing but a 'state of siege' in respect to the numerous sources of *political vagueness*. It is special laws, even if they are emergency laws, that are needed as measures against vagueness, and the step taken by the Congress has correctly indicated the political direction to be followed, by having created a firm basis for *such* laws and *such* measures.[8]

The congress endorsed Lenin's policy and elected his supporters to the Central Committee. It also appointed Plekhanov, Lenin and Martov to the Central Organ. The resolutions on these two matters were both carried *nem. con.*, as Martov and his supporters abstained from voting; and Martov himself announced that 'the decisions of the Congress are lawful'. But in fact a split had taken place, and the congress was fairly evenly divided into a majority and a minority. From these words the two groups got their nicknames, Bolsheviks (majoritarians) and Mensheviks (minoritarians). The split was never really healed and the names stuck.

*One Step Forward, Two Steps Back*, written in Geneva between February and May 1904, betrays the state of tension Lenin was in when he wrote it: it is ultra-polemical in argument and shrill in tone. The period after the end of the London congress was confused and exhausting. Most members of the party in Russia and abroad thought the split temporary and unnecessary and wanted it healed as quickly as possible. Lenin did not agree. He thought the split was on a fundamental matter. He had a clear vision of what the Party should be; and he was determined that it should be this and that he should control it. This meant a sharp conflict between different parts of his nature: between his affections and his pugnacious temperament and his love of intellectual rigour. He was fonder of Martov than of any of the other revolutionaries. Krupskaya records his delight in July 1917 when Martov took a 'correct' line, 'not because it was of any advantage to the Bolsheviks, but because Martov was acting worthily—as behoved a revolutionary'. And when he was already seriously ill, Lenin said to Krupskaya 'somewhat dolefully, "Martov is dying too, so they say" '.[9]

But Krupskaya also quotes a passage from *One Step Forward, Two Steps Back*, where Lenin wrote:

[8] *Collected Works*, Vol. 6, 507–8
[9] N. K. Krupskaya, *op. cit.*, Vol. 1, 108–9

I cannot help remembering a conversation of mine at that Congress [the London congress] with one of the 'Centre' delegates. 'What a depressing atmosphere prevails at our Congress,' he complained to me. 'All this fierce fighting, this agitation one against the other, these sharp polemics, this uncomradely attitude!' 'What a fine thing our Congress is,' I replied to him. 'Opportunity for open fighting. Opinions expressed. Tendencies revealed. Groups defined. Hands raised. A decision taken. A stage passed through. Forward! That's what I like! That's life! It is something different from the endless, wearying intellectual discussions, which finish, not because people have solved the problem, but simply because they have got tired of talking.' The comrade of the 'Centre' looked on me as though perplexed and shrugged his shoulders. We had spoken in different languages.

'That quotation sums up Ilyich to a "t",' she adds.[10]

Various attempts were made to heal the split but they all broke on the rock of Lenin's intransigence. The congress had adopted the party programme and rules and that was that. It was a matter of principle to obey the congress decisions and work on their basis. But also Lenin had won and he was determined not to allow the ex-editors back on to the board of *Iskra* and so give them an influence on policy and the chance to turn the Central Organ into a rival of the Central Committee. When in October 1903, Plekhanov had come over to the conciliationists and was putting pressure on Lenin to agree to the ex-editors rejoining the *Iskra* board, Lenin brought things to a head by resigning himself. Plekhanov at once brought back Martov and company, and in the next number of *Iskra* wrote an article, criticizing Lenin, entitled *What is not to be done*.

Lenin immediately declared war on *Iskra* and wrote endless, acrimonious attacks on it and all its works. He also tried to retain his grip on the Central Committee as a weapon in the fight, but this too eluded him. By the summer of 1904 his nerves were in shreds and in July Krupskaya and he went off into the mountains with their rucksacks for a month. This restored his balance, and in August, at a little village on the Lac de Bré, he began making plans for the next step. He decided to set up a Bolshevik committee, to start a new paper as a rival to *Iskra* and to press for a new congress to endorse his line.

When he got back to Geneva in September he began to put

[10] N. K. Krupskaya, *op. cit.*, Vol. 1, 102–3

this plan into action. Before the end of the year he had got a Bureau of Majority Committees set up, with the task of preparing and convening a third congress of the party, and announced the publication of a Bolshevik newspaper probably to be called *Vpered* ('Forward').

# 4  *The 1905 revolution*

It was at the beginning of January 1905 that it became apparent that there was a revolutionary situation in Russia. The war against Japan, that had begun the previous February, had been a series of defeats, and on 2 January Port Arthur fell after a siege of five months. At the same time strikes broke out in St Petersburg and other towns, and those in St Petersburg merged into a general strike. On 9 January a huge crowd of workers led by Father Georgi Gapon went in procession to the Winter Palace to present a petition to the tsar. When it reached the square in front of the palace, troops opened fire and killed several hundred people. These shots riddled not only the bodies of the workers but the image of the tsar as the 'little father' of his people, and created the opportunity for revolutionary action.

Lenin in Geneva immediately recognized the symbolic importance of 'Bloody Sunday', as it came to be called, in two articles in *Vpered* under the headings, *The Beginning of Revolution in Russia* and *Revolutionary Days*. He accepted Father Gapon as a sincere Christian Socialist and quoted his appeal to the Russian people.

> 'Comrades, Russian workers!' Father Georgi Gapon wrote, after that bloody day ... 'We have no longer a tsar. Today a river of blood divides him from the Russian people. It is time for the Russian workers to begin the struggle for the people's freedom without him. For today I give you my blessing. Tomorrow I shall be with you. Today I am busy working for our cause.'
> This is not Father Georgi Gapon speaking. This is the voice of those thousands upon thousands, of those millions upon millions of Russian workers and peasants who until now could believe naively and blindly in the Tsar Father and seek alleviation for their unbearable lot from Our Father the Tsar 'himself'. . . .[1]

The Russian people was stirring and what Lenin hoped and believed rapidly came to pass. Both the lawyers and students in St Petersburg protested to the tsar against the government's

[1] *Collected Works*, Vol. 8, 111–2

behaviour and declared their sympathy with the workers. The war went from bad to worse. The Russian armies suffered a crushing defeat at Mukden in February and after the naval disaster of Tsushima in May there was no further hope; the fighting virtually came to an end and the morale of the soldiers in the Far East began to collapse. The strikes spread, especially to railway workers. From the beginning of March there was massive unrest among the peasantry amounting to revolt in a number of provinces. There was revolt in Finland, Poland and the Baltic provinces. At the weekly meeting of his ministers on 18 February the tsar remarked to Bulygin, the minister of the interior, that they seemed to fear a revolution; to which Bulygin replied: 'The revolution has already begun.'

The autocracy was frightened into making concessions, but its conduct reveals the increasingly contradictory position it was in as well as the weak and hesitant character of Nicholas II. At the beginning of February he had ordered Bulygin to draft proposals for summoning representatives of the Russian people to take part in the deliberations of his council, but almost at the same time the Grand Duke Serge was murdered; the result was that at the same council on 18 February he issued the Bulygin Rescript announcing his intention of summoning the worthiest and most trusted representatives of the people to advise him on reform, and a manifesto 'on the disorders' drafted by Pobedonostsev that called for the annihilation of Russia's internal and external enemies and for God's blessing on the strengthening of the autocracy. This was only a dramatic instance of a persistent state of affairs. For while the tsar appointed mildly reformist ministers of the interior like Svyatopolk-Mirsky and Bulygin, he gave his confidence to the staunchly conservative General Dmitri Trepov, whom he appointed Governor-General of St Petersburg and associate minister of the interior with special privileges and direct access to himself.

In this revolutionary situation everyone was laying his plans. The *zemstvos* were organizing themselves to put pressure on the tsar to grant a real constitution. The various professional unions were negotiating to unite, an aim which they achieved in May with the Union of Unions. The peasant representatives were organizing an All-Russian Peasant Union, whose first congress met in Moscow at the end of July. The different nationalist organizations were considering how best to turn the weakness of the autocracy to their advantage.

The Social-Democrats were not behindhand. Trotsky went at once to Russia, where he lived under an assumed name and put out a steady stream of propaganda for the socialist cause. The Menshevik leaders remained in exile and held a conference to declare the party line on the situation. Lenin did likewise. He made no attempt to go to Russia and there is nothing in his writings to suggest that he was impatient to get there. He presumably thought the risk of arrest too great to justify his going. He could do more for the cause from outside.

But, characteristically, what he wanted was action. He criticized the Menshevik line for being mere description, when what was needed was a call to action. He quotes from the resolution of the Menshevik conference:

> The final abolition of the entire regime of monarchy and social estates in the process of mutual struggle between the elements of politically emancipated bourgeois society for the satisfaction of their social interests and for direct acquisition of power—such is the task in this new phase which the objective conditions of social development spontaneously evoke.
>
> Therefore, a provisional government that would undertake to carry out the tasks of this revolution, bourgeois in its historical nature, would, in regulating the mutual struggle between antagonistic classes of a nation in the process of emancipation, not only have to advance revolutionary development, but also to combat factors in that development threatening the foundations of the capitalist system.[2]

He labels this a mere *description* of a process and not a call to action; and contrasts it with the resolution of the Third Party Congress (Bolshevik) held in London in April.

Lenin had quickly made up his mind that a new congress was necessary to define party tactics in the new situation, and he had busied himself convening it and drafting resolutions to put before it. He was concerned to give practical guidance to revolutionaries on the spot and to sharpen the differences with the Mensheviks, partly from his love of a sharp clash and partly from a clear-sighted view that the Bolsheviks could in this way exploit the situation tactically to their great advantage. All but one of the resolutions dealt with specific aspects of the revolutionary situation: and this last resolution defined the authority of the Central

[2] *Collected Works*, Vol. 9, 38–9

Committee of the party over the local committees, establishing what the resolution called a single centre.

The first resolution called for an armed uprising and laid down the role of the party as explaining it to the workers, arming them for it and planning its execution. This pointedly contradicted *Iskra's* contention that 'a people's revolution cannot be timed in advance'. To this Lenin replied that a strike and an uprising can be timed, though both arise out of 'revolutions in social relations that have already taken place'.[3]

The second resolution committed the party to joining a provisional revolutionary government to prevent a return to autocracy and to defend the independent class interests of the proletariat. This was based on the strongly held belief that tsarism was identified with autocracy and feudalism and that its overthrow was an essential part of the bourgeois revolution: if the tsar kept his throne and there was a constitutional monarchy, as the liberals wished, it would be a bastard government and not even the bourgeois revolution would have attained its objectives. As a Marxist Lenin wanted this as a necessary preliminary to the socialist revolution, but he wanted also to take part in the government to push it towards the future and force it to take as many practical measures as possible in the interests of the proletariat.

The third resolution dealt with the peasant movement. Lenin grasped more quickly and firmly than most people the significance of the peasant uprisings. If they spread all over Russia and kept up their momentum they would lend irresistible force to the blow to knock the tsar off his throne. It was therefore the party's first duty to back them to the hilt and to make the proletariat understand the vital part the peasants had to play in the revolution. On the other hand the peasants were not wholly bourgeois or wholly proletarian, nor were they a homogeneous class. Lenin regarded the larger part, the small landholders, as petty bourgeois, and the wage labourers as proletarians. The party was to work for revolutionary peasant committees to assume the task of directing the revolutionary movement locally, and within these committees to organize representatives to work for the peasant proletariat and push the revolution in the direction of confiscation of all landed estates and of nationalization (itself not at this stage

[3] *Collected Works*, Vol. 8, 153

carefully defined). These revolutionary peasant committees were
clearly in his mind replicas in miniature of the provisional revolu
tionary government in St Petersburg.

Finally, the fourth resolution urged the party to create as many
local proletarian organizations as possible and promote as many
local proletarians as possible to lead these organizations. The
intellectuals in the party should concentrate on developing in
them full, revolutionary Social-Democratic consciousness.

Lenin elaborated these points in a long pamphlet written with
great gusto and buoyancy, published in July: *Two Tactics o*
*Social-Democracy in the Democratic Revolution*. The main argument is
that only a provisional revolutionary government can guarantee
maximum freedom: the provisional government is 'the organ of a
popular rising', its formal purpose to convene a constituent
assembly and 'the content of its activities ... the immediate
implementation of the minimum programme of proletarian
democracy ...'.[4] Accordingly the party should strive in every
way to have it set up, and not be content to see it 'emerge from a
victorious popular insurrection'[5] as the Mensheviks proposed
Furthermore the party should join in its deliberations in order
to exert the maximum possible influence on the course of
the revolution. Here again was a contrast with the Menshevik
line, which was that it was correct for the bourgeois revolution to
be led by an exclusively bourgeois government: the Social
Democratic party would only do itself harm by entering such a
government and could exert a far stronger and better influence on
the revolution from outside.

In an epilogue Lenin posed the question: 'what is revolution
from the Marxist point of view?' and went on to give the answer

> The forcible demolition of the obsolete political superstructure
> the contradiction between which and the new relations of production
> have caused its collapse at a certain moment. The contradiction
> between the autocracy and the entire structure of capitalist Russia
> and all the needs of her bourgeois-democratic development has
> now caused its collapse. .... The slogan 'the democratic dictatorship
> of the proletariat and the peasantry' ... defines the classes upon
> which the new 'builders' of the new superstructure can and must
> rely, the character of the new superstructure (a 'democratic' as
> distinct from a socialist dictatorship), and how it is to be built

[4] *Collected Works*, Vol. 9, 28
[5] *Ibid.*, 74

(dictatorship, i.e. the forcible suppression of resistance by force and the arming of the revolutionary classes of the people).[6]

Lenin backed up his argument with Marx's strictures on Camphausen for not acting dictatorially in 1848 and on the Frankfurt national assembly for its feebleness.

Lenin wound up the main part of the pamphlet by quoting a saying of Marx: 'Revolutions are the locomotives of history', to which he added: 'Revolutions are festivals of the oppressed and the exploited.'[7] Here is Lenin's whole belief. Revolutions are spontaneous, active and creative. But if they are not to run into the sand they need control and direction. Lenin was determined that the party should provide the engine-driver.

Throughout the summer and early autumn the unrest intensified. Army morale deteriorated so rapidly that it looked as if the tsar might not be able to rely on the troops. In June the sailors of the battleship *Potemkin* mutinied. In August Bulygin published his proposals for a purely consultative assembly elected by indirect franchise. These were already out of date and their publication a sign of how pathetically out of touch the government was with public opinion. At the same time it decreed the autonomy of the universities, which meant that a stream of students and workers poured into the universities and used them as revolutionary stamping-grounds. A joint congress of representatives of *zemstvos* and the Union of Unions met in September to reject the Bulygin proposals and reaffirm their demand for a real, democratic constitution.

On 8 October began a nationwide railway strike which led on to general strikes in many towns including St Petersburg. Chaos loomed. The tsar gave in and appointed Witte as president of the council of ministers and, in effect, a sort of prime minister. Witte had been a highly successful minister of finance, who had been responsible for balancing the Russian budget and raising the huge loans on the French money market that were necessary for industrial development and for building the Trans-Siberian railway. He had just returned to Russia after conducting with great skill the negotiations that led to the signing of the Treaty of Portsmouth, which brought the war with Japan to an end. He was a man of great ability and power of decision, loyally devoted

[6] *Ibid.*, 128
[7] *Ibid.*, 113

to the service of the tsar, but he never won the trust of the tsar or of the court.

When he took office in October Witte wrote a memorandum on the situation which confirms in amplified form what Lenin had written at the end of May after the disaster of Tsushima:

> Everything [wrote Lenin] is up in arms against the autocracy: the wounded national pride of the big and petty bourgeoisie, the outraged pride of the army, the bitter feeling over the loss of hundreds of thousands of young lives in a senseless military adventure, the resentment against the embezzlement of hundreds of millions from public funds, the fears of an inevitable financial collapse and a protracted economic crisis as a result of the war, and the dread of a formidable people's revolution ...[8]

> A general feeling of profound discontent with the existing order [wrote Witte] was the most apparent symptom of the corruption with which the social and political life of Russia was infested. It was this feeling that united all the classes of the population. They all joined in a demand for radical political reforms, but the manner in which the different social groups visioned the longed-for changes varied with each class of people.

> The upper classes, the nobility, were dissatisfied and impatient with the Government. They were not averse to the idea of limiting the Emperor's autocratic powers, but with a view to benefiting their own class. Their dream was an aristocratic constitutional monarchy. The merchants and captains of industry, the rich, looked forward to a constitutional monarchy of the bourgeois type and dreamed of the leadership of capital and of a mighty race of Russian Rothschilds. The 'intelligentzia' [sic] i.e. members of various liberal professions, hoped for a constitutional monarchy, which was eventually to result in a bourgeois republic modelled upon the pattern of the French state. The students, not only in the universities, but in the advanced high school grades, recognized no law—except the word of those who preached the most extreme revolutionary and anarchistic theories. Many of the officials of the various governmental bureaus were against the régime they served, for they were disgusted with the shameful system of corruption which had grown to such gigantic proportions during the reign of Nicholas II. The *zemstvo* and municipal workers had long before declared that safety lay in the adoption of a constitution. As for the workmen, they were more concerned about filling their stomachs with more food than had been their wont. For this reason they revelled in all manner of socialistic schemes of state organization. They fell completely under the sway of the revolutionists and rendered assistance without stint wherever there was need of physical force.

> Finally, the majority of the Russian people, the peasantry, were

anxious to increase their land holdings and to do away with the unrestrained arbitrary actions on the part of the higher landed class and of the police throughout the extent of its hierarchy, from the lowest gendarme to the provincial governor. The peasants' dream was an autocratic Czar, but a people's Czar, pledged to carry out the principle proclaimed in the reign of emperor Alexander II, to wit, the emancipation of the peasants with land in violation of the sacredness of property rights. The peasants were inclined to relish the idea of a constitutional monarchy and the socialistic principles as they were formulated by the labourite party, which party emphasized labour and the notion that labour alone, especially physical labour, is the foundation of all right. The peasants, too, were ready to resort to violence in order to obtain more land, and, in general, to better their intolerable condition.

It is noteworthy that the nobility was willing to share the public pie with the middle class, but neither of these classes had a sufficiently keen eye to notice the appearance on the historical stage of a powerful rival, who was numerically superior to both, and possessed the advantage of having nothing to lose. No sooner did this hitherto unnoticed class, the proletariat, approach the pie than it began to roar like a beast which stops at nothing to devour its prey.[9]

Witte concluded from his analysis of the situation that there were only two alternatives: a constitution that took real heed of the popular movement or a dictatorship of suppression. He placed them before the tsar. Nicholas hesitated but finally signed, with slight modifications, the manifesto that Witte had drafted. The October Manifesto was greeted with joy. It foreshadowed a real constitution: it granted the basic freedoms of person, conscience, speech, meeting and association; it suggested a widening of the franchise; and laid down that no law would be effective without the sanction of the Duma (parliament) and that the people's representatives would have effective control of the administration.

But the granting of a constitution did not mean that the tsar had been converted to the idea of a constitutional monarchy; still less the tsarina or the court. Trepov kept his post at the ministry of the interior and the confidence of the tsar; and on the very day on which the October Manifesto appeared he pasted up posters threatening the citizens of St Petersburg in case of trouble in the streets. The tsar had had to make concessions to keep his throne, but it was only a matter of time before troops were in

[9] *Memoirs of Count Witte* (1921), 266–8

action to crush the risings. Lenin's summary of the situation was much to the point: on the one hand—the Manifesto, Witte, a constitution, on the other—Trepov, shootings, prisons full, Black Hundred pogroms.[10]

Meanwhile, on 13 October, about thirty deputies from factories in St Petersburg had met in the Institute of Technology and set up the Soviet of Workers' Deputies. This is the first appearance of the Soviet (Committee), since made famous by the 1917 revolution and its name incorporated in the title of the Communist state: the Union of Soviet Socialist Republics (U.S.S.R.) The St Petersburg Soviet was a committee of representatives of the St Petersburg factories, by no means all of them factory workers. Its core was a number of workers who had been chosen by their fellows as deputies to the Shidlovsky Commission that the government had announced in January to investigate the grievances of the industrial workers in St Petersburg. In the event it never met, as the workers' deputies put forward terms for their participation unacceptable to the government. But the various independent organizations that had chosen deputies remained in being and it was they, and their deputies, who now in October constituted the Soviet.

Some of them had links with Social-Democracy, but rather with the Menshevik than the Bolshevik wing. The two dominant personalities, in turn chairmen of the Soviet, were both more or less independent: G. S. Khrustalev-Nosar, a radical lawyer, who had been prominent in the elections to the Shidlovsky Commission and had helped to organize the printers' union in St Petersburg and Moscow; and Trotsky, who had taken the 'hard' line at the Second Party Congress but had since co-operated to some extent with *Iskra*; after his return to Russia from his refuge in Finland he found in the Soviet an admirable field for his talents as an orator and organizer.

The Bolshevik attitude was reserved and suspicious. Once the Soviet had come into being and shown it would last for at least some time, the local Bolshevik leaders ordered party members to enter it and if possible capture it, or, if this proved impossible, to disrupt it. Lenin's attitude was different. Still in exile in Stockholm, he welcomed the Soviet as likely to provide what he

[10] The shady wing of the extreme reactionary movement, the Union of the Russian People, that was responsible for the pogroms.

*Lenin*

Lenin talking with a marcher in the May Day Demonstration in Red Square 1919.

*Lenin and Stalin, 1922*

*Sketches of Lenin by Leonid Pasternak,*
*the father of Boris Pasternak.*

*The Ulyanov family. Alexander standing between his mother and his father; Lenin sitting on extreme right.*

*Lenin and the St. Petersburg Union of Struggle for the Emancipation of the Working Class, 1895. Sitting (left to right): V. V. Starkov, G. M. Krzhizhanovsky, Lenin, Y. O. Martov (the Menshevik leader). Standing: A. L. Malchenko, P. K. Zaporozhets, A. A. Vaneyev.*

*Lenin speaking. On the right of the platform, Trotsky.*

*Lenin and A. A. Bogdanov playing chess on Capri, 1908. Gorky and his wi*
*look on.*

called 'a solid centre' and the embryo of a provisional revolutionary government, and told Bolsheviks to co-operate with other revolutionary groups even if they did not fully agree with them; though he admitted that his attitude was based only on newspaper reports and might be mistaken. After his arrival in St Petersburg at the beginning of November, Lenin approved the Soviet decision to reject an application of the anarchists for representation on the Soviet. One of his reasons for this was that the Soviet was not a labour parliament or organ of proletarian self-government (in which case it would only be right to admit anarchists), but 'a fighting organization for the achievement of definite aims'[11] which the anarchists did not share. Lenin regarded the Soviet as a weapon in the fight to overthrow the autocracy and to realize the bourgeois revolution, but he evidently did not regard it as the only weapon or the most important one. He attended a number of meetings of the executive committee and spoke once at a plenary session of the Soviet; but he devoted far more time and thought to the party and to the congress being planned to bring about party unity.

There was in fact an uncertainty about the role of the Soviet. On the one hand it sprang from and represented the workers of St Petersburg, on the other it contained leading revolutionaries like Trotsky. The workers on the whole wanted practical reforms like the eight hour day, the revolutionaries wanted revolution. The Soviet tried both lines. It backed the sailors' mutiny at Kronstadt and sent out agents to the provinces to organize the rising, but this last was a failure. It backed the workers' demand for the eight hour day by organizing another general strike for the end of October. This too was more or less a failure, and alienated middle class opinion: the atmosphere was much more favourable for the government to dissolve the Soviet. A Soviet resolution calling on all citizens not to pay taxes and to withdraw their savings provided Witte with an excellent ground for acting. He arrested Nosar on 26 November and the other members of the Soviet on 3 December.

The same day in Moscow there was a mutiny in one of the garrison regiments, the Rostov grenadiers; though this was over by the next morning, it led to a general rising. Meetings of the Moscow Soviet, of the Bolshevik and Menshevik wings of the

[11] *Collected Works*, Vol. 10, 72

C

party and of a congress of railwaymen's delegates that was in session all endorsed the rising, and there were meetings in all the factories which were stormily enthusiastic for the idea. It is quite clear that the rank and file were in a revolutionary mood and that pressure for a rising came from below. What is not so clear is how far this mood was spontaneous and how far stimulated by party agitators. The Social-Democratic Party was strong in Moscow, and especially the Bolshevik wing of it. Members of the party were prominent in the debate before the rising and in the rising itself, but the course of events makes a strong impression of lack of leadership and of formlessness. Men of the local party militia fought in small bands. Barricades appeared in the streets. There was much sniping. Troops remained loyal and did not come over to the revolutionaries as they had hoped. Fighting began on the 7th and was over by the 17th: the final stage was the storming of the working class suburb of Presnaya, now known as Red Presnaya, where the revolutionaries were led by a Bolshevik, Sedoy, and an anonymous Social-Revolutionary known by his nickname, 'The Bear'.

This was the turning point in the revolution. There were still risings in various parts of Russia and there was still danger from the unrest in the armies of the Far East. But the back of the revolution was broken and the government was regaining control. The scene of action contracted from the whole of Russia to the floor of the Duma called into being by the October Manifesto.

# 5 *The aftermath, 1906-1907*

It was not immediately clear to any of the Social-Democrats that the revolution had in fact failed. Until at least the spring of 1907 they believed that the Moscow defeat was only temporary and that another revolutionary wave would overwhelm the autocracy. They were accordingly preoccupied with the correct tactics in this situation. The Mensheviks, true to their belief that the revolution was essentially bourgeois, were in favour of co-operating with the Duma and taking part in the elections for it. They did not regard the Duma as satisfactory in its present form or value it for itself, but they thought it would be fundamentally hostile to the government and, under continuous pressure from the masses, would be able to effect the overthrow of the autocracy and initiate a true liberal-bourgeois regime.

Lenin and the Bolsheviks disagreed. They thought that any Duma elected under the existing law was bound to be fundamentally friendly to the monarchy. It might indeed transform the autocracy into a so-called constitutional monarchy, but this would be a sham: behind a parliamentary facade the tsar, his ministers and the governing class would continue to exercise real power. More immediately important, taking part in the elections would distract the workers and peasants from the urgent task: to keep up the revolutionary pressure by constant action. Lenin therefore came out for a boycott of the elections. He devoted much of his writing at this time to arguing this case and much of his time to organizing partisan combat activities.

The main purpose of these activities was to weaken the army, the police and the other agents of the government, and so prepare the way for its overthrow. But they also served to train the participants in direct action and so fit them to lead the masses in the rapidly approaching climax of the revolution. Some of the actions brought in money too. Combat groups staged a number of bank hold-ups: the most successful were at the Bank of Mutual Mercantile Credit in Moscow in March 1906, which netted

875,000 roubles, and at the State Bank at Tiflis in Georgia in June 1907, where the haul was 341,000 roubles. 'The confiscated funds', wrote Lenin, 'go partly into the treasury of the Party, partly for the special purpose of arming and preparing for an uprising, and partly for the maintenance of persons engaged in the struggle.'[1] Other sources of money were forging bank-notes, and gifts and legacies from rich businessmen.

The most notorious case of this is the so-called Schmitt Case. Nicholas Schmitt, a Moscow business man and Social-Democrat supporter, committed suicide in 1906 and left his money to the party. As this happened at the moment when the party had just achieved formal unity at the Stockholm Congress, with a Menshevik majority, this meant that the money would effectively be at the disposal of the Mensheviks. Lenin was determined to prevent this. So he fixed up a marriage between Schmitt's elder daughter and a Bolshevik lawyer, and then claimed the money on her behalf. The claim was successful but the husband proceeded to hand over to the party only a little of the money. Thereupon Lenin married another Bolshevik to the younger daughter, who then demanded and gained her share of the inheritance and duly handed it over to the party. Not content with this coup, Lenin's agent Victor threatened the elder daughter and her husband with violence unless they handed over more of their share.

This ruthless and unscrupulous conduct shows very clearly that Lenin and the Bolsheviks thought that any methods and tactics were fair in war. It also shows his utter disregard for party discipline. For the Stockholm Congress had condemned partisan actions and expropriations, as the hold-ups were called, forbidden party members to take part in them and ordered the special combat groups attached to party organizations to be dissolved. Lenin took no notice whatever of this resolution.

While the congress was in session in April 1906 the elections for the Duma took place and the first results began to come in. From these it was clear that large numbers of workers had ignored the order to boycott the elections and had managed to elect several Social-Democrats and almost a hundred vaguely 'Labour' deputies. Furthermore, the elections had not yet taken place in the Caucasus where the local party, largely Menshevik in colour, was known to be conducting a vigorous campaign and to stand a good

[1] *Collected Works*, Vol. 11, 216

chance of getting a number of its candidates home. This situation affected the attitude of the Bolsheviks at the Congress. They voted against the resolution to participate in the Duma and to form a Social-Democratic group in it, but they split on whether to take part in the elections that had not yet been held: eleven of their delegates voted against this too, but sixteen abstained and Lenin and sixteen others voted for it.

The Duma met on 27 April and it very quickly became apparent that there was a great gulf of incomprehension and distrust between it and the tsar and his ministers. In particular their views on the compulsory redistribution of land were diametrically opposed. On 20 June the government put out a statement of its land policy firmly rejecting compulsory redistribution. This stung the Duma into issuing a proclamation to the Russian people declaring that the land question could not be solved without the co-operation of the Duma and appealing to them to wait peacefully for legislation on the subject. The government chose to regard this as a deliberate challenge to its authority, and dissolved the Duma on 9 July.

The Duma had achieved nothing. But it had shown itself independent and highly critical of the government. This altered Lenin's attitude to it. Still convinced that the revolution had not reached its climax and that the most vital activity was organizing armed uprising, he now thought that parliamentary activity was a useful adjunct to this, and came out in favour of conducting a vigorous, independent Social-Democrat campaign in the elections for a second Duma held in February 1907, and for organizing the Social-Democratic deputies elected to the Duma in the most effective way possible. As he put it:

> Marxism differs from all other socialist theories in the remarkable way it combines complete scientific sobriety in the analysis of the objective state of affairs and the objective course of evolution with the most emphatic recognition of the importance of revolutionary energy, revolutionary creative genius, and revolutionary initiative of the masses—and also, of course, of individuals, groups, organizations, and parties that are able to discover or achieve contact with one or another class.[2]

Therefore there is a need to foster revolutionary devotion to the great revolutionary 'moments' of history and to build up

[2] *Collected Works*, Vol. 13, 36

revo luionary traditions, but it is all the more important not to make a fetish of a particular mode of action (in this case the boycott) taken out of its historic context. Any mode of action is possible, as is any place: 'in a pigsty if necessary'.

The Social-Democratic party did well in the elections and won 65 seats against eighteen in the first Duma. But the relations between the Duma and the government were quite as bad as they had been in the first Duma. The new chief minister Stolypin made himself bitterly unpopular by his methods of stamping out the remains of the revolution. He set up field courts-martial with power to impose and execute the death sentence on the spot. This was something peculiarly abhorrent to Russians, who took any amount of casual violence and brutality, including even beating to death, but were shocked to the core by the formal imposition of the death penalty and by its formal execution. These courts-martial had executed 683 death sentences by April 1907.

Stolypin also had a positive land policy which he was determined to push through at the earliest possible moment. The Duma, however, had other ideas and would not help him. So he seized on an alleged Social-Democratic plot on the tsar's life to dissolve the Duma on 3 June 1907. He then unconstitutionally altered the election laws in favour of the landowners and rich business men in order to ensure a docile Duma in future. This measure and the dissolution were violations of the Fundamental Laws of 1906. Stolypin's action was a *coup d'état* and was so regarded at the time.

In analysing the revolutionary changes of the period 1905–8 in an article in *Proletary No. 38*, Lenin put first Stolypin's land policy, which he described as agrarian Bonapartism. By this he meant that it was a dictated policy and not a democratic one springing from the grass roots, and that, like Napoleon's, it was designed to create a class of peasant landowners who would be staunch supporters of the existing social order. He went on to say that a 'Black Hundred' Duma had replaced the old, rigged local bodies (the *zemstvos*), for the Duma was unconstitutional and the government had flagrantly gerrymandered the franchise to keep power in the hands of the governing classes. This was so obvious that the Duma did not clothe the nakedness of the autocracy, but simply revealed it. This from Lenin's point of view was an advantage, as it meant that the class-party lines were more sharply drawn and, to his eye at least, the liberals were revealed as counter-revolutionary. Finally, millions of people had gained practical experience of revolution, and in due course this would be of the greatest value in bringing the revolution to a successful conclusion. When this would be it was impossible to say. The immediate task was to strengthen the party illegal organizations and to step up agitation.

Lenin showed his instinct and knowledge in fixing on Stolypin's land policy as the most important single result of the revolution. Like Marx and Engels, Lenin was extremely conscious of history and referred frequently in his writings to historical events, and especially to the great revolutionary 'moments' of the past like 1789 and 1848. Moreover he was extremely well read in the history of the French Revolution, and knew as well as any academic historian that one of Napoleon's strongest appeals to Frenchmen had been his guaranteeing security of title to all who had become owners of land in the course of the revolution, and that this had in fact established a predominant class of small peasant landowners in France. Lenin feared that Stolypin might do the same.

This was indeed the aim of Stolypin's policy. Like the majority of the landowners themselves he had become convinced that the system of communal land tenure was holding back Russian agriculture and as a result economic progress in general, and that the communes encouraged socialistic rather than individualistic ideas: so they were at the same time archaic and revolutionary bodies. What was wanted was to break them up and make it legally practicable for individual peasants to own and inherit land, and, wherever possible, to consolidate separated strips of land into a single, compact holding. The law of 9 November 1906 laid down that a peasant householder could claim ownership of all the pieces of land actually in his possession. Another law set up Land Organization Commissions to supervise the process thus initiated. (Further laws of 1910 and 1911 completed the process by abolishing communes in which there had been no redistribution since 1861 and forcibly converting the communal tenants into landowners with a hereditary title to their lands, and by consolidating the law on land allocation.)

All this applied only to the lands allocated to the peasants when they were emancipated in 1861. It did not touch land owned by the tsar, the state and the church (about 39 per cent of usable land in European Russia but largely forest) or land owned by private landowners (about 26 per cent as against about 35 per cent for allotment land). So it affected only a little over a third of all land.

Here Stolypin's policy differed sharply from that of all the opposition parties. They were all agreed on the confiscation of landed estates of all kinds and all except the Cadets (liberals) agreed that this should be without compensation. This was in accordance with the wishes of the peasants, who expressed themselves quite clearly through their deputies to the first and second Dumas. 'As for our being ignorant,' said one deputy, 'well, all we are asking is for some land in order, in our stupidity, to grub about in ...'[3]. The peasant needed land; he was desperate for it. 'And so, gentlemen, when the peasants sent me here they instructed me to champion their needs, to demand land and freedom for them, to demand that all state, crown, private and monastery lands be compulsorily alienated without compensation ... I want you to know ... that a hungry man cannot keep quiet when he sees that, in spite of his suffering, the government is on the side of the landed gentry. He cannot help demanding land, even if it is against the law; want compels him to demand it.'[4] He was determined to get rid of the landlord. 'The landlords', cried an SR peasant deputy, 'must be thrown off not because there are not enough "norms" [of land] to go round, but because the farmer does not want to be burdened with donkeys and leeches.'[5] But the peasant wanted land not only from a desperate need but from a sense of justice. 'Man is justice. When a man is born—it is just that he should live, and to live it is just that he should have the opportunity to earn his bread by his labour.'[6] Or, put even more forcefully by a peasant from the province of Saratov: 'Nowadays we talk of nothing but the land; again we are told: it is sacred, inviolable. In my opinion it cannot be inviolable; *if the people wish it, nothing can be inviolable.* (A voice from the Right: "Oh-ho!") Yes, oh-ho! ... Gentlemen of the nobility, do you think we do not know when you used us as stakes in your card games,

[3] *Collected Works*, Vol. 13, 381
[4] *Ibid.*, 383–4
[5] *Ibid.*, 392
[6] *Ibid.*, 395–6

when you bartered us for dogs? We do. It was all your sacred, inviolable property ... You stole the land from us ... The peasants who sent me here said this: The land is ours. We have come here not to buy it, but to take it.'[7]

All the opposition parties were further agreed that the individual peasants should occupy and farm the land. Where they differed was over who was to own it. The Cadets, true to their liberal principles wanted the peasants to be not only occupiers but owners: they proposed that the confiscated estates should be divided among the poor peasants. The SRs, who still believed it was possible to leap the bourgeois revolution and go straight from a feudal society to a socialist one, were alone in wanting to preserve the *mir*: it was after all the village community in its economic aspect and could be the agent of a revolutionary government just as much as of a tsarist one. The Social-Democrats thought this antiquarian nonsense. The revolution was essentially bourgeois. This was inevitable and right. The question was how to speed up the bourgeois phase of the revolution and, more narrowly, how the peasants could contribute to this speed-up. Here there was a split. The Mensheviks' primary thought was that the bourgeois phase must complete itself through industrialization, the agent of which was the liberal bourgeoisie. The best way to speed up the process was to overthrow the autocracy, for the bourgeoisie to form a bourgeois-capitalist government and for the proletariat to bring continuous pressure to bear on this government to hasten the transformation from capitalism to socialism. The peasantry played no part in this process, except in so far as the landless peasants could be considered proletarians. This reflected the Mensheviks' relative unconcern for the peasantry. But they were, after all, Russians as well as Social-Democrats and had worked out an articulate peasant policy. This was that the crown and church lands should be nationalized, i.e. owned and run by the central government, but that the private lands should be municipalized, i.e. owned and distributed to the individual farmers by the *zemstvos*. The idea behind this was to strengthen the local authorities *vis-à-vis* the central government and so provide stronger popular organs which could help to bring popular pressure to bear on the government in its bourgeois phase.

The Bolsheviks, largely under Lenin's guidance, were for

[7] *Ibid.*, 398

nationalization of both kinds of land. The state would become the sole landowner in Russia. The peasant would pay a rent to the state for his land and a steeply progressive land tax would equalize holdings and income. This in Lenin's eyes had the advantage of strengthening the state economically at the expense of the crown, the church and the private landowners. This would directly weaken the forces of autocracy and feudalism and indirectly strengthen the forces of capitalism by making farming rapidly more capitalistic and by tending to favour the development of industry at the expense of agriculture: a good thing at this stage as it must speed up the process of capitalization as a whole.

This policy also had tactical advantages in Lenin's eyes. More than any of the Social-Democratic leaders except Trotsky, he distrusted and despised the liberal bourgeois. He thought they were bound to be traitors: their class interest made them enemies of the autocracy and to that extent in the present situation revolutionaries; but as soon as they had achieved their objectives their class interest would equally make them turn on their working-class supporters and allies. They would have to do this willy-nilly. They were bound to be traitors. But Lenin also despised them. He despised them because they were bourgeois: their ideas and institutions and habits were Philistine; bourgeois society was Philistine through and through. He further despised them because they were weak and flabby: they were economically weak, because they were still so small a fraction of Russian society and because capitalism was still so relatively undeveloped in Russia; and they were spiritually flabby, because they had not the self-confidence born of an inherited culture and an inherited set of values, both deeply embedded in tradition.

By contrast Lenin, alone among his colleagues, set real store by the peasant. He remarked, it will be remembered, how strange it was that of all Russian writers Tolstoy, the aristocrat and the army officer, understood the peasant best of all. It is perhaps even stranger that Lenin, the son of a civil servant and a doctor's daughter, town-born and town-bred, should have understood the peasant so well. But so it was. He had a deep intuitive feeling for the peasant and for his feelings and beliefs. From the start of the revolution in 1905 he had grasped the fact that the peasantry was a revolutionary class and believed that it would be the most dependable ally of the proletariat in the revolution. He put his conviction into words in the slogan: *the revolutionary democratic dictatorship of the peasantry and the proletariat*. He embodied his conviction in his land policy: nationalization. The state should own the land; the peasant would farm it. The peasants locally would decide how to run things: how to grub about in the land. For this purpose there should be 'revolutionary-democratic land committees'. As far as possible these should be dominated by the poorest peasants, landless and therefore truly proletarian; with them would be the not-so-poor peasants, who owned a little land and possibly a horse, who were strictly not proletarian but petty bourgeois, but for the moment allies.

# 6   Party quarrels, 1908-1914

When the revolution was clearly finished and the government again in control, the revolutionary parties had to reconsider their positions. Lenin and the Mensheviks differed fundamentally. The Mensheviks came to the conclusion that an armed rising was for the time being out of the question and that it was therefore best to disband the illegal organizations of the party and concentrate on building up a strong legal party based on trade unions and other workers' groups, which would act energetically on behalf of the workers in the country and in the Duma. Lenin accused the Mensheviks of wanting to liquidate the revolutionary class struggle on the ideological plane and the illegal Social-Democratic Party on the plane of organization. He was convinced they were betraying Marxism and the proletariat, and would be seduced into playing the same role in the history of Russian Social-Democracy as had been played by Bernstein and the revisionists in Germany and by Millerand and other socialists, who had entered coalition ministries in France and ended up indistinguishable from their bourgeois colleagues. He labelled them 'liquidators' and attacked them relentlessly and with the utmost bitterness in innumerable articles and in his letters.

'Like men who know how to appreciate the fashion and the spirit of the times as accepted in liberal parlours,' the liquidators, writes Lenin, 'tittered condescendingly over this antiquated ... eccentric striving to formulate answers to vexed questions.'[1] They are 'conducting a campaign of slander against the Party Conference with an easy shamelessness which might well be envied by the Bulgarins and Burenins' (slanderous, reactionary journalists).[2] 'Potresov and Co. ... are *a model of unprincipledness* among Russian Marxists to-day.'[3] 'It is impossible to imagine a more disgusting, a more dishonest trick than the one played by L.

[1] *Collected Works*, Vol. 17, 147
[2] *Ibid.*, Vol. 18, 22
[3] *Ibid.*, Vol. 17, 75

Martov.'[4] Nor does Lenin even spare the revered Vera Zasulich. 'Vera Zasulich, like all liquidators, does her best to calumniate the Party ...'.[5] But it should be added that in using such words and phrases Lenin was only handling the common coin of controversy in party circles.

For these attacks Lenin was accused by many of his opponents of confusing the trivial with the important, of making mountains out of molehills. But the critics were surely wrong.

Lenin was self-righteous and abusive and at times slightly hysterical in tone, but he was right in thinking the cause of the quarrel a matter of substance. He believed emphatically that party doctrine and tactics must grow out of the actual social-economic situation. In 1910 he wrote:

> Our ... doctrine is not a dogma, but a guide to action ... by losing sight of it, we turn Marxism into something one-sided, distorted and lifeless; we deprive it of its lifeblood; we undermine its basic theoretical foundations—dialectics; the doctrine of historical development, all-embracing and full of contradictions; we undermine its connection with the definite practical tasks of the epoch, which may change with every new turn of history.[6]

One of the party's main tasks was to analyse the turn of history correctly. Both Bolshevik and Menshevik analyses took full note of the decisive change in Russian history, the rapidly accelerating process of industrialization; but they drew opposite conclusions from this observation. The Mensheviks thought that Russian history would follow more or less the path of German history since 1870, and therefore the history of the Russian Social-Democratic Party would follow more or less the path of its opposite number in Germany: the steady building-up despite capitalist opposition and government persecution of a parliamentary party capable at the decisive moment of overthrowing the bourgeois-capitalist regime and leading the proletariat to victory in the revolution. The Bolsheviks thought this an illusion. In Russia the autocracy was too strongly entrenched, as the events of 1905–7 had proved, and would remain strong enough to prevent capitalism developing a liberal-democratic form of state, as it had done in Western Europe, even in Germany. This would at the

[4] *Ibid.*, Vol. 17, 152
[5] *Ibid.*, Vol. 19, 394
[6] *Ibid*, Vol. 17, 39

same time prevent any form of gradual revolution and necessitate an armed, bloody revolution at the moment of revolutionary climax. It was not then clear which analysis was right. Nor is it now. For the first World War cut clean across the pattern of history and made it a matter for argument, even now, how the pattern would have developed had the war not occurred. What is however clear is that this is not a trivial matter; nor can the analysis of the pattern be trivial.

This has been recognized subsequently not only by Lenin but by one of the leading Mensheviks, Theodore Dan, who writes:

> The traditionally critical attitude of Menshevism towards the Party organization as it had taken shape historically, and the attempt to reform it, to make it, not only in its mass foundations but also in its apex, genuinely 'worker' (the Workers' Congress!) began to take the form, among broad circles of Russian 'legal' Mensheviks, of a special trend, both theoretically and organizationally amorphous, but completely definite in its attempt to break the evolutionary continuity of the Party and re-create it from the ground up, quite independently of its old and still surviving organizations and authorities. The intellectual inspirer of this trend, which the Bolsheviks called the 'liquidation' of the Party (this also gave rise to the polemical epithet 'liquidationism', accepted . . . by those it had been aimed at) was A. N. Potresov, editor of *Nasha Zarya*, who had stayed on in Russia. . . .[7]

At the time some Social-Democrats, of whom Trotsky was the most active, thought the quarrel was only one of personalities and organization, and made great efforts to end it. These were greeted with scorn and derision by Lenin, who went so far as to entitle one of his articles 'Judas Trotsky's Blush of Shame'.

But much more alarming to Lenin was a group of Bolsheviks, led by Bogdanov, Bazarov and Lunacharsky, who formed a 'school' with the writer Maxim Gorky on Capri to propagate their views. They were nicknamed *otzovists* (from the Russian verb *otzovat*, to recall) because they wished to recall the Social-Democratic deputies from the Duma and to withdraw from all legal organizations. In their uncompromising support for illegal activities they balanced the liquidators and their support for a legal party. On this account Lenin called them 'liquidators of the left' and sharply criticized their tactics as exclusive and self-indulgent. They misjudged the attitude of the masses to the work

[7] Theodore Dan, *The Origins of Bolshevism* (1964), 394

of the Social-Democratic deputies in the Duma and shirked the drudgery of legal work:

> During the revolution we learned to speak French, [as he put it picturesquely], i.e. to introduce into the movement the greatest number of rousing slogans, to raise the energy of the direct struggle of the masses and extend its scope. Now, in this time of stagnation, reaction and disintegration, we must learn to 'speak German', i.e. to work slowly . . . systematically, steadily, advancing step by step, winning inch by inch. Whoever finds this work tedious, whoever does not understand the need for preserving and developing the revolutionary principles of Social-Democratic tactics *in this phase too, on this bend of the road*, is taking the name of Marxist in vain.[8]

But this disagreement on tactics was a comparatively minor matter. What was really serious in Lenin's eyes was an apparent disagreement on basic theory, and to this he devoted one of his major works: *Materialism and Empirio-Criticism*, written in the course of 1908 and published in Moscow in May 1909.

Lenin takes as his starting point some articles by Bazarov, Bogdanov and Lunacharsky in a symposium entitled *Studies in the Philosophy of Marxism* published in St Petersburg in 1908. He shows that they have abandoned Marxism in favour of Machism, materialism for idealism. Ernst Mach, a very distinguished Austrian physicist whose studies of motion led him to a position which to some extent anticipated that formulated by Einstein in his theory of relativity, was much concerned with the problem of knowledge and with the nature of physics. He devoted a book to perception. He came to the conclusion that all we know at first hand is sense-perceptions. Events in the physical world are complexes of sensations; and physics is the science of discovering the laws governing the complexes and their interconnections. 'Sense-perceptions are ultimate elements, whose relations we have to establish empirically. Physics has only to deal with sense-perceptions and their functional relations.'[9] Mach clearly believed that as a scientist he was dealing with reality, and that it was possible by experiment to establish certain aspects of reality beyond doubt. But in his own words he was dealing with 'sense-perceptions and their functional relations', so there is a doubt whether he was in fact dealing with things, objects, events in the real world, for it is not self-evident that the functional relations

[8] *Collected Works*, Vol. 15, 458–9
[9] Mach quoted in Hugo Dingler, *Geschichte der Naturphilosophie* (1932), 150

of sense-perceptions are external to the perceiving body in a way that sense-perceptions themselves are not. On this ground Lenin argued that fundamentally Mach's theory did not differ from Berkeley's and was, therefore, idealist, not realist.

Lenin himself, following Engels, believed that sense-perceptions are copies or images or reflections of the real objects perceived. Whatever its merits, this is certainly a realist theory; and Lenin set the greatest store by realism.

He relied on two main arguments to prove the reality of the world and the objects in it. The first is that our actions prove or disprove the reality. The burnt child fears the fire. The parachutist whose parachute opens sails to the ground and lives to jump another day; he whose parachute does not open drops like a stone and is dead: 'stone dead hath no fellow.' The second argument is the continued existence of nature. Before we existed the natural world existed. The best proof of this is fossils: petrified witnesses to a time when there were organisms of such a size and shape but no human beings. Therefore the natural world is independent of the existence of human observers.

From these two premises Lenin goes on to argue that causality is real: law exists in nature and in mind; and that causality is dialectical:

> cause and effect are conceptions which only hold good in their application to individual cases; but as soon as we consider the individual cases in their general connection with the universe as a whole, they run into each other, and they become confounded when we contemplate that universal action and reaction in which causes and effects are eternally changing places, so that what is effect here and now will be cause there and then and vice versa.[10]

Equally real are space and time: 'The basic forms of all being are space and time, and being out of time is just as gross an absurdity as being out of space.'[11] Lenin supports this by quotations from Lloyd Morgan on the necessity for physics to treat space and time as real.

Nature is real; matter is real; but both are dynamic, not static; dialectical in their mode of operation:

> But dialectical materialism insists on the approximate, relative character of every scientific theory of the structure of matter and its

[10] Engels, *Anti-Dühring*, Moscow (1959), 36, quoted by Lenin, in *Collected Works* Vol. 14, 156.
[11] Engels, *op. cit.*, quoted by Lenin, *ibid.*, 176

properties; it insists on the absence of absolute boundaries in nature, on the transformation of moving matter from one state into another, that from our point of view is apparently irreconcilable with it, and so forth. However bizarre from the standpoint of 'common sense' the transformation of imponderable ether into ponderable matter and vice versa may appear, however 'strange' may seem the absence of any other kind of mass in the electron save electro-magnetic mass, however extraordinary may be the fact that the mechanical laws of motion are confined only to a single sphere of natural phenomena and are subordinated to the more profound laws of electro-magnetic phenomena, and so forth—all this is but another *corroboration* of dialectical materialism ... [The physicists wrongly fought meta-physical] materialism and its one-sided 'mechanism' and, in so doing threw out the baby with the bathwater. Denying the immutability of the elements and of the properties of matter known hitherto, they ended by denying matter, i.e. the objective reality of the physical world. Denying the absolute character of some of the most important and basic laws, they ended by denying all objective law in nature and by declaring that a law of nature is a mere convention. ...

From Engels' point of view, the only immutability is the reflection by the human mind (when there is a human mind) of an external world existing and developing independently of the mind. No other 'immutability', no other 'essence', no other 'absolute substance', in the sense in which these concepts were depicted by the empty professorial philosophers, exist for Marx and Engels. The 'essence' of things . . . is *also* relative; it expresses only the degree of profundity of man's knowledge of objects; and while yesterday the profession of this knowledge did not go beyond the atom, and today does not go beyond the electron and ether, dialectical materialism insists on the temporary, relative, approximate character of all these *milestones* in the knowledge of nature gained by the progressing science of man. The electron is as *inexhaustible* as the atom, nature is infinite, but it infinitely *exists*.[12]

Freedom is the knowledge of necessity:

'Necessity is *blind* only *in so far as it is not understood.*' (Hegel) Freedom does not consist in an imaginary independence from natural laws, but in the knowledge of these laws, and in the possibility this gives of systematically making them work towards definite ends. ... Freedom ... consists in the control over ourselves and over external nature, a control founded on knowledge of natural necessity.[13]

It is therefore vital for us, says Lenin, to exercise our freedom

[12] *Collected Works*, Vol. 14, 261–2
[13] Engels, *Anti-Dühring*, 5th German edn., 112–3, quoted by Lenin, *ibid.*, Vol. 14 187–8.

correctly. It is necessary to be partisan in matters of philosophy: non-partisanship leads to shamefaced idealism; idealism leads to religion and religion is the ultimate prop of the forces of reaction. 'I would not give a farthing for a political freedom that allows man to be a slave of religion.'[14]

> Recent philosophy is as partisan as was philosophy two thousand years ago. The contending parties are essentially—although this is concealed by a pseudo-erudite quackery of new terms or by a weak-minded non-partisanship—materialism and idealism. The latter is merely a subtle, refined form of fideism, which stands fully armed, commands vast organisations and steadily continues to exercise influence on the masses, turning the slightest vacillation in philosophical thought to its own advantage. The objective, class role of empirio-criticism consists entirely in rendering faithful service to the fideists in their struggle against materialism in general and historical materialism in particular.[15]

Lenin seems to have in mind two separate arguments here: phenomenalism and idealism are as a matter of historical fact linked with fideism (religion); and they are logically connected. There is something in the first argument. Whereas Hume and the Utilitarians were sceptics in religion as well as in philosophy, Berkeley was an Anglican bishop who actually spent a good many years engaged in pastoral work in his Irish diocese, by no means a common practice of eighteenth-century bishops; and Locke, Kant and Hegel, though not strictly orthodox, all supported the established branch of the Christian church to which they belonged.

The second argument is not only not true but seems to be almost the opposite of the truth. The idealist and the phenomenalist ('empirio-criticist') recognize sense-perceptions alone as incontrovertible data. But no one has been so bold as to claim God as a sense-perception: indeed the definition of God is an absolute person (or 'the absolute') existing infinitely and eternally, independently of the world and of ourselves. The idealist, therefore, *qua* idealist is strictly unable to say whether God exists or not; he has no means of telling. On the other hand the realist accepts the reality of the objective world existing in itself and independent of any single individual. There does not seem to be any reason, in principle, why this world should not include or be created by

[14] *Collected Works*, Vol. 38, 74
[15] *Ibid.*, Vol. 14, 358

God or even *be*, in some sense, God. Idealism is radically agnostic, realism may be theist.

Lenin was so much in earnest about this controversy that he at first refused to go to Capri to see Gorky and visit the 'school'. Gorky had written early in January 1908 to invite Lenin and Krupskaya to stay, and Lenin had answered that they could not get away at the moment, though 'It is amazingly tempting, damn it, to come to you to Capri!'[16] But during February Lenin was reading the articles in *Studies in the Philosophy of Marxism* and wrote several letters to Gorky criticizing the studies pretty sharply and pressing Gorky not to contribute articles about the philosophic dispute to Bolshevik journals. Finally he wrote in April positively refusing to come to Capri. 'I cannot and will not talk with people who have begun to advocate combining scientific socialism with religion ... We must not argue, it is stupid to strain the nerves unnecessarily. Philosophy must be *separated* from Party (factional) affairs.'[17] Lenin stuck to this decision for a long time, and it was not until December 1909 that he visited Gorky.

Lenin and Gorky had first met at the London congress in 1907. 'When we were introduced, he shook me heartily by the hand, and, scrutinizing me with his keen eyes and speaking in the tone of an old acquaintance, he said jocularly: "So glad you've come. I believe you're fond of a good scrap? There's going to be a fine old scuffle here." '[18] They took to one another. Gorky, the son of a peasant and brought up in conditions of the utmost poverty and brutality, was impressed by Lenin's frugality and simplicity. In a cheap restaurant Lenin had only 'two or three fried eggs, a small piece of ham, and a mug of thick, dark beer.'[19] Some of the worker delegates to the congress were discussing Lenin in Hyde Park, and one of them said: 'For all I know there may be other fellows as clever as he in Europe on the side of the workers. But I don't believe you'll find another one who could get you on the spot like that fellow.'[20] And a little later in his memoirs Gorky adds this comment: 'In the autumn of 1918 I asked a worker from Sormovo, Dmitry Pavlov, what he thought

[16] *Letters of Lenin*, 256
[17] *Ibid.*, 271
[18] M. Gorky, *Days with Lenin*, 5
[19] Gorky, *op. cit.*, 18
[20] *Ibid.*, 17

was Lenin's most striking feature. He answered: "Simplicity. He is as simple as truth itself." '[21]

Lenin and Gorky went to the music hall together. (Lenin did not much care for the theatre, which he found too artificial, though he was observed in tears at Sarah Bernhardt in *La Dame aux Camélias*.) Lenin 'laughed gaily and infectiously at the clowns and comedians and looked indifferently at the rest'.[22] Never indeed was there anyone who laughed so infectiously as Lenin, 'like a child, till the tears came, till he choked with laughter. To laugh like that one must have the soundest and healthiest of minds. . . .'[23] On this Gorky, Lenin himself and the simplest fisherman were agreed.

Lenin speaking to someone in trouble said: 'It's a good thing you can meet failure with humour. Humour is a splendid, healthy quality. And really life is as funny as it is sad, just as much.'[24] And when he eventually got to Capri he was instinctively appreciated by the local fishermen, one of whom said of him: 'Only an honest man could laugh like that.'[25] They went out fishing. Lenin asked:

'Cosi: drin, drin. Capisce?' A second later he hooked a fish, drew it in and cried out with child-like joy and a hunter's excitement, 'Drin, drin.' The fishermen roared with laughter . . . and nicknamed [him] 'Signor Drin-Drin'. After he had gone away, they continued to ask: 'How is Drin-Drin getting on? The Tsar hasn't caught him yet?'[26]

Lenin thoroughly enjoyed the holiday spirit.

With equal enthusiasm he would play chess, look through 'A History of Dress', dispute for hours with comrades, fish, go for walks along the stoney paths of Capri, scorching under the southern sun, feast his eyes on the golden colour of the gorse, and on the swarthy children of the fishermen. In the evening, listening to stories about Russia and the country, he would sigh enviously and say, 'I know very little of Russia—Simbirsk, Kazan, St Petersburg, exile in Siberia and that is nearly all.'[27]

Lenin's two visits to Capri, in December 1909 and July and

[21] Gorky, *op. cit.*, 19
[22] *Ibid.*, 19
[23] *Ibid.*, 23
[24] *Ibid.*, 23
[25] *Ibid.*, 28
[26] *Ibid.*, 28
[27] *Ibid.* 38

August 1910, were happy interludes in what was probably the gloomiest period of his life. By 1908 it was clear that the revolution had failed; the Russian workers were cowed, and whether another revolutionary opportunity would arise was quite uncertain. Lenin and Krupskaya were again in exile. They had escaped from Russia to Sweden and then gone back to Geneva. From there they moved to Paris in November 1908. They remained there till the summer of 1912 when they moved to Cracow to be nearer Russia, as there seemed to be signs of a revival of revolutionary activity.

Lenin's time and energies were much occupied with party quarrels which exasperated his nerves. He was also engaged in trying to sustain and build up the party inside Russia. He had several valuable agents there, like Krasin and Bukharin, but he himself largely undermined his own work by being taken in by the police spy Malinovsky. Lenin was a good judge of men, and was evidently himself puzzled by his failure to see through Malinovsky. 'But I never saw through that scoundrel Malinovsky,' he remarked to Gorky. 'That was a very mysterious affair, Malinovsky.'[28]

Malinovsky and Lenin met for the first time in January 1912 in Prague at the congress at which, under Lenin's guidance, the Bolshevik party finally broke with the Mensheviks, formally constituted itself *the* Social-Democratic Party and elected a new central committee. Malinovsky had made such a good impression on Lenin that he was elected a member of this committee. He came as a representative of the Moscow trade unions and of the Bolshevik underground in Russia, with a reputation as a hard worker and a violent, effective speaker.

Malinovsky was born in Poland in 1878, a worker of Polish peasant stock. As a young man he moved to St Petersburg, where he worked as a metal turner. He already had a police record for petty crime and from 1899 to 1902 served a prison sentence for breaking and entering. About 1902 he began to take an energetic part in St Petersburg trade union affairs and became a police agent. He established himself rapidly in both spheres, was arrested a number of times and jailed. After his release from prison in 1910 he disappeared from St Petersburg to avoid suspicion, and moved to Moscow. By 1912 he was high enough in the

[28] *Ibid.*, 58

counsels of the Moscow trade union movement to be elected one
of their delegates to the Prague congress and in the counsels of the
police to be especially chosen to make contact with Lenin and to
become his confidant.

In this he succeeded to admiration. He was much helped in his
task by being known as a worker who was thought 'rather a
Menshevik' in Zinoviev's words. But there is no doubt that he
made the best possible impression on Lenin as a live wire with a
flair for political leadership: he was a man of vitality, talent and
immense ambition with something of the 'card' in his make-up:
a Khlestakov of the labour movement.

Co-operation between them was easy in another way too:
they had the same aim, to split the Social-Democratic party
once and for all. This was Lenin's first political task at the time;
and it was what Malinovsky had been ordered to achieve by his
bosses, for they had come to the conclusion that there was again
some danger to the regime from the workers, and that the best
way to avert it was to disrupt the Social-Democratic movement by
splitting the party and then embittering the factions, if indeed
they needed any embittering. The culmination of this policy
and of the mutual support of the police and the party was the
election of Malinovsky to the Fourth Duma as a Social-Democratic deputy. As a deputy he made an impression on the Duma
as an eloquent speaker and a leader of great resource and intransigence. Under orders from his two chiefs he succeeded in
defying the strong current of opinion in favour of party unity
and in splitting the party into two formally recognized factions
in the Duma, the Bolshevik and Menshevik. In the spring of 1914
he took a prominent part in a joint Social-Democratic demon-
tration in the chamber against the prime minister, for which
those involved were suspended for a fortnight. When they
returned to the chamber after this, each deputy in turn tried to
read a formal protest which would then have to be incorporated
in the minutes. The chairman ruled each of them out of order.
Malinovsky was the most violent and impassioned of them all.
Next day he went to the chairman and handed in his resignation as
a deputy.

This sudden action, taken without his having consulted anyone, caused a sensation. Why had he done it? He himself went
straight to Lenin in Cracow and gave his explanation: after

much beating about the bush and contradictory explanation he finally let out under questioning that in his youth he had been sentenced for rape and that the police were now threatening to expose him unless he resigned from the Duma. There had in fact been rumours for some time past that Malinovsky was a police agent, and as early as November 1912 Bukharin had warned Lenin of his suspicions. Then in February and March 1913 the arrest of Sverdlov, Stalin and the wife of another Bolshevik, Troyanovsky, all after contact with Malinovsky, sharpened these suspicions to the point where the Central Committee had to investigate the matter. Malinovsky, however, diverted suspicion from himself by directing it on to the editor of *Pravda*, Chernomasov, also a then-undetected police agent, who was forced to resign.

Now the rumours swelled into an accusation that Malinovsky was an agent, and a demand for a non-party enquiry was put forward by Martov and Dan. Lenin naturally refused to agree to this, but the Central Committee set up its own tribunal of enquiry. It consisted of Lenin, Zinoviev and Hanecki, a staunch supporter of Lenin. It exonerated Malinovsky and declared that the rumours were malicious inventions of the Mensheviks put about for their own shameful purposes. This verdict seemed so convenient for the Bolsheviks and so contrary to the evidence produced that many people thought then, and still think, that Lenin knew the truth about Malinovsky and had deliberately and dishonestly engineered a whitewashing acquittal.

There were certainly two strong reasons for this. First, the bulk of the rumours and the demand for an enquiry came from the Mensheviks, so that a verdict of guilty would be seized on by them as proof of their virtue and of the gullibility, or worse, of the Bolsheviks. Second, and more important still, the confidence of the rank and file in the Bolshevik leadership, and especially in Lenin, would be severely and perhaps fatally shaken. What would they think of a man who had been taken in by such a rogue, and had given him his complete confidence? What would be their reactions to the thought of two such staunch comrades as Sverdlov and Stalin languishing in Siberia as the direct result of Malinovsky's action? What would be the consequences to the party and the revolution of Lenin and his closest colleagues being totally discredited?

But there are as it happens a number of small pieces of evidence that contradict this conclusion. During the first World War Malinovsky was a prisoner of war in Germany and throughout his imprisonment Lenin sent him things to read and material for propaganda among his fellow prisoners, and Krupskaya sent him food parcels and coped with his laundry.

In a letter to Kamenev dated 29 March 1913, just after Stalin's arrest, Lenin wrote: 'There are heavy arrests at home. Koba (Stalin) has been arrested. We have discussed with Malinovsky what measures to take.'[29] Could Lenin have written these words to one of his most trusted lieutenants about a colleague whom he knew at the time of writing to be an agent?

Krupsakya discusses Malinovsky in a passage in her memoirs in which she records that the tribunal of investigation could not get definite proof of his guilt. She then goes on: 'Only once did a doubt flash across Lenin's mind. I remember one day in Poronino [outside Cracow where Lenin and Krupskaya spent the summer], we were returning from the Zinovievs and talking about these rumours. All of a sudden Ilyich stopped on the little bridge we were crossing and said: "It may be true!" and his face expressed anxiety.'[30] The incident bears the stamp of actuality, and this can only mean that at the time of the investigation Lenin was genuinely uncertain.

Finally there is Lenin's remark to Gorky quoted at the beginning of this discussion: 'That was a very mysterious affair, Malinovsky.' This could have more than one meaning, but it appears to exclude the possibility that Lenin was convinced of Malinovsky's guilt and deliberately smothered the conviction and the guilt.[31]

During these gloomy and troubled years Lenin was much fortified by his love for Inessa Armand. Born in Paris in 1879 of a French father and Scotch mother, Elizabeth d'Herbenville had been taken as a girl to St Petersburg by an aunt who got a job as governess in the household of a well-to-do business man called Armand. Aged eighteen Elizabeth had married the second son, Alexander Evgenevich, to whom she bore five children. At the same time she was drawn towards advanced ideas through the

[29] *Collected Works*, Vol. 35, 93
[30] N. K. Krupskaya, *Memories of Lenin*, Vol. 2, 132
[31] For the detailed story of Malinovsky see Bertram D. Wolfe, *Three Who Made a Revolution*, Chapter 31.

influence of Alexander's elder brother, and gave more and more of her time to social work, especially with prostitutes. Finally she left her husband and went abroad. There she became a Bolshevik, adopted the pseudonym Inessa, went back to Russia on a mission for the party, was twice arrested and eventually in April 1907 sentenced to two years' exile. She managed to escape and went to Paris. She got to know Lenin early in 1910. In the same year she kept house for the Bolshevik 'school' at Longjumeau just outside Paris. In 1911 she and two of her children went to live next door to Lenin and Krupskaya at number 2 Rue Marie-Rose.

She was described at this period as having a 'somewhat asymmetrical face, unruly, dark chestnut hair, great hypnotic eyes, and inextinguishable ardour of spirit'.[32] She spoke French, English, Russian and German. She was musical, with a special love for Beethoven, and played the piano well. At the Longjumeau 'school' she alternated with Lenin in giving the course on political economy.

When Lenin and Krupskaya moved to Cracow in 1912 Inessa went on a tour of Bolshevik 'cells' in Russia. She was again arrested and imprisoned, but after a while she was released at her husband's instance, as she had developed tubercular symptoms, and joined Lenin in Cracow. On the outbreak of war in 1914 she had to go to a sanatorium at Les Avants, but on her discharge she again joined Lenin and Krupskaya in Berne, where they went for long walks in the woods together. She was Lenin's representative at the conference of the International Socialist Bureau in July 1914 and a delegate to the conferences of the bureau held at Zimmerwald in 1915 and Kienthal in 1916. She returned to Russia with Lenin in the same train in 1917.

Lenin admired her brain and her accomplishments, and loved her deeply. According to Alexandra Kollontay, Krupskaya was fully aware of Lenin's love for Inessa and schooled herself to accept it; she expected him to leave her and, when he did not, offered to go away herself, but Lenin asked her to stay.

But characteristically Lenin did not allow his admiration or love to interfere with his respect for truth. In a passage in a letter to Inessa written in January 1915 about a pamphlet she was

---

[32] Quoted in Bertram D. Wolfe, 'Lenin and Inessa Armand', in *Encounter*, February 1964, q.v. for further details; also the same author's *Strange Communists I Have Known* (1966).

writing for working-class women on sex and marriage, Lenin picked up a quotation from her draft:

> 'Even a fleeting passion and intimacy' are 'more poetic and cleaner' than 'kisses without love' of a (vulgar and shallow) married couple. That is what you write. And that is what you intend to write in your pamphlet. Very good.
>
> Is the contrast logical? Kisses without love between a vulgar couple are *dirty*. I agree. To them one should contrast . . . what? . . . One would think: kisses *with* love? While you contrast them with 'fleeting' (why fleeting?) 'passion' (why not love?)—so, logically, it turns out that kisses without love (fleeting) are contrasted with kisses without love by married people. . . . Strange. For a popular pamphlet, would it not be better to contrast philistine-intellectual-peasant . . . vulgar and dirty marriage without love to proletarian civil marriage with love (adding, *if you absolutely insist*, that fleeting intimacy and passion, too, may be dirty and may be clean). What you have arrived at is, not the contrast of class *types*, but something like an 'incident', which of course is possible. But is it a question of particular incidents? If you take the theme of an incident, an individual case of dirty kisses in marriage and pure ones in a fleeting intimacy, that is a theme to be worked out in a novel (because there the whole *essence* is in the *individual* circumstances, the analysis of the *characters* and psychology of *particular* types). But in a pamphlet?[33]

Lenin is here making his point in terms of the orthodox Marxist view of sex and marriage worked out by Engels in *The Origin of the Family, Private Property and the State*. Marriage like all other institutions is a function of the social ownership of property. In a capitalist society marriage is essentially an institution for the inheritance of private property: woman is a chattel and man an owner. Because he is the owner he has a freedom of action denied to the woman. Adultery and prostitution are the twin complements of bourgeois marriage. It will disappear with the overthrow of capitalism. In communist society, society itself will own the means of production, manage and supervise the process of production and look after its members' children. So in this society woman will regain her sexual freedom. Marriage will be based on love, not money, and the partners will be on an equal footing: a given marriage may last for a long or a short time; either way it will be terminable by a simple civil act without the need for the tedious and degrading proceedings of the divorce court.

[33] *Collected Works*, Vol. 35, 183–4

This accounts for the opposition of 'philistine ... marriage without love to proletarian civil marriage with love' that looks at first sight as illogical and tendentious as Inessa's contrast that Lenin is criticizing. But he may also, perhaps even unconsciously, be making a contrast between what might be called the late nineteenth-century 'Tristan and Isolde' view of love, suggested by Inessa's words 'a fleeting passion and intimacy ... more poetic and cleaner' than a marriage, and the communist view that true love may, yet, run smooth, when the artificial obstacles to its course have been swept away by revolution.

> I know nothing that is greater than the Appassionata. I would like to hear it every day. It is marvellous superhuman music. I always think with pride—perhaps it is naive of me—what marvellous things human beings can do. But I can't listen to music too often. It affects your nerves, makes you want to say stupid, nice things, and stroke the heads of people who could create such beauty while living in this vile hell. And now you mustn't stroke anyone's head—you might get your hand bitten off. You have to hit them on the head, without any mercy, although our ideal is not to use force against anyone. H'm, h'm, our duty is infernally hard.[34]

In this remark to Gorky, Lenin's emotions can be felt welling up in his normally dry speech; and his feeling for music, his feeling for suffering human beings and his love for Inessa flow into one another in his passion for the Beethoven sonata.

Something of the same passion can be felt in his attitude to Tolstoy. In a short article, *Leo Tolstoy as the Mirror of the Russian Revolution*, written in 1908, Lenin admits that it is odd to identify Tolstoy with a revolution 'which he has obviously failed to understand, and from which he obviously stands aloof', but he goes on to argue that it is precisely in this contradictory and bewildered attitude that Tolstoy so faithfully reflects the revolution:

> The contradictions in Tolstoy's works, views, doctrines, in his school, are indeed glaring. On the one hand, we have the great artist, the genius who has not only drawn incomparable pictures of Russian life but has made first-class contributions to world literature. On the other hand we have the landlord obsessed with Christ. On the one hand, the remarkably powerful, forthright and sincere protest against social falsehood and hypocrisy; and on the other, the 'Tolstoyan', i.e. the jaded, hysterical sniveller called the Russian intellectual, who publicly beats his breast and wails:

[34] Gorky, *op. cit.*, 52

'I am a bad ... man, but I am practising moral self-perfection; I don't eat meat any more, I now eat rice cutlets.' On the one hand, merciless criticism of capitalist exploitation, exposure of government outrages, the farcical courts and the state administration, and unmasking of the profound contradictions between the growth of wealth and achievements of civilisation and the growth of poverty, degradation and misery among the working masses. On the other, the crackpot preaching of submission, 'resist not evil' with violence. On the one hand, the most sober realism, the tearing away of all and sundry masks; on the other, the preaching of one of the most odious things on earth, namely, religion, the striving to replace officially appointed priests by priests who will serve from moral conviction, i.e. to cultivate the most refined and, therefore, particularly disgusting clericalism. Verily:

> 'Thou art a pauper, yet thou art abundant,
> Thou art mighty, yet thou art impotent—
>    —Mother Russia!'
>    (Nekrasov: Who can be Happy and Free
>    in Russia?)[35]

Mighty but impotent. This might serve as a summary of Russia's apparent and real power: the reality not revealed until the first World War. One of the main reasons for this contradiction was the nationalities: the Poles, the Finns, the Georgians, the numerous Asiatic peoples, perhaps the Ukrainians. All these were non-Russians and all were oppressed by the autocracy, which from the reign of Tsar Alexander III intensified its efforts to Russify them.

Lenin was increasingly concerned with the nationalities question in the years after 1912, and in 1913 he produced a draft programme on the question for the party. This recognized the right of self-determination and secession but insisted at the same time that: 'The right of nations to self-determination (i.e. the constitutional guarantee of an absolutely free and democratic method of deciding the question of secession) must under no circumstances be confused with the expediency of a given nation's decision.'[36] This must be determined with regard to proletarian interests. The programme also condemned 'cultural national autonomy' on the ground that it led to the division of a state's educational affairs, whereas proletarian interests demanded that the workers should all be united in proletarian organs, like

[35] *Collected Works*, Vol. 15, 205
[36] *Ibid.*, Vol. 19, 429

trade unions or co-operatives or educational associations and not separated into exclusively national organizations of this type.

This is a real attempt to produce a sensible, workable Marxist programme on this question, a question of the utmost importance for Russian Social-Democrats as well as for many others, e.g. the Austrians. But it barely conceals a centrifugal tendency based on two separate though closely related contradictions. First is the fact that the existing leaders of the national communities were for the most part middle-class nationalists. They agreed with the Rissian liberals and the Social-Democrats in wanting to end the autocracy and to urge on the bourgeois revolution; but they did not in the least want a classless, nationless society. On the contrary they made no bones about wanting secession from Russia and the setting-up of new nation states, which would clearly at this stage of historical development be bourgeois states. As democrats the Bolsheviks were wholeheartedly, almost unconsciously, in favour of self-determination; but the most clear-headed could not but be aware of how self-determination would throw back the cause of the proletariat. Secondly, much more fundamentally though still almost invisibly, the proletariat itself could not be relied on to know its own interests: to feel deeply and before all else proletarian, and not national. And if they did in the event feel first and foremost national, what was the party to do? The decision or lack of decision is embodied in the phrase 'the expediency of a given nation's secession'.

This contradiction was to be fully revealed first on the international stage, when the various socialist parties of Europe split on the outbreak of the first World War and most of their leaders and members backed their own governments and not the Socialist International. This was not yet revealed by 1912, but the increase of international tension was already very clear, and from 1912 Lenin wrote increasingly about international affairs. He ranged over the whole world: Australia, India, Persia, Turkey, Italy, France, England, the U.S.A. He called Sun Yat-Sen a Chinese narodnik; he denounced Lloyd George's land reforms as humbug; he praised Jim Larkin and Harry Quelch as labour leaders; he explained that Theodore Roosevelt's progressive party was designed to rescue American capitalism from its inevitable contradictions. He paid much attention to the trouble spots of the world, Persia, Libya, and above all the Balkans, and gave out the first notes of the theme he was to develop in full in *Imperialism, the Highest Stage of Capitalism:* capitalism leads to imperialism, imperialism leads to war.

# 7 *1914-1917*

The outbreak of war in 1914 placed the international socialist movement in a cruel dilemma and in a lightning flash revealed to the members and to the world at large the contradictions in its attitude to war. The International had been consistently opposed to war, and from 1900 onwards its congresses had passed resolutions condemning militarism. It believed that action on an international scale by the working class would prevent a major war developing. It had formulated this belief most fully in a resolution passed at the Stuttgart Conference in 1907. This declared that war derived from capitalism and would not cease until capitalism was replaced by socialism. Meanwhile socialists should strive by all means to prevent war breaking out, especially by securing the reduction in size of the armed forces of the Powers and by voting against war credits. Instead they should aim at arming the whole people, who as workers would use their arms against their own governments to stop them going to war. If, however, a war should break out, the parliamentary representatives of Social-Democracy, 'aided by the International Bureau as an active and co-ordinating power', should use all means to stop it.

The International reaffirmed its attitude at Copenhagen in 1910. It further enlarged it by urging its members to demand the end of secret diplomacy and the publication of all secret treaties, the compulsory arbitration of international disputes and the autonomy of all peoples, who should be defended against warlike interests and oppression. Some extreme left-wing socialists wanted to add a general strike and insurrection to the means to be used to stop war breaking out, but this was left out of the official programme in deference to the German Social-Democratic party which was unalterably opposed to them.

This typifies the socialist dilemma: the stronger the party, the less international and revolutionary. By 1914 the German Social-Democratic Party represented over four million voters, a third of the total number of voters, and shared their emotions and aspirations. When war broke out they felt as Germans, not as international socialists, and their parliamentary representatives, with the exception of a handful of deputies, joined their fellow members in voting for war credits. The same story repeated itself in the other countries of Europe: in France the veteran Marxist doctrinaire Jules Guesde even entered the cabinet as Minister of War.

Of those who steadfastly opposed the war most were pacifists. They regarded war as evil in itself and therefore wanted to bring it to an end as quickly as possible and to use the working class to achieve this.

Lenin shared neither of these attitudes. He was not a pacifist either in theory or in temperament, so he was not under the emotional strain of those socialists who had a horror of war and had unconsciously hoodwinked themselves into believing that it would never come. Nor was he a patriot. As he himself said, he knew very little of Russia, and his years of exile had made him a true internationalist. On top of this his hatred of tsarism made him actively welcome a war that must hasten its overthrow. Lenin was far from indifferent to the suffering that the war was bound to bring to ordinary men and women in every country, but he never believed for one moment that the suffering would be in vain. On the contrary, in the suffering was hope; out of the suffering would come victory for the socialist revolution and a new life for the people.

When the war broke out Lenin and Krupskaya were in the country in Galicia and were arrested by the local police. But with the help of the Austrian Social-Democratic leader, Victor Adler, they were able to gain their release and permission to leave Austria-Hungary.

As soon as they were settled in Berne, Lenin set out his attitude to the war in an article written before October 1914 entitled: *The War and Russian Social-Democracy.* The war, he argued, was an imperialist war. It had wrecked the socialist policy embodied in the resolutions passed at successive international congresses: Stuttgart, Copenhagen and Basle; and it had broken up the old Socialist International (the Second International) for ever. The main task of true Social-Democrats was now to expose the chauvinism of each individual country: Russian Social-Democrats should concentrate on Russian chauvinists, especially Smirnov, Maslov and Plekhanov.

Lenin expanded this in a forty-page pamphlet *Socialism and War*, written in July and August, 1915. In this he lays stress on the fact that socialists are not pacifists. The class war is *war*. In the past, and especially in the period 1789–1871, there were just wars: wars against absolutism and feudalism that Marx and Engels strongly supported. Now the imperialist war has broken out.

The nature of this war had been foreseen by Engels in a prophetic passage written in 1887:

> Eight to ten millions of soldiers will mutually massacre one another and in doing so devour the whole of Europe until they have stripped it barer than any swarm of locusts has ever done. The devastation of the Thirty Years War compressed into three or four years, and spread over the whole Continent; famine, pestilence, general demoralization both of the armies and of the mass of the people produced by acute distress; hopeless confusion of our artificial machinery in trade, industry and credit, ending in general bankruptcy; collapse of the old states and their traditional state wisdom, to such an extent that crowns will roll by dozens on the pavement and there will be nobody to pick them up; absolute impossibility of foreseeing how it will all end and who will come out of the struggle as victor; only one result absolutely certain: general exhaustion and the establishment of the conditions for the ultimate victory of the working class.[1]

Lenin does not quote this passage but he makes the same point as Engels. The imperialist war has broken out. This is a grim event but there is no sense in sitting and bewailing it. Nor is it the task of Marxists to try and end it as soon as possible. On the contrary it is the task of all Marxists to do all they can to develop it into a civil war. They must work to stir up insurrections in their own countries and to bring about the defeat of their own governments. No true socialist can possibly be a social-chauvinist, but no more can he be a half-hearted, pseudo-pacifist like Kautsky, emptying Marxism of all its revolutionary content. The test of a true socialist is his attitude to self-determination. The socialist of the oppressor countries must champion the oppressed countries' right to self-determination. Their acting on this right will lead not to the Balkanization of Europe but 'to the freer, fearless and therefore wider and more universal formation of large states and federations of states, which are more to the advantage of the

[1] Marx-Engels, *Selected Correspondence, 1846–1895* (1936), 456–7

D

masses and more in keeping with economic development'.[2] The socialist of the oppressed countries must work for the unity of the *workers* of the oppressed and oppressor states: the 'juridical separation of one nation from another (the so-called "cultural-national autonomy" ...) is reactionary.'[3] Lenin is here foreseeing the danger of new national states, or perhaps autonomous federal states, coming into being, dominated and ruled by bourgeois governments. Lenin then applies this analysis to the party situation in Russia and shows that the Bolsheviks alone were solid for the correct party line.

In furtherance of his policy Lenin joined with other internationalist socialists in following up the initiative of a group of Italian socialists who in the course of 1915 took soundings about holding a conference to define their attitude to the war and the International. This met at Zimmerwald in Switzerland in September. There were 38 delegates present from the belligerent and the neutral countries. It condemned the war and the socialists who had voted for it, and called on the workers to unite 'across frontiers, battlefields, devastated cities and countries'. But it also set up a commission to stimulate the International Bureau into new activity, and the majority had the firm intention of re-animating the International, not of breaking with it. Lenin had submitted a series of resolutions calling for the end of the Second International and the establishment of a new one, but these the conference rejected by nineteen votes to twelve. Nevertheless Lenin and his friends signed the conference manifesto: it was a compromise but a step forward and, in Lenin's opinion, held out hope of international co-operation on genuine Marxist lines, even if on a miniature scale.

By 1916 the war had gone on so long and the casualties had been so heavy for so little result that there were everywhere people who were wondering if there would not have to be a compromise peace. President Wilson had sent his confidential emissary Colonel House to Europe in January to test the opinion of both sides on a set of proposals he had drawn up. Both sides rejected these and prepared for a knock-out blow in the next year. Either way attention was being concentrated on the end of the war and, to some extent, on the subsequent peace.

[2] *Collected Works*, Vol. 21, 316
[3] *Ibid.*, Vol. 21, 316–7

This shift of attention affected the socialist movement too. At the international conference held at Kienthal in Switzerland in April 1916 the emphasis was not so much on simply ending the war as on the basis for a lasting peace: this was the international socialist revolution without which no peace would be either tolerable or lasting. The conference had in fact come round to Lenin's position.

In the first half of 1916 Lenin was also engaged in working out his thought on imperialism in a long pamphlet that he wrote for a popular audience, though it was not published until after the Russian revolution in 1917. In this work, *Imperialism, The Highest Stage of Capitalism*, Lenin first sets out with a considerable array of statistics the tendency towards monopoly shown by capitalism in all the most advanced countries of the world in the last fifty years. He then goes on to analyse the various ways in which this tendency shows itself. Within each country concentration eliminates the smaller, weaker firms and produces giant combines, trusts and cartels. The same process takes place in banking as in industry, and then the banks, through their control of finance, begin to take over control of industry, a process so far most marked in Germany and France. This control by finance capital leads to the formation of a financial oligarchy, which further extends its grip on the world economy by the large-scale export of capital. This leads to the division of the world supplies of raw materials and the world market between them, e.g. in the electrical industry, where the General Electric Company of the U.S.A. and the Allgemeine Elektrizitäts Gesellschaft of Germany have agreed to divide the world between them, or in the oil industry, where the Standard Oil Company forced the German group, Rothschild and Nobel, to accept a minor place in the Rockefeller oil empire. This process is accompanied by the final stage of colonialism, in which the great powers are occupying the last remaining independent parts of the world and dividing the world between them.

Some bourgeois economists like J. A. Hobson and some renegade socialists like Kautsky have argued that this process will culminate in an ultra-imperialism or inter-imperialism which will supersede capitalist and national rivalries and bring a hope of peace to the world. Lenin will have none of this and treats this argument as dope for the masses. As the war had been in progress for nearly two years and had engulfed nearly the whole of Europe, it is possible to feel the strongest sympathy with Lenin; but he does not in fact produce much in the way of argument to support his point of view. He defines imperialism, reasonably enough, as the final stage of capitalism, or as 'in its essence ... monopoly capitalism', and goes on to say that the idea that ultra-imperialism could lead to world peace is absurd, because imperialism is the final stage of capitalism, which is its own gravedigger. But this is only a striking metaphor of Marx's to crown his argument that the inherent contradictions of capitalism must produce violent clashes which will finally disrupt it. Lenin is therefore assuming the conclusion he is supposed to be proving and his argument is circular.

He goes on to point out that because of its colonies Great Britain has increased its railway network four times as much as Germany, but that Germany has increased its production of coal and iron to give it 'an overwhelming superiority over Britain ... The question is what means other than war could there be *under capitalism* to overcome the disparity between the development of productive forces and the accumulation of capital on the one side, and the division of colonies and spheres of influence for finance capital on the other?'[4] The validity of this question depends on the axiom that in its final stage capitalism must export capital abroad, and not invest it at home, in order to maximize profits. This in turn is a deduction from the Marxist form of the labour theory of value, which denies the possibility of raising the standard of living of the workers, and is therefore inextricably bound up with the whole theory of Marxism. So Lenin's question is a good one to any other Marxist, especially an acknowledged Marxist authority like Kautsky, but it glances harmlessly off the skin of any bourgeois theorist.

Finally Lenin points to China and asks how long an inter-imperialist alliance would work there. The great powers had certainly treated China like a colony and imperialist rivalry between Japan and Russia had led to the war of 1904; but this had remained a local war, and imperialist U.S.A. had played the largest part in settling the terms of peace. It is quite possible that clashes of interest between the powers in the Far East might have brought about a world war, but the fact is that

4 *Collected Works*, Vol. 22, 275–6

they did not. So this speculation is not too strong a point of support.

At about the same time Lenin developed his thought on the vital question of self-determination in a set of theses: *The Socialist Revolution and the Right of Nations to Self-Determination.* He begins by noting that the most advanced nations of the world have reached the imperialist stage of history and that therefore the socialist revolution is on the agenda of history. The socialist revolution implies democracy and the right of nations to self-determination: 'In the same way as there can be no victorious socialism that does not practise full democracy, so the proletariat cannot prepare for its victory over the bourgeoisie without an all-round, consistent and revolutionary struggle for democracy.'[5] It is not true that it is impossible to realize self-determination under capitalism, for it has been realized, for example by Norway; but it is only in a partial and distorted form. So one of the tasks of the socialist revolution is to push self-determination beyond bourgeois legality and to incorporate it in the revolution.

But self-determination does not automatically lead to the setting up of innumerable small states. The right to secession does indeed exist, but

[it] is not the equivalent of a demand for separation, fragmentation and the formation of small states. It implies only a consistent expression of struggle against all national oppression. The closer a democratic state system is to complete freedom to secede the less frequent and less ardent will the desire for separation be in practice, because big states afford indisputable advantages, both from the standpoint of economic progress and from that of the interests of the masses and, furthermore, these advantages increase with the growth of capitalism.[6]

Federation is better than national inequality, though democratic centralism is better still. Thus Marx preferred independence for Ireland from Great Britain to its forcible subordination; but Lenin implies that it would have been better for Ireland to have remained within a truly democratic Britain. The events of the next few years were to provide a caustic commentary on this thesis.

Lenin goes on to repeat that it was the duty of socialists in

[5] *Ibid.*, 144
[6] *Ibid*, 146

both the oppressor and the oppressed countries to work for the freedom of peoples to choose their own governments and for the solidarity of the workers, otherwise they would find themselves the victims of trickery employed by the bourgeois for their own oppressive purposes: for example, the Poles, if they achieved independence, would use it to oppress the Jews and Ukrainians, and the various Balkan governments, backed up by the great powers, would incorporate and oppress national minorities.

At this moment in time there were, according to Lenin, three types of country with respect to self-determination: the advanced countries of western Europe and the U.S.A.; the countries of eastern Europe; and the semi-colonial countries like China, Persia and Turkey. In the first type the progressive bourgeois movement was long over, and the proletariat must now act, e.g. by the English proletariat backing the Irish demand for freedom. In the second, the progressive bourgeois movements were typical of the early twentieth century and the proletariat must complete the bourgeois reforms and merge them into the socialist revolution. 'The most difficult and most important task ... is to unite the class struggle of the workers of the oppressor nations with that of the workers of the oppressed nations.'[7] In the third, bourgeois progressive movements have hardly begun and socialists must demand self-determination and support the more revolutionary elements in the struggle for national liberation.

The concrete tasks of the proletariat in the immediate future are: if the revolution has actually begun, to seize the commanding heights of power and then 'to proclaim and grant liberty to *all* oppressed peoples';[8] if on the other hand the revolution is not coming about for five or ten years, then to educate the masses. In particular English socialists must advocate liberty for Ireland and the colonies, German socialists liberty for Alsatians, Danes, Poles and the colonies, and Russian socialists liberty for Finland, Poland, the Ukraine etc. Russian socialists affirmed this as long ago as 1903 and repeated their affirmation at the Prague congress in 1912; and Polish socialists have taken the same line at the Zimmerwald Conference with a resolution that only socialism *'will break the fetters of national oppression* and destroy *all forms of foreign* rule, will ensure for *the Polish people* the possibility of

[7] *Collected Works*, Vol. 22, 151
[8] *Ibid.*, 153

free, all-round development as an *equal* member of a concord of nations.'[9]

Lenin repeated these themes throughout 1916 in pamphlets, in newspaper articles, in speeches and in his letters. To them he added one more: the illusion of disarmament, which had been increasingly preached as part of socialist policy, especially by socialists in the neutral countries:

> Disarmament is the ideal of socialism. There will be no wars in socialist society; consequently, disarmament will be achieved. But whoever expects that socialism will be achieved *without* a social revolution and the dictatorship of the proletariat is not a socialist. Dictatorship is state power based directly on *violence*. And in the twentieth century . . . violence means neither a fist nor a club, but *troops*. To put 'disarmament' into the programme is tantamount to making the general declaration: we are opposed to the use of arms. There is as little Marxism in this as there would be if we were to say: we are opposed to violence . . . the dream of disarmament [is] nothing but an expression of despair. . . .[10]

But, Lenin went on, there is no need to despair. We know all about trusts and the employment of women and children in factories; we know all about the Commune of 1871 and the revolution of 1905. We recognize the horror of the trusts driving women and children into the factories as industrial fodder, but we don't say: back to domestic industry and the hand loom. We recognize the heroism of the women and children fighters in 1871: we are inspired by it. The proletarians will **imitate them.** Forward into socialism!

[9] *Ibid.*, 155
[10] *Collected Works*, Vol. 23, 95, 97

## 8  The February revolution

In the early part of February 1917 bread got scarcer and scarcer
in St Petersburg, and the queues got longer and slower. There
were demonstrations in the streets with workers carrying placards
demanding 'Bread!' and proclaiming 'Down with Autocracy!'
On 21 February the political and economic journalist, Sukhanov,
was sitting in his office when he overheard two typists 'gossiping
about food difficulties, rows in the shopping queues, unrest among
the women, an attempt to smash into some warehouse. "D'you
know," suddenly declared one of these young ladies, "if you ask
me, it's the beginning of the revolution!" '[1] They did not mean
this seriously, but they had sensed what was in the air.

The 22nd was quiet. But there was a lock-out at the Putilov
works, over a wage dispute, and the locked-out workers went
from factory to factory to bring the men out on strike. On the
23rd about 90,000 workers were out and there were street demonstrations in connexion with the strike. On the 24th more workers
were out, 240,000 according to government figures. They surged
about the streets carrying placards: 'Bread!' 'Down with Autocracy!' and 'Down with the War!' Soldiers in the hospitals waved
at the demonstrators and ordinary people showed them much
sympathy. The police kept breaking up the crowds, but not with
any ferocity; as soon as they moved on the crowds filtered back
again. The police called on the available troops for help, but
they were dubious allies as they were inclined to look on the
crowds with a friendly eye. Their stocks of ammunition were low
and they had orders to shoot only in self-defence. On the workers'
side the Bolsheviks used their influence to stop their having arms
for fear they might let them off in excitement and so provoke the
troops. Nevertheless tension was increasing. Bombs were thrown
at some of the troops, perhaps by police *agents-provocateurs;* and,
though there is no evidence of it, it was widely believed that the
police had machine-gunned the crowds from the roofs.

[1] N. N. Sukhanov, *The Russian Revolution 1917* (1955), 3

The next day, 25 February, was much the same, though yet more workers were on strike. Crowds gathered round the statue of Alexander III in Znamensky Square and listened to revolutionary speeches. At about three in the afternoon a detachment of mounted police under its officer appeared on the scene. He pushed through the crowd to seize a Red Flag in its midst, and was killed. It is not clear if he was killed by a bullet or a knife, by a member of the crowd or by a Cossack standing by; but what is clear is that both the crowd and the police were under the impression that the Cossacks had joined the workers. That night Khabalov, the commander of the St Petersburg military district, on orders from the tsar, briefed his officers and the police on putting an end to the demonstrations: they were to break up small, peaceful crowds by mounted charges and large, aggressive ones by shooting them, afterfi ring three warning shots over their heads.

Sunday 26 February began quietly. In the morning the tsarina telegraphed to the tsar: 'The city is quiet.' The government appeared to have taken the measure of the disturbances and to have nerved itself to put them down. But in the afternoon there was serious rioting in Znamensky Square and Kazansky Square. The rioters were dispersed by shooting but only at the cost of heavy casualties—according to official figures 40 dead and as many wounded. By the evening it looked as if the government was regaining control and the riots fizzling out. But this superficial appearance was misleading, for there were two phenomena of importance, both of them noted by the police, that contradicted the appearance: the behaviour of the crowds and the behaviour of the troops. The crowds would disperse under fire but they were not panic-stricken. 'When preliminary shots were fired into the air, the crowd not only did not disperse but answered these volleys with laughter. Only when loaded cartridges were fired into the very midst of the crowd, was it found possible to disperse the mob, the participants of which, however, would most of them hide in the yards of nearby houses, and as soon as the shooting stopped come out again into the street.'[2]

'The overwhelming majority of the soldiers' wrote General Martynov, 'were disgusted with the role assigned to them in quelling the riots and fired only under compulsion.'[3] 'Since the

[2] Police report quoted in L. Trotsky, *History of the Russian Revolution* (1965), 133
[3] Quoted in G. Katkov, *Russia 1917, The February Revolution* (1967), 269, which gives the best narrative of these events.

army units have not opposed the crowd', wrote the *agent-provo-cateur* Shurkanov, 'and in individual cases have even taken measures paralysing the initiative of the police officers, the masses have got a sense of impunity, and now ... have become convinced that the revolution has begun, that success is with the masses, that the authorities are powerless to suppress the movement, because the troops are with it, that a decisive victory is near, since the troops will openly join the side of the revolutionary forces ...'.[4] Prophetic words! For towards evening the fourth battalion of the Pavlovsky Regiment had mutinied. The men were surrounded by a unit of the Preobrazhensky Regiment, arrested and disarmed; some were imprisoned. But when their rifles were checked a number were missing.

27 February was the critical day. During the previous night soldiers of the Volynsky Regiment had stayed awake discussing the events of the day. Early in the morning the very unpopular commanding officer, Lashkevich, appeared, lectured the men on their duty and quoted the tsar's orders. One of the NCOs, Kirpichnikov, told Lashkevich the men were refusing to go on duty. '[Lashkevich] went pale, shrank back and hurried out. We rushed to the windows, and many of us saw the commanding officer suddenly fling his arms wide and crash to the ground face down ... He was killed by a well-aimed stray bullet.'[5] (It was reported to the director of police that Kirpichnikov himself had fired the shot though there is no evidence of this.) This led to a general mutiny. The mutineers went at once to the barracks of the Litovsky and Preobrazhensky regiments and persuaded the soldiers of these units to join them. They then marched to the Duma where they were welcomed with speeches by representatives of the Left, Kerensky, Chkheidze and Skobelev. Meanwhile more regiments had mutinied, and there was sporadic shooting, clashes and skirmishes. The government and military authorities seemed to be dazed and ignorant of which units were still loyal: they gave no orders until it was too late. A force sent to punish the Volynsky mutineers got cut off in the streets and eventually vanished into the crowds in the darkness. The crowd, helped by soldiers with machine guns and even an armoured car, fired the barracks and the police headquarters, beat up police stations and freed the

[4] Trotsky, *op. cit.*, 134–5
[5] Katkov, *op. cit.*, 273

prisoners from the city jails, especially of course the political prisoners. By the evening the organized garrison of St Petersburg had dissolved into individual armed soldiers at one with the workers.

The political leaders released from prison combined with trade union and co-operative leaders and the Left deputies Chkheidze and Skobelev to set up a Provisional Executive Committee of the Soviet of Workers' Deputies. This had in turn sent out notices of a meeting of the Soviet to take place in the Tauride Palace (the Duma building) at 7 p.m. In the meantime it began the task of organizing and feeding the soldiers who were homeless as well as revolutionary. It also set up a military committee consisting of a handful of officers known to be democrats which combined that very day with the military committee of the Duma to form the Military Commission.

The Soviet met in the evening in one wing of the Tauride Palace, which was packed with soldiers, prisoners brought in for safety, members of the Duma, and casual bystanders who surged through the halls and corridors or stood about among the guns, the boxes of ammunition and the bags of flour on the floor made slushy by the mud and snow brought in on their boots. With Skobelev in the chair the Soviet managed to transact a certain amount of business. It set up a supply commission to organize the capital's food supplies, and a literary commission to draft a proclamation to the people. There was considerable debate whether the newspapers should be free to appear or not. One side argued that there should be a temporary ban to prevent enemies of the revolution spreading lies about the events and undermining the morale of the people; the other that it was vital to the revolution to uphold the principle of liberty and that the newspapers coming out in the ordinary way and the information which they gave would help to calm people and give them confidence. In the end it was decided to leave the decision to the individual editors. Most important of all, the Soviet set up an Executive Committee to take general control of the situation. It consisted of representatives of all shades of socialist opinion— SR, Menshevik and Bolshevik—and of various non-party men. It held its first meeting immediately in the Press Gallery of the Duma chamber and in about an hour had 'worked out instructions for the city districts concerning militia, planned the location of assembly points, and nominated Commissars. [It communicated its] decisions on to the district representatives, who set off at once.'[6] It also took steps to see that its representatives on the Military Commission understood that they were responsible to it, so that it could be sure of having a hold over the Commission's activities.

The Soviet had managed to arrive at these decisions in a grossly overcrowded room and despite constant interruptions by soldiers stammering out fraternal greetings from the various regiments. 'The audience listened as children listen to a wonderful, enthralling fairy-tale they know by heart, holding their breaths, with craning necks and unseeing eyes.'[7] The climax came when

> a young soldier burst through the flimsy barrier at the doors, and rushed to the centre of the hall. Without asking for the floor or waiting for permission to speak he raised his rifle above his head and shook it, choking and gasping as he shouted the joyful news:
> 'Comrades and brothers, I bring you brotherly greetings from all the lower ranks of the entire Semyonovsky Regiment of Life Guards. All of us to the last man are determined to join the people against the accursed autocracy, and we swear to serve the people's cause to the last drop of our blood!'
> In his emotion, bordering on frenzy, the youthful delegate of the mutinous Semyonovskys, who had plainly attended a school of party propaganda, was really, in these banal phrases and stereotyped terminology, pouring out his soul, overflowing with the majestic impressions of the day and consciousness that the longed-for victory had been achieved. In the meeting, disturbed in the midst of current business, there gushed forth once again a torrent of romantic enthusiasm. No-one stopped the Semyonovsky from finishing his lengthy speech, accompanied by thunderous applause. The importance of this news was obvious to everyone: the Semyonovsky Regiment had been one of the most trustworthy pillars of Tsarism. There was not a man in the room who was not familiar with the 'glorious' traditions of the 'Semyonovsky boys' and in particular did not remember their Moscow exploits in 1905.[8]

On this same day, 27 February, the Duma had been impelled into action. In the morning an imperial decree was published dissolving the Duma. This put its members in a dilemma: were

[6] Sukhanov, *op. cit.*, 72
[7] *Ibid.*, 61
[8] *Ibid*, p. 63

they to accept this and disperse or to reject it? It was pretty clear that the government had lost all authority and control of the situation, so if they dispersed it meant handing over control to the Soviet and therefore to the various working-class parties. If on the other hand they refused a perfectly correct decree signed by the tsar they would be acting illegally and committing themselves to a revolutionary course of action with all the risks which that entailed for legally constituted parliamentary parties. They formed a provisional committee in the morning and later in the day decided to remain in St Petersburg.

The leading man in the committee was Milyukov. He was more intelligent, more experienced and more determined than any of his colleagues. A democrat and a parliamentarian, he wanted to keep control of the revolution and to keep it constitutional. It was therefore his policy to get a government formed as quickly as possible and then to get it legalized. The government came into being on 1 March with Prince Lvov as prime minister, Milyukov as foreign minister, a forceful business man Guchkov as minister of war and Kerensky as minister of justice. Kerensky was included as a socialist to give the ministry as broad a character as possible; he accepted office because he longed to be a minister and because he saw himself as the link between the governing and the working classes and from that very fact the vital link in the revolutionary chain.

The government at once sent off Guchkov and a monarchist, Shulgin, to persuade the tsar to abdicate. Unkown to them he had in fact already decided to do so but not in favour of his son Alexis, whom he could not bear to part with, but in favour of his brother Michael. This news got a bad reception from railway workers to whom Guchkov announced it on his way back on 3 March. But in St Petersburg Milyukov still tried to get the other members of the provisional government to accept it. Finally Grand Duke Michael himself killed the plan by refusing to accept the throne. The government postponed a decision on what form the state should take, monarchy or republic, until such time as a constituent assembly could meet, but meanwhile its constitutional authority was shaky and it would need to justify it by its actions.

Its effective authority had already been challenged by the Soviet. The Soviet had issued on the very day the government had been formed, 1 March, its now famous Order No. 1. This instructed the soldiers and sailors to elect soviets throughout the army and the navy; to elect representatives to the Soviet; to keep control of all weapons, which were on no account to be handed over to the officers; only to obey orders of the Duma that were endorsed by the Soviet; and to conduct themselves as disciplined units when on duty, and as revolutionary citizens when off. The crucial clause is that relating to the Duma; by it the Soviet denied the Duma sovereign power and arrogated to itself the last word. In fact it set itself up as a rival and superior government. Which government the workers, soldiers and sailors would obey would depend on how quickly either could create an efficient means of getting its orders carried out, and, more important, which could capture and hold their loyalties. At first the advantage lay with the Soviet. It had in the soviets a method that had proved its value in the 1905 revolution and could be quickly and easily re-created. The collapse of the authority of officers and factory-owners had opened the way for some other authority; the Soviets could step in. Against this the provisional government had no channel of communication or chain of command. In the same way, the events of the February days gave the Soviet a tremendous claim on the loyalty of the workers, while the provisional government was a vague, grey affair with very little reality for them. But the Soviet could forfeit this loyalty if it failed to satisfy the workers' deepest desires: food and peace. Contrariwise the provisional government could capture this loyalty if it could provide them (and it alone could make peace) and if it could harness the imaginative energy released by the revolution.

Life was difficult: food was getting shorter, bread was rationed, prices kept on rising, workers came out on strike and bosses locked them out, the Germans might attack again at any moment, all kinds of undesirables were knocking about in disguise: ex-Pharaohs (police), German agents, anarchists, Bolsheviks. People in the streets were continually talking and listening to someone or other holding forth, and continually cursing: cursing the weather, for the spring was late and cold, and hailstorms kept sweeping down on the streets and squares; cursing their lot; cursing other people for getting in their light, for having got hold of some extra food, for advocating the continuance of the war, or for being what they were not: an aristocrat, an officer, a soldier, a spiv, an agent of some sort, or God knows what.

But, at the same time, life was creative. The tsar was gone. The tyranny of ages was ended for ever. The war would soon come to an end and the land would once again belong to the people. 'My holy of holies', wrote Chekhov to a friend, 'is the human body, health, intelligence, talent, inspiration, love and the most absolute freedom—freedom from violence and lying, whatever forms they may take.'[9] That was just it. Men could look forward in hope, they were free to make anything they liked out of life.

The provisional government reflected this ambiguity. Kerensky defines its main tasks 'in order of priority: 1. To continue the defence of the country; 2. to reestablish a working administrative apparatus throughout the country; 3. to carry out a number of basic political and social reforms; 4. to prepare the way for the transformation of Russia from a highly centralized state into a federal state.'[10] Further it was vital in Russia's critical position, as Kerensky points out, to complete its tasks as quickly as possible.

It is easy to understand why the government wanted to continue the war. Its members were liberal democrats whose sympathies were wholly with the allies and whose imaginations pictured Russia transformed from an autocracy into a bourgeois society much like that of France or England. They were constitutionalists who believed themselves bound by the existing treaties with the allies. Above all they feared the consequences of military defeat or a separate peace with Germany. These were not plain to see. But they would almost certainly include the loss of territory on the western frontier and German control, or occupation, of the oil wells of the Caucasus, and they might well mean the overthrow of the government itself and the relapse of Russia into complete anarchy. The glorious opportunity to create a free society would have been lost, perhaps for ever.

Nevertheless the decision to continue the war was a mistake. It was not based on a realistic assessment of the military and economic situation, or on an understanding of the people's feelings.

What the ordinary Russian wanted was peace, bread and land. Philips Price, the *Manchester Guardian's* correspondent in Russia,

---

[9] Quoted in W. H. Bruford, *Chekhov and his Russia* (1947), 203–4
[10] *The Kerensky Memoirs* (1966), 219

noted in March that in St Petersburg there was 'one main topic:
. . . bread and peace'.[11] And on a visit to barracks he heard the
soldiers discussing: 'Should they go up to the front if ordered to do
so? What were the objects of the war? . . . Could the war be stopped
with honour now? . . . "What we want is land, as soon as we
return home. We took up our rifles for our mother earth, and we
will not put them down till we get it." Thunderous applause.'[12]
The British Ambassador Sir George Buchanan, who had been
at his post since 1911 and was a shrewd observer, said much the
same thing. In a private letter to the Foreign Office on 2 April
he wrote: '. . . perfect order . . . reigns in the town . . . In certain
country districts, however, the peasants have been cutting down
the woods of the landed proprietors and are talking of dividing
up their lands. But, so far as I am aware, there has been no
incendiarism nor anything in the shape of an organised *Jacquerie*.'[13]
And a week later he wrote: 'Not only are the relations of officers
and men most unsatisfactory, but numbers of the latter are
returning home without leave. In some cases they have been
prompted to do so by reports of an approaching division of the
land and by the desire to be on the spot to secure their share of the
spoils.'

Moreover Russia was not far from industrial breakdown. This
was widely recognized, but it was thought to be due to inefficiency,
corruption and war weariness. It was hoped that the revolution
would inject a new spirit into bosses and workers alike and inspire
them with a feeling that Russia now belonged to them and so a
passionate desire to supply everything that was needed to bring
the revolutionary war to a victorious conclusion. But this did not
happen. Instead production declined, factory discipline went to
pieces, and neither factory-owners nor Workers' Soviets nor the
government seemed able to get a grip on the situation. In May
Konavalov, the minister of trade and industry, resigned in
despair. His temporary successor, Stepanov, wrote in a memorandum he submitted to the government in June: 'The disruption
of Russia's national economy has reached its peak at the present
moment. The country is facing economic and financial bank-
ruptcy. These menacing symptoms appear with special vividness

[11] M. Philips Price, *Reminiscences of the Russian Revolution* (1921), 13
[12] *Ibid.*, 16
[13] Sir George Buchanan, *My Mission to Russia* (1923), Vol. 2, 110–1

in the main branches of industry, which have completely lost their equilibrium.'[14]

The government also recognized the need for land reform, to satisfy the peasants and to produce the desperately needed food. But it felt that as a provisional government it did not have the necessary authority to put forward, still less to impose, a solution of its own. This must await the constituent assembly which would set up a permanent, constitutional government and hammer out a lasting scheme of land reform.

But the first essential was to end the war. Without this it was impossible to get the solid backing of the Russian people; it was impossible to prevent economic chaos; it was impossible to tackle the land problem or the national problem. It was impossible in time of war to grant autonomy to, say, Finland or the Ukraine, when there was a real possibility of the autonomous governments taking their peoples out of the war, and therefore in effect, if not formally, out of the Russian federal state. Grappling with the overwhelming problems of military discipline and supply left too little time and energy for re-establishing a working administrative apparatus throughout the country; or, put the other way round, the attempt to re-establish a working administrative apparatus kept breaking down because the apparatus had simultaneously to grapple with problems which were almost insoluble and which it was quite untrained to solve. More fundamentally, the apparatus did not work because the people did not feel the authority of the government behind it. This was to begin with not the government's fault. The essence of the revolution was freedom. Peasants stopped working for their landlords and sat on their backsides on their own land smelling the sweet spring air; factory workers stayed at home; soldiers fraternized with their enemies or downed tools and wandered away from the trenches; intellectuals talked all night and greeted the dawn with poems; exiles bit their fingers with impatience to be home again and free. The government shared this feeling and wholeheartedly introduced the basic political and social reforms, so that Lenin when he arrived in April could say that the revolution had already brought Russia politically up to the level of the advanced countries.

But its belief in freedom had a certain mystical quality about it, which made it belittle authority as such, and disincline it to

[14] Browder & Kerensky, *The Russian Provisional Government 1917* (1961), Vol. ii, 672

exert its own authority except where absolutely necessary. The prime minister, Prince Lvov, embodied this belief. 'He believed "blindly", as Guchkov said of him, in the eventual triumph of democracy, in the capacity of the Russian people to play a constructive part in the affairs of state; and he was always saying, both in public and in private, "Do not lose heart, have faith in Russian freedom!" '[15]

[15] Kerensky, *op. cit.*, 220

# 9  Lenin and the April Theses

Lenin arrived at the Finland Station in St Petersburg on the night of 3 April. The local Bolshevik leaders had gone to meet him in Finland and travelled on the train with him to give him first-hand news of the situation as they travelled. In the imperial waiting-room was a small delegation of the Soviet to welcome him.

> The train was very late. . . . But at long last it arrived. A thunderous *Marseillaise* boomed forth on the platform, and shouts of welcome rang out. We stayed in the imperial waiting-rooms while the Bolshevik generals exchanged greetings. Then we heard them marching along the platform, under the triumphal arches, to the sound of the band, and between the welcoming rows of troops and workers. The gloomy Chkheidze [chairman of the Soviet], and the rest of us after him, got up, went to the middle of the room, and prepared for the meeting . . .
>
> Shlyapnikov, acting as the master of ceremonies, appeared in the doorway, portentously hurrying, with the air of a faithful old police chief announcing the Governor's arrival. Without any apparent necessity he kept crying out fussily: 'Please, Comrades, please! Make way there! Comrades, make way!'
>
> Behind Shlyapnikov, at the head of a small cluster of people behind whom the door slammed again at once, Lenin came, or rather ran, into the room. He wore a round cap, his face looked frozen, and there was a magnificent bouquet in his hands. Running to the middle of the room, he stopped in front of Chkheidze as though colliding with a completely unexpected obstacle. And Chkheidze, still glum, pronounced the following 'speech of welcome' with not only the spirit and wording but also the tone of a sermon:
>
> 'Comrade Lenin, in the name of the Petersburg Soviet and of the whole revolution, we welcome you to Russia. But—we think that the principal task of the revolutionary democracy is now the defence of the revolution from any encroachments either from within or from without. We consider that what this goal requires is not disunion, but the closing of the democratic ranks. We hope you will pursue these goals together with us.'
>
> Lenin . . . stood there as though nothing taking place had the slightest connexion with him—looking about him, examining the persons round him and even the ceiling of the imperial waiting-room,

adjusting his bouquet . . . and then, turning away from the Executive Committee delegation altogether, he made this 'reply':

'Dear Comrades, soldiers, sailors, and workers! I am happy to greet in your persons the victorious Russian revolution, and greet you as the vanguard of the world-wide proletarian army ... The piratical imperialist war is the beginning of civil war throughout Europe ... The hour is not far distant when at the call of our comrade, Karl Liebknecht, the peoples will turn their arms against their own capitalist exploiters ... The worldwide Socialist revolution has already dawned ... Germany is seething. ... Any day now the whole of European capitalism may crash. The Russian revolution accomplished by you has prepared the way and opened a new epoch. Long life the worldwide Socialist revolution!'[1]

So in a few words Lenin immediately announced his attitude to the war and the revolution: the war would turn into civil war, the revolution was not the bourgeois revolution but the socialist revolution, the crisis of European capitalism was at hand.

Lenin left the waiting-room.

To another *Marseillaise*, and to the shouts of the throng of thousands, among the red-and-gold banners illuminated by the searchlights, Lenin went out by the main entrance and was about to get into a closed car, but the crowd absolutely refused to allow this. Lenin clambered on to the bonnet of the car and had to make a speech.[2]

He then climbed on to an armoured car and the procession moved off, a searchlight mounted on one of the armoured cars stabbing the darkness of the night, and 'it sliced out ... sections of excited workers, soldiers, sailors—the same ones who had achieved the great revolution and then let the power slip through their fingers.'[3] 'From the top of the armoured car Lenin "conducted a service" at practically every street-crossing, making new speeches to continually changing audiences. The procession made slow progress. The triumph had come off brilliantly, and even quite symbolically.'[4]

The procession arrived at Bolshevik headquarters in Kshesinskaya's palace. Lenin went in. But very soon he had to come out and speak to the crowd from the balcony. He spoke again of the imperialist war: a war between rival gangs of capitalist exploiters,

[1] Sukhanov, *The Russian Revolution 1917*, 272–3
[2] *Ibid.*, 274
[3] Trotsky, *History of the Russian Revolution*, 312
[4] Sukhanov, *op. cit.*, 275

in which defending the fatherland was in fact defending one of them.

' "Ought to stick our bayonets into a fellow like that," a soldier suddenly shouted out, in a lively reaction. "Eh? The things he says! Eh? If he came down here we'd have to show him! ... Must be a German ... he ought to be ...!" '[5]

Lenin went back into the palace, and eventually to the dining-room for a meal. On the way he ran into Sukhanov and greeted him affably, ragging him a bit about their disputes on the land question. They sat down at a table together and went on talking. Lenin pitched into the Executive Committee of the Soviet and its Soviet line on the war, repeatedly condemning what he called 'revolutionary defencism' and attacking Tsereteli, Chkheidze and Steklov for this. Their chat was interrupted by shouts to Lenin to hurry up and finish, as there were about two hundred party workers downstairs waiting for him.

Lenin went down and spoke to them for about two hours. He again began by saying that the crisis of imperialism was at hand and the imperial war would turn into civil war and open the way to the worldwide socialist revolution. He fiercely attacked the peace policy of the Soviet and jeered at its leaders. He went on to attack the provisional government and to call on the Bolshevik party to be an opposition minority to 'enlighten, explain, persuade'.[6] He then startled his audience by saying: 'We don't need a parliamentary republic, we don't need bourgeois democracy, we don't need any Government except the Soviets of Workers', Soldiers' and Farm-labourers' deputies.'[6] Nor was legislation needed on the land question: there was simply to be 'organized seizure'. In the towns the 'armed workers [were to] stand at the cradle of production, at the factory benches'.[7] He ended by anathematizing all the false European socialists who by supporting the war had betrayed the proletariat and Social-Democracy and made its name stink: the very name

had been desecrated by treason. It was impossible to have anything in common with it, impossible to purge it: it had to be cast aside as the symbol of the betrayal of the working class.

I shall never forget that thunder-like speech, which startled and

[6] Sukhanov, *op. cit.*, 276
[5] *Ibid.*, 282
[7] *Ibid.*, 284

amazed not only me, a heretic, who had accidentally dropped in, but all the true believers. I am certain that no-one had expected anything of the sort. It seemed as though all the elements had risen from their abodes, and the spirit of universal destruction, knowing neither barriers nor doubts, neither human difficulties nor human calculations, was hovering around Kshesinskaya's reception-room above the heads of the bewitched disciples.[8]

Next day there was a meeting of Social-Democrats (Bolsheviks, Mensheviks and independents) at the Tauride Palace organized by a group of members who thought the time ripe for a re-unification of the party. Lenin dashed their hopes. He made much the same speech as the day before but took care to emphasize the irreconcilable difference of his line from that of the majority:

> [He] was the living incarnation of schism ... each new word of [his] filled [his hearers] with indignation. Protests and exclamations of outrage began to be heard. It wasn't only a question of the in-appropriateness of such a speech at a 'unifying' conference, it was also that together with the idea of unity the foundations of the Social-Democratic programme and of Marxist theory were spat upon ... I remember Bogdanov [a Menshevik member of *Ex. Com.*] shouting: 'This is the raving of a madman! It's indecent to applaud this clap-trap!' and livid with rage and contempt, turning to the audience, 'You ought to be ashamed of yourselves! Marxists!'[9]

The same day Lenin gave the Bolsheviks a written précis of his main points *On the Tasks of the Proletariat in the Present Revolution*, now known as the 'April Theses': no support for the war, which was still what it always had been, an imperialist war; complete renunciation of annexations 'in deeds, not merely in words'; no support for the bourgeois government of 'revolutionary defencism'—it was capitalist through and through, and it was an illusion to think it could be converted into a socialist govern-ment. The present stage of the revolution was a transition from the first, bourgeois stage to the second, socialist stage, 'which is to place power in the hands of the proletariat and the poorest strata of the peasantry'.[10] There was to be no parliamentary republic; the only possible form of revolutionary government was the Soviet. But as this was in the hands of traitors to the proletariat who had given in to the bourgeois, their errors must be exposed and the masses educated to 'learn from experience how to rid

[8] *Ibid.*, 280
[9] *Ibid.*, 286
[10] 'April Theses' in *A Handbook of Marxism* (1935), 784–5

themselves of errors'.[11] Furthermore he advocated abolition of the police, the army, the bureaucracy, and the arming of the whole people; confiscation of all private land; nationalization of all land and its management by Soviets of Agricultural Labourers' and Peasants' Deputies; organization of separate soviets of the poorest peasants; merger of all banks into one national bank to be run by the Soviet; an immediate party congress to change the party programme on the war, on its attitude to the state, its antiquated minimum programme and its name. The name Social-Democratic had been betrayed and besmirched by the Socialist leaders of the Second International. It was anyway unscientific and had been attacked by Marx in the *Critique of the Gotha Programme* and by Engels; and the word Democratic hinted at a form of state, whereas Marxists were against all forms of state. A more scientific term would have been Communist. This was derived from *The Communist Manifesto* and looked forward to a society based on the Communist motto: *From each according to his ability, to each according to his needs.*

> We want to rebuild the world. We want to end this imperialist World War in which hundreds of millions of people are involved and billions of dollars are invested, a war which cannot be ended in a truly democratic way without the greatest proletarian revolution in history.
> And here we are, afraid of our own shadow. Here we are, keeping on our backs the same old soiled shirt . . .
> It is high time to cast off the soiled shirt, it is high time to put on clean linen.[12]

The theses 'produced the impression of an exploding bomb'.[13] Lenin was alone in his views, and the local Bolsheviks attributed them to his long exile and consequent ignorance of Russian conditions.

Exile was if anything, however, an advantage to Lenin. Living in Switzerland he was far better informed about the war and the affairs of the world than Bolsheviks in Russia, still more than those who had been sent to Siberia. He was right in thinking that the crisis of the war was at hand. The strain on nerves and resources was beginning to tell. The casualties of the Russian offensive and retreat of 1916 and of Verdun and the Somme

[11] 'April Theses' in *A Handbook of Marxism*, 786
[12] *Ibid.*, 791
[13] Zalezhsky, quoted by Trotsky, *op. cit.*, 326

had been astronomical. Jutland had decided the German government to embark on unrestricted U-boat warfare. The day before Lenin arrived in St Petersburg the government of the United States had declared war. A fortnight later the first of the mutinies in the French army broke out. The apparently imminent ruin of the old order in Europe drove Lord Lansdowne to write his celebrated letter pleading for a negotiated peace, published in *The Daily Telegraph* on 29 November 1917:

> We are not going to lose this war, but its prolongation will spell ruin for the civilized world. ... What will be the value of the blessings of peace to nations so exhausted that they can scarcely stretch out an arm with which to grasp them? In my belief, if the war is to be brought to a close in time to avert a world-wide catastrophe, it will be brought to a close because on both sides the peoples of the countries involved realize that it has already lasted too long.

Could words more accurately describe the feelings of the Russian people or more completely confirm Lenin's diagnosis from the angle of 'a disillusioned Conservative'?[14]

What Lenin said when he got to St Petersburg was only what he had been saying since the outbreak of the war and had developed at length in *Socialism and War* and *Imperialism, the Highest Stage of Capitalism*. Only the expression of his views was terser and more lapidary.

The 'revolutionary defencists' had no cause to be shocked at Lenin's line, for it was consistent and orthodox. But it is understandable that they were. Though the Russian Social-Democrats as a whole had voted against war credits, there was from the very beginning a strong minority of 'social patriots', and Plekhanov himself had come out in favour of the defence of the fatherland, despite the tsar and the autocracy. With their overthrow in 1917 the Kaiser and Hindenburg stood out as symbols of imperialism, and it was easy to slip into feeling that their victory would not inaugurate the world revolution but clamp the fetters of imperialism on the workers of the world for an unforeseeable length of time. Moreover, while Lenin had been in neutral Switzerland the members of the party in Russia were exposed to the feverish atmosphere there. There had been a million casualties in the 1916 campaign, and it was estimated that there were another million deserters living peacefully in their

[14] Cruttwell, *A History of the Great War* (1934), 373

homes. The widespread disgust at the incompetence and corruption in high places had relieved itself in the murder of Ras-
putin, but this had come too late to save the tsar and the dynasty:
'the old emotional loyalties had been used up or worn thin.'[15]
The emotions were powerful, volatile, unfocused. It is not
surprising if for many people they focused on Russia and lent
drive to a last effort to defend her, to break the German war
machine to pieces, and to bring peace and freedom to the war-
weary workers and peasants.

There was a wide measure of agreement on land policy.
Bolsheviks and Mensheviks (and SRs) had been determined
since 1905 to confiscate all land, whether it belonged to private
landowners or the tsar, the state or the church. They all favoured
the public ownership of all land, but differed over the form of
ownership: the Bolsheviks wanted the state as such to own it,
the Mensheviks favoured the *zemstvos* and the SRs the *mirs*.
They all approved of the peasants individually occupying and
farming the land. But they also all favoured equality of holdings
and wanted to move towards this. As long ago as 1906 Lenin had
drafted the resolution on land adopted at the London congress,
which proclaimed party backing for peasant seizure of the land or,
better, nationalization, i.e. state seizure of the land, which would
then be rented to the peasants. This alternative had the further
merit of facilitating the collection of a steeply progressive land
tax which could be used to achieve equality of holdings quite
quickly.

The only new feature in Lenin's land policy in 1917 was the
function of the soviets. This brought it decidedly closer to the
policy of the Mensheviks and SRs. The soviets would be *local*
managers of the land just as the *zemstvos* or *mirs* would be. But
there is a decisive difference too. The *mir* consists, by definition, of
the entire village community and is therefore a normally conservative force. It was a fair guess that once the peasants actually
occupied all the land it would be just that: to get changes in the
use of land, in technique and in marketing would be very difficult.
The *zemstvos*, even reformed according to Menshevik wishes,
would tend to consist of *kulaks*. The soviets, on the other hand,
would consist of 'Agricultural Labourers' and Peasants' Deputies',
some of whom would be zealous party members; and from the

[15] Sumner, *Survey of Russian History*, 70

word go there were to be separate soviets of the deputies of the poorest peasants. Lenin meant the theoretical distinction he had already drawn between the mass of peasants, who were petty-bourgeois, and the poorest peasants, who were proletarian, to be embodied in practice at the grass roots. It could be widened as opportunity offered.

This distinction also implied Lenin's attitude to the revolution, the state and the government. All Marxists agreed that the revolution would overthrow capitalism and the bourgeois state. Marx and Engels had argued that the inherent contradictions of capitalism would rend it asunder and that it would be its own grave-digger. The revolution was inevitable. But it was at the same time the task of the party to work for revolution and to intervene at the decisive moment to make and direct it. There was an inherent contradiction here too. Naturally enough Social-Democrats emphasized one or other of these aspects of Marxist dialectic according to their temperament and circumstances. In general Mensheviks tended to rely on the inevitability of revolution and Bolsheviks expected and longed for the day of action: Lenin had been doubtful in January if 'we the old would see the revolution', but there is no doubt that it came as a glorious climax of his life which he welcomed with his whole being; and it is significant that Trotsky, who had been on Martov's side in the *Iskra* split and counted as a Menshevik at the time of the 1905 revolution, joined the Bolsheviks on his return from exile in the U.S.A. in May.

The peculiar conditions of Russian life led to another difference connected with this, and even more important in practice: whether Russia had undergone the bourgeois, capitalist revolution. Social-Democrats from Marx onwards, including Lenin, had expected the revolution to break out in Western Europe, probably in Germany. In comparison Russia was a backward country almost wholly unindustrialized before 1860, and therefore, according to Marx's scientific analysis, a country in which the revolution could not occur. After 1860 and still more after 1880, Russian industry grew with comparative rapidity, though its output was still far below that of Germany, Britain or the U.S.A. But it grew in a peculiar form. Most of the capital was imported from abroad, as were many technicians. The state owned by far the largest number of factories, and the factory workers were the equivalent of the earlier state serfs. All this had another important consequence: a large and powerful middle class did not develop. There were not thousands of busy, hard-headed entrepreneurs. There were few bankers, managers or skilled craftsmen. In a word there was scarcely a bourgeoisie.

So long as the tsar was autocratic and the government little more than a set of bureaucrats obedient to his will this situation presented no theoretical problem. But after the revolution of 1905 and the summoning of the Duma the problem arose whether the regime was still autocratic or had become, or at least started to become, bourgeois/capitalist. After the overthrow of the tsar this problem was more acute and of immediate practical importance. If the regime had been more or less bourgeois since 1905, it could be plausibly argued that Russia had passed, albeit pretty rapidly, through the bourgeois stage of revolution and was ripe for the socialist revolution. If however the regime had remained autocratic until the tsar's abdication, Russia had clearly only just embarked on the bourgeois revolution, and some time must elapse before it could move on to the next stage. The practical test of the theory for an individual was whether he supported the provisional government or not.

It might seem that this was a decision to be taken on the strength of straightforward, political judgment. But this would be to underrate the importance for Marxists of *correct* action. The underlying theory of political action must be scientific and correct; for if it were not, it followed that the action was bound to be inappropriate and therefore futile. Equally the action must be correctly conceived and executed in relation to the concrete situation it was dealing with. Strategy and tactics must be correct. And a very large number of the disputes between different Social-Democratic groups, and especially between Lenin and his opponents, turned on questions of tactics. The Mensheviks took the view that only with the tsar's abdication did Russia enter on the bourgeois revolution, and that the provisional, liberal government was the correct government to preside over this stage. It was the task of the party to use the freedom given to all political parties to educate and prepare the proletariat as thoroughly as possible for the inevitable next revolution and the seizure of power. Most Bolsheviks before Lenin's arrival agreed with them and the most prominent of them on their arrival from Siberia,

Kamenev and Stalin, cautiously advocated backing the government.

The decision was further complicated by two other factors that might be regarded as accidental: what Trotsky called the 'flabbiness' of the leading Russian bourgeois, and the Soviet.

The first meant that many Social-Democrats, even though they recognized the necessity of the bourgeois revolution, hated, despised and distrusted the bourgeois and liberal politicians, and thought them totally unfit to govern Russia for even a short time, and especially at the crisis of the war. This was most true of Lenin and Trotsky, and was yet another factor dividing them from the Mensheviks and stimulating them to make the transition stage between the two revolutions as short as possible.

Lenin regarded the Soviet as 'an organization of the workers [and] the embryo of a workers' government'.[16] It is characteristic of him that he is thinking of the immediate situation and the correct tactics to employ in it, and of how to transform it: how to convert the 'revolutionary-democratic dictatorship of the proletariat and the poorest peasantry' into the 'dictatorship of the proletariat'. He had grasped at once that the provisional government had no real authority. Only the Soviet had it, backed by the workers, soldiers and sailors. On the other hand the Bolsheviks were in a minority in the Soviet, and could not at once use it as the correct form of the dictatorship of the proletariat. The first task was to draw the mass of the people to the Bolshevik side and thereby capture the soviets. They would then be poised to act as 'organs of insurrection' to overthrow the provisional government. In overthrowing it they would automatically transform themselves into 'organs of revolutionary power'; and the St Petersburg Soviet would exercise the dictatorship of the proletariat and guide the Russian people, in alliance with the revolutionary European proletariat, through the socialist revolution to the communist society.

These ideas were not unique, for Trotsky had already put them forward in his book, *The Year 1905*. Nor were they radically new, for Lenin had welcomed the St Petersburg Soviet in an article written for *Novaya Zhizn* at the very beginning of November 1905, and had moved a resolution on the role of the soviet at the Fourth (Unity) Congress of the party in April 1906. He had taken

[16] *Collected Works*, Vol. 23, 304

up and reiterated his thought in the *Letters From Afar* that he had written in March 1917 just before leaving Switzerland. But the 1905 article had not been published and was unknown, and there had only been time for one of the *Letters From Afar* to be published by this time. Between 1905 and 1917 Lenin had not thought or written much about the soviets, nor had anyone else. Their attention and thought had been concentrated on the Duma and then on the war. Moreover there had been little contact between Lenin and the Bolsheviks inside Russia during the war: he complained constantly of this in his letters and urged the need to establish regular links. Lenin was not an original thinker, but he had a creative political intelligence and an abnormally sensitive 'feel' for a situation, so it is not so surprising as it looks at first sight that his hearers were so shattered by what he said. His mind had made a great creative leap; theirs had stood still. They were like a pack of mongrels lumbering after a whippet.

When Lenin arrived in St Petersburg in April he was greeted by the Bolsheviks as their leader. But to the Russian people as a whole he was quite unknown, and his arrival did not cause the government any alarm. The Bolsheviks constituted a small minority group among the Socialists and on the Soviet and represented only a tiny fraction of the people. They did not appear to be of great political consequence.

What seemed much more important was the continuous political effervescence in St Petersburg that crystallized at intervals into political demonstrations. The first of these, on 23 March, was the most united and the most joyful.

On the 23rd of March the United States entered the war. On that day Petrograd was burying the victims of the February revolution. The funeral procession—in its mood a procession triumphant with the joy of life—was a mighty concluding chord in the symphony of the five days. Everybody went to the funeral: both those who had fought side by side with the victims, and those who had held them back from the battle, very likely also those who killed them—and above all, those who had stood aside from the fighting. Along with workers, soldiers, and the small city people here were students, ministers, ambassadors, the solid bourgeois, journalists, orators, leaders of all the parties. The red coffins carried on the shoulders of workers and soldiers streamed in from the workers' districts to Mars Field. When the coffins were lowered into the grave there sounded from Peter and Paul fortress the first funeral salute, startling the innumerable masses of the people. That cannon had a new sound: our cannon, our salute. The Vyborg section carried fifty-one red coffins. That was only a part of the victims it was proud of. In the procession of the Vyborg workers, the most compact of all, numerous Bolshevik banners were to be seen, but they floated peacefully beside other banners. On Mars Field itself there stood only the members of the government, of the Soviet, and the State Duma—already dead but stubbornly evading its own funeral. All day long no less than 800,000 people filed past the grave with bands and banners. And although, according to preliminary reckonings by the highest military authorities, a human mass of that size could not possibly pass a given point without the most appalling chaos and fatal whirlpools, nevertheless the demonstration was carried out in complete order—a thing to be observed generally in revolutionary processions, dominated as they are by a satisfying consciousness of a great deed achieved, combined with a hope that everything will grow better and better in the future It was only this feeling that kept order, for organisation was still weak, inexperienced and unconfident of itself. The very fact of the funeral was, it would seem, a sufficient refutation of the myth of a bloodless revolution. But nevertheless the mood prevailing at the funeral recreated to some extent the atmosphere of those first days when the legend was born.[1]

Less solemn, more in a holiday mood, were the processions all over Russia to celebrate May Day. 'The holiday of proletarian anti-militarism blended with the revolution-tinted manifestations of patriotism.' But a demonstration against the government defined this patriotism much more sharply.

One of the first acts of the Provisional Government had been to issue a proclamation on war aims. The original draft read:

> The Provisional Government considers it its right and duty to declare now that the ideal of free Russia is not rule over other peoples, nor the seizure of their national property, but the establishment of a stable peace based on national self-determination. However, the Russian people will not allow its homeland to emerge from the great struggle humbled and with its vital energies sapped. These principles will underlie the foreign policy of the Provisional Government, unswervingly guiding the people's will and guarding the rights of our fatherland, while the obligations undertaken towards our Allies will be fully observed.[2]

Under pressure from the Soviet it added that there would be no violent seizure of foreign territory. So it was in black and white that Russia not only had no wish to rule over other peoples, e.g. the Poles, who did not wish to be ruled, but renounced all foreign conquests. But the foreign minister, Milyukov, did not genuinely approve this decision, and in a note to the Allies on 18 April interpreted it in such a way as to suggest that Russia stood by the terms of its agreements with the Allies and was not averse to certain territorial gains which would guarantee the settlement arrived at after the war. This put the fat in the fire. The Soviet believed it had been double-crossed by Milyukov, and the man in the street vaguely sensed that the war might drag on for the sake of Armenia or Constantinople. Two days later on 20 April the

[1] Trotsky, *History of the Russian Revolution*, 345–6
[2] Sukhanov, *The Russian Revolution*, 249

masses demonstrated all day long in St Petersburg and demanded Milyukov's resignation.

This precipitated a double crisis: a crisis inside the government and a crisis in the relations between the government and the Soviet. Most of the ministers thought that Milyukov by his action had violated the principle of cabinet responsibility and forfeited the confidence of his colleagues as well as of the Soviet and the public, and must be transferred from the foreign office. Milyukov would not tolerate this and resigned. This created an opportunity to reconstruct the government in such a way as to end the Dual Power and give the government real authority. If there was a coalition government with an adequate number of socialist ministers in it, it was hoped that the Soviet would steadfastly back the government. There would be only one source of authority, not two; and one set of orders flowing from this source. There would be the very important consequence in the provinces that the local authorities would receive only one set of orders, and there would be no need for two or more sets of authorities: local *zemstvos* and soviets could amalgamate, or, in the short run, at least co-operate. The majority of the Soviet thought much the same. From the time of Order No. 1 the Soviet had proved its authority over the troops, and Kronstadt, the naval base, was firmly in the hands of the local sailors' soviet. Milyukov's resignation showed the Soviet's power over high policy. With socialist ministers in the government the Soviet could hope to control and direct policy in a consistent socialist direction. The Executive Committee of the Soviet resolved to join the coalition by a large majority. But all the Bolshevik members and a few left-wing Mensheviks and SRs voted against joining. The socialists got six posts. Kerensky got the Ministry of War and Marine; Tsereteli, the Menshevik leader and the dominant figure in the Executive Committee, got the Ministry of Posts and Telegraphs; and Chernov, the SR leader, the Ministry of Agriculture. So the socialists not only had six posts, but two crucial ones: War and Agriculture.

Success in these posts could win the government the support of the vast majority of the Russian people and perhaps save the country from disintegration. But meanwhile by entering the government the Mensheviks and SRs had exposed themselves to Bolshevik attack.

E

The 1st All-Russian Congress of Soviets opened in St Petersburg on 3 June. Lenin showed at once that he was not afraid of responsibility. On 4 June Tsereteli made a speech justifying the Executive Committee's decision to join the government, in the course of which he said that there was no political party willing at the present time to assume full power. From the floor Lenin interjected 'There is!' and in his speech immediately following Tsereteli's he elaborated this. 'He [Tsereteli] said there was no political party in Russia expressing its readiness to assume full power. I reply: "Yes, there is. No party can refuse this, and our party certainly doesn't. It is ready to take over full power at any moment".'[3] There was applause and laughter. The laughter is easy to understand. Governing Russia at this moment was no picnic, and here was a small party without a majority in the St Petersburg Soviet or the Congress of Soviets, let alone the country, saying quite calmly that the party was ready to take over full power, apparently without fear or bravado or irony. This was either awe-inspiring or ridiculous.

Lenin did not regard it as either, for he believed that the tide was running the Bolshevik way and that the party was equipped to take it. The events of June and July strongly reinforced his belief. The soldiers, sailors and factory workers in St Petersburg were more and more coming to the Bolshevik line. How far this was spontaneous and how far under the influence of steady Bolshevik propaganda is a matter of dispute. What is clear is that by the beginning of June there was great pressure from the rank and file, especially in certain regiments, for a mass demonstration against the government and for the Soviet, a demonstration to force the Soviet to take power even against its own will. The Bolshevik party decided, after considerable hesitation among the leaders, to take control of this movement, and on 9 June put up posters signed by the party Central Committee and by the Central Bureau of Factory Committees calling for a mass demonstration the next day, and sending its representatives to the factories and barracks to make the necessary arrangements. This alarmed the Soviet, which insisted that the demonstration should be called off. The Bolsheviks accepted this decision and worked throughout the night of the 9th to get it obeyed by the rank and file. The Soviet thereupon decreed an all-party demonstration for 18 June

[3] *Collected Works*, Vol. 25, 20

which would show the solidarity of the working class and the Soviet. The Bolsheviks by numbers and by good organization turned this into a Bolshevik triumph. Hundreds of banners proclaimed 'Down with the Ten Capitalist Ministers!' 'Down with the Offensive!' and 'All Power to the Soviets!'

A fortnight later on 3 July there was a much more formidable movement which looked to the government like an armed uprising to overthrow it, inspired and led by the Bolsheviks. In the second half of June the Russian army had launched an offensive against the Germans. At first this gained some ground and looked as if it might be a success, but it quickly petered out and was followed by swift and steady German advance. Morale in the army sank back. In the capital there was great excitement and anger. Machine-gun units refused to leave for the front and inspired the regimental committees to insist on an armed demonstration through the heart of the city. Troops began to move in the afternoon of 3 July, and were joined by workers from the Putilov and other factories. At the same time they sent a message to the Kronstadt sailors telling them of their actions. They marched first to the Kshesinskaya Palace, the Bolshevik headquarters, where they were joined by various Bolshevik leaders, and then in the evening to the Tauride Palace where the workers' section of the Soviet was in session. There was great confusion, with disorganized bodies of men rushing about; eventually soldiers and workers camped for the night in the courtyard of the palace. Early next morning all was quiet and there was no sign of a disciplined rising. But about 11 a.m. disorders began again. At noon the sailors began to disembark. They too went first to the Kshesinskaya Palace, and called insistently for Lenin. He came out on to the balcony and made a speech which 'consisted of a few simple phrases: a greeting to the demonstrators; an expresion of confidence that the slogan, "All Power to the Soviets", would conquer in the end, an appeal for firmness and self-restraint'.[4] They then moved on to the Tauride Palace. On the way firing broke out and some sailors were wounded. They believed they had been deliberately fired on and were in an ugly mood when they reached the palace. Chernov went out to greet them and was surrounded immediately and in grave danger of being lynched. Trotsky had to use all his eloquence and

[4] Trotsky, *op. cit.*, 547

histrionic talent to rescue him. Later in the evening some of the Putilov workers broke into the palace looking for Tsereteli. A crowd of about forty workers burst in to the hall tempestuously.

> The deputies leaped from theirs eats. Some failed to show adequate courage and self-control.
>
> One of the workers, a classical *sans-culotte*, in a cap and a short blue blouse without a belt, with a rifle in his hand, leaped up on to the speakers' platform. He was quivering with excitement and rage, stridently shouting out incoherent words and shaking his rifle:
>
> 'Comrades! How long must we workers put up with treachery? You're all here debating and making deals with the bourgeoisie and the landlords ... You're busy betraying the working class. Well, just understand that the working class won't put up with it! There are 30,000 of us all told here from Putilov. We're going to have our way. All power to the Soviets! We have a firm grip on our rifles! Your Kerenskys and Tseretelis are not going to fool us.'
>
> Chkheidze, in front of whose nose the rifle was dancing about, showed complete self-control. In answer to the hysterics of the *sans-culotte*, pouring out his hungry proletarian soul, the chairman tranquilly leaned down from his height and pushed into the worker's quivering hand a manifesto, printed the evening before:
>
> 'Here, please take this, Comrade, read it. It says here what you and your Putilov comrades should do. Please read it and don't interrupt our business. Everything necessary is said there.' ...
>
> The baffled *sans-culotte*, not knowing what else to do, took the appeal and then without much difficulty was got off the platform. His comrades too were quickly 'persuaded' to leave the hall.[5]

The workers left the hall and the workers outside the palace milled around, but that was all. As Sukhanov says of the incident in the hall, 'Order was restored and the incident liquidated'.

In the early hours of the next morning loyal troops began to arrive to protect the government and the Soviet and to break up the demonstrators. There was some shooting in the streets and some tussles when loyal troops disarmed parties of demonstrators. But in the main the demonstrators ebbed back to the suburbs. When the demonstration was to all intents and purposes over, the Bolshevik Central Committee passed a resolution 'to end the demonstration, in view of the fact that the workers' and soldiers' actions of 4 July and 5 July have forcefully emphasized the danger in which the country has been placed by the disastrous policy of the Provisional Government'.[6]

[5] Sukhanov, *op. cit.*, 449–50
[6] *Ibid.*, 457

Everything was over. It had been an alarming and exhausting two days for the government and the Soviet, and it was natural that they thought the Bolshevik party had engineered the demonstrations, intending to turn them into an armed rising to seize power for itself under the banner 'All Power to the Soviets'. But it is doubtful if this is true.

Lenin had stated publicly that the party was ready to take full power, and this was of course known not only to the Congress of Soviets but in the barracks and factories. Bolshevik agitators were continually ramming home the lesson of their slogans: 'Down with the War', 'Down with the Ten Capitalist Ministers' and 'All Power to the Soviets'; and this had some effect at the front and in St Petersburg. The demonstrators were Bolshevik in spirit if not in name, and on each day made straight for the Kshesinskaya Palace, as though to 'home' where they expected to receive instructions. But their expectations were disappointed. Lenin gave them no clear instructions. All that happened was that members of the party went with the demonstrators to the Tauride Palace. The shooting and clashes in the streets, by all accounts, were sporadic and haphazard. The behaviour of the demonstrators at the Tauride Palace was passionate and threatening, but largely chaotic and purposeless. They all but lynched Chernov but made no attempt to murder or arrest the leading members of the Soviet, or to occupy the building until they had achieved their ends. Nor did other groups occupy strategic points like the Marian Palace (the seat of the government), the Central Post Office or the main railway stations. All this is in such contrast to Bolshevik action in October that it suggests that the party did not believe the time was yet ripe for taking power and had not worked out a plan to do this in July. It is just possible that it planned and launched the mass demonstrations to show its power and to embarrass the government, with instructions to convert the demonstrations into an armed rising if it looked as if events were going that way. But this is to allow enormous scope to spontaneity and accident and seems out of keeping with Lenin's insistence on efficiency and discipline. It is more likely that Trotsky is right in his account, that the initiative lay with the rank and file, and that the party, unable to stop the demonstrations, decided to do its best to control them and prevent their leading to useless violence which would give the government an excuse to attack the party.

If this was indeed its policy it was a failure. The governmen
was frightened into action. It sent troops to break up the *Pravd*
printing press. It arrested Trotsky, Lunacharsky and others. I
would have arrested Lenin and Zinoviev but they had botl
gone into hiding. It started a campaign against Lenin as a Germai
agent and produced a series of telegrams between Stockholm an
St Petersburg to prove that he had received German money
These telegrams between Helphand (alias Parvus) and Haneck
(alias Fürstenberg) in Stockholm, and Lenin, Kollontay, Koz
lovsky and Sumenson in St Petersburg showed that money ha
been transferred from the Nye Bank in Stockholm to Sumenson'
account in the Siberian Bank in St Petersburg. This was ostensibl
payment for business transactions carried on by an expor
company which Helphand had founded in Copenhagen, an
which did in fact do good business. There is no direct proof tha
the money was used for other than business purposes. But Help
hand had got well over five million roubles from the Germai
government for use in anti-war propaganda inside Russia and ha
met secretly with Radek in Stockholm on 13 April, and it seem
almost certain that they arranged how the money should be mad
available to the Bolsheviks in Russia. None of this of cours
makes Lenin a German agent. Helphand was technically such a
agent. But his life makes clear that he was working during th
war for a German victory because he thought this the indispensabl
prelude to a socialist revolution in Germany and so to the worl
revolution. On the outbreak of the revolution in Russia h
naturally wanted Russia to withdraw from the war to speed up th
German victory and he used his established position as a Germai
agent to help any Russian groups that were anti-war and activel
campaigning to force Russia out of it. In practice this meant th
Bolshevik party. Lenin had no scruples about accepting th
money. It was a godsend. If the German government cared t
provide money, well and good. For the moment their purpose
ran in tandem; once the war was at an end they would diverge
Lenin meant to set up a Soviet socialist government to transforn
Russia into a communist society, not a puppet government of th
Germans to extend and prolong the imperial *Reich*.

At the time Lenin and his colleagues flatly denied the charg
that they had received money, and this was prudent. The charg
was plausible, and rumours that Lenin was a German agent ha

already stirred up popular hostility to him. But it is hard to see why later Bolsheviks have persisted in this denial, for receiving the money, if Lenin did receive it, does not seem to be a dirty action either by bourgeois or communist standards of value.

Partly because of these rumours and partly because of the apparent failure of an attempt to seize power in the July days, but still more because of an indefinable but definite loss of confidence in the Bolsheviks, there was during July a marked ebb of the Bolshevik tide: large numbers of workers and peasants turned to one of the other revolutionary parties or ceased to be attached to any recognized group.

Now was the moment for the government to assert its authority and get a grip on the country and its urgent problems. This it failed to do. The troops had no confidence in the government or the military high command. Kerensky on his tour of the front in May and June had inspired the soldiers with momentary enthusiasm by his bursts of frenetic oratory, but their enthusiasm expired the minute he had vanished to another part of the front. Despite this and the disquieting lack of supplies, the government persisted in its plan for a major offensive in June. It was a complete failure, and after it morale was naturally lower than before. Moreover the Germans had the sense to realize that the one thing that might restore it was a major offensive aimed at St Petersburg or Moscow. So they refrained from mounting a counter-attack. Inactivity and fraternization would serve their turn better.

To these was added an even more powerful solvent of discipline: land hunger. Just as the government refused to make peace, so it refused to execute an immediate land settlement; that must wait for the constituent assembly. But it had already twice postponed the date of the assembly, and the peasants by July were sceptical and impatient.

They would wait no longer. They began to act. They seized land: meadow, ploughland and forest. They seized crops, foodstuffs, fodder and farm implements. In many cases they attacked manors and farm buildings.

During July the government counter-attacked and had some success in repressing disorder. But in September and October unrest again increased and there was more destruction of property than before, much of it of an elemental character.

On a night about the 8th of September, [writes Trotsky] the peasants of the village Sychevka in Tombov province, going from door to door armed with clubs and pitchforks, called out everybody, small and great, to raid the landlord, Romanov. At a village meeting one group proposed that they take the estate in an orderly fashion, divide the property among the population, and keep the buildings for cultural purposes. The poor demanded that they burn the estate, leaving not one stone upon another. The poor were in the majority. On that same night an ocean of fire swallowed up the estates of the whole township. Everything inflammable was burned, even the experimental fields. The breeding cattle were slaughtered. 'They were drunk to madness.' The flames jumped over from township to township.[7]

The peasants owed loyalty to the SRs more than to any other political group and still voted in large numbers for SR candidates in the elections for the constituent assembly. But during this period this loyalty was waning. When the SR leader Chernov became minister of agriculture peasant hopes rose. They believed he would act and give them land. But his inaction and their idealism combined to disillusion them. As Trotsky puts it:

It was not for nothing that Chernov dubbed himself Rural Minister! But it was not for nothing, either, that the strategy of the villages brusquely parted company with Chernov's strategy. Their industrial isolation makes the peasants, so determined in struggle with a concrete landlord, impotent before the general landlord incarnate in the state. Hence the organic need of the muzhiks to rely upon some legendary state as against the real one. In olden times they created pretenders, they united round an imagined Golden Edict of the czar, or around the legend of a righteous world. After the February revolution they united round the Social Revolutionary banner 'Land and Freedom', seeking help in it against the liberal landlord who had become a governmental commissar. The Narodnik programme bore the same relation to the real government of Kerensky, as the imagined edict of the czar to the real autocrat.[8]

To the disillusioned peasants came the soldiers from the front. Even before the February revolution there had been a million deserters, now they began to flow like a tide. The army melted away: it 'was reverting to its peasant origin'.[9] But the soldiers were peasants with a difference. Their experiences had made them not merely disillusioned but revolutionary. Each one, as he came

[7] Trotsky, *op. cit.*, 865
[8] *Ibid.*, 871
[9] Cruttwell, *A History of the Great War*, 424

home to his village, bore in himself the seeds of revolution; each one was an unconscious agent of Bolshevism. 'As air currents carry seeds, the whirlwinds of the revolution scattered the ideas of Lenin.'[10]

[10] Trotsky, *op. cit.*, 877

## 11    *The October revolution*

The peasants were not alone in their feelings. During the summer more and more people in official circles, military as well as civilian, had lost all confidence in the Provisional Government and indeed in democratic, parliamentary government. They began to yearn for a 'strong man', a saviour. Right-wing extremists, active since the spring, worked on the new commander-in-chief, General Kornilov, to proclaim himself dictator and seize power. Simultaneously Kerensky, who had come to despise his colleagues and to delude himself that he was the predestined saviour of Russia, was planning to use Kornilov and the army to establish himself as dictator.

After a good deal of manoeuvring Kornilov came into the open on 27 August and marched on St Petersburg. By the next day his attempted coup had landed in mid-air. He had no real backing from the rank and file of the army, and workers had torn up the railway line between his headquarters and St Petersburg. It was a victory for the workers and soldiers and not for Kerensky.

Lenin, who had been living unobtrusively in Finland, was taken by surprise by the coup, which he described as 'a most unexpected ... and downright unbelievably sharp turn of events'.[1] But he grasped its significance at once. He wrote a short letter to the Central Committee of the party on 30 August urging that the moment for action had come. They must use it not only to fight against Kornilov and his backers but against Kerensky. By mobilizing the opinion of workers, soldiers and peasants they must force him to grant their demands: dissolve the Duma, arm the St Petersburg workers, legalize the transfer of land to the peasants, and introduce workers' control of grain, factories etc. A few days later Lenin followed this up with a draft resolution on the political situation in which he argued that the Kornilov coup had shown that 'the entire army *hates the general staff*',[2] and

[1] *Collected Works*, Vol. 25, 285
[2] *Ibid.*, 314

that only the urban working class could lead the people to victory, make a real peace and guarantee the immediate transfer of land to the peasants.

The tide had in fact already begun to flow for the Bolsheviks before the Kornilov coup. During the previous months politicians on the left were as disillusioned with the government as those on the right. In particular many of the Left SRs were disgusted with the performance of their ministers in the government, and were being drawn steadily towards the Bolsheviks on the decisive issues of peace and land.

During July large numbers of local soviets had come into being, most of them dominated by the Bolsheviks. Voices began again to be heard demanding the dissolution of the Duma and the transfer of power to the soviets. At the end of July and the beginning of August there were elections held in many soviets and for the most part the Bolsheviks were successful.

> The Moscow Soviet created ... a fighting group of six, which alone should have the right to deploy armed forces and make arrests. The regional congress of Kiev, which met at the end of August, advised its local soviets not to hesitate to replace unreliable representatives of the power, both military and civil, and take measures for the immediate arrest of counter-revolutionists and the arming of the workers. In Vyatka the soviet committee assumed extraordinary rights, including the disposition of the armed forces. In Czaritsyn the whole power went over to the soviet staff. In Nizhni-Novgorod the revolutionary committee established its sentries at the post and telegraph offices. The Krasnoyarsk Soviet concentrated both the civil and military power in its hands.[3]

The Kornilov coup deepened and accelerated this flow.

> The news of the bourgeois *coup* profoundly stirred the surface and the depths of Russia. The entire organized democracy rose to its feet. All Soviet Russia bristled and took up arms, not only metaphorically but quite literally. Hundreds of thousands and millions of workers, soldiers and peasants rose up in arms, for defence and for attack, against the class enemy.
>
> Their desire for a decisive battle grew irresistibly, hour by hour. Here there was class instinct, a small portion of class consciousness, and the influence of the ideas and organization of the gigantically growing Bolsheviks: but more than that there was weariness of war and other burdens; disappointment in the fruitlessness of the revolution, which up to then had given the masses of the people nothing;

[3] Trotsky, *History of the Russian Revolution*, 802

bitter resentment against the masters and the wealthy rulers; and a yearning to make use of the sovereignty that had been won.[4]

The government continued to flounder. In August it had postponed the elections for the Constituent Assembly from September to November. It suddenly released Trotsky on 4 September. The Executive Committee of the Soviet, still dominated by the Mensheviks and SRs supporting the coalition, called a democratic conference for the middle of September to discuss the continuance of the coalition and to rally support for the government. After a week of debate the conference voted in favour of the coalition and of summoning a Council of the Republic (Pre-Parliament), which was to be a general consultative body pending the elections for the Constituent Assembly.

The Bolsheviks took part in the democratic conference and the Central Committee of the party decided by 70 votes to 55 to take part in the Pre-Parliament. Lenin was against this from the first. He thought it futile and irrelevant. Early in September the Bolsheviks had won a majority on the Executive Committee and on that of the Moscow Soviet. Trotsky had become Chairman of the St Petersburg Soviet. On 17 September Lenin moved to Vyborg to be nearer St Petersburg. On 1 October he wrote another short letter to the Central Committee of the party, to the St Petersburg and Moscow committees of the party and to the Bolshevik members of the St Petersburg and Moscow Soviets urging the immediate seizure of power. Kamenev and Zinoviev were against this and strongly resisted the proposal in the debates within the party. On 7 October, the day on which the Pre-Parliament met, Lenin moved secretly to St Petersburg to press his case. Trotsky as leader of the Bolshevik delegates to the Pre-Parliament made a speech deriding its proceedings and then led the delegation from the chamber. The Bolsheviks took no further part in the proceedings.

On 10 October Lenin, without his beard and wearing a wig, attended a meeting of the Central Committee and argued his case. His resolution in favour of an immediate armed rising was carried by ten votes to two. During the next week Lenin secretly met members of the Committee, a representative of the Moscow Committee and other leading Bolsheviks to make plans for the rising.

[4] Sukhanov, *The Russian Revolution 1917*, 522

In this the Bolsheviks were inadvertently helped by their opponents in the Soviet. The Soviet was at this time deeply suspicious of the government's military plans and in particular suspected it of a plot to smash its political opponents by bringing back reliable troops from the front to replace the doubtful garrison of St Petersburg and by handing over the capital to the Germans. Accordingly, on a Menshevik motion the Soviet set up a committee of revolutionary defence with the main task of organizing the defence of St Petersburg. The Bolsheviks saw how they could make use of this to organize the rising, and voted for the motion. The committee came into being on 12 October with the title of the Revolutionary Military Committee, with Trotsky as its president and the SR Lazimir as head of its bureau—an appointment deliberately designed to camouflage Bolshevik intentions. Its terms of reference were equally ambiguous. They were to set up under the Committee departments of defence, supplies, communications and intelligence; to make contact with the northern front, the St Petersburg District HQ, the Baltic fleet and the Finnish Soviet, in order to ascertain the facts of the military situation and take the necessary measures in the light of them; to take a census of the composition of the St Petersburg garrison and of its military supplies; and to take measures for maintaining discipline in the soldier and worker masses. These objectives were unexceptionable for the purpose of defending St Petersburg, but they could equally well be used for staging the armed rising. This possibility was reinforced by the composition of the Committee. This consisted of the presidiums of the St Petersburg Soviet and of the soldiers' section, and of representatives of the fleet, of the Finnish Soviet, of the trade unions, including most importantly the railway and postal unions, of the factory committees, of the party military organizations and of the Red Guard.

Another new formation of this period was no less important. Under the direction of the Military Revolutionary Committee, [the form prefered by Trotsky's translator], there was created a Permanent Conference of the Garrison. The soldiers' section represented the garrison politically, the deputies being elected under the party symbols. The Garrison Conference, however, was to consist of the regimental committees which guided the daily lives of their units and thus constituted a more immediate practical 'guild' representation. The analogy between the regimental and the factory committees is obvious. Through the mediation of the workers' section of the Soviet the Bolsheviks were able upon big political questions to rely confidently upon the workers. But in order to become masters in the factories it had been necessary to carry the factory and shop committees. The composition of the soldiers' section guaranteed to the Bolsheviks the political sympathy of the majority of the garrison. But in order to get the practical disposal of the military units it was necessary to rely directly on the regimental committees. This explains why in the period preceding the insurrection the Garrison Conference naturally crowded out the soldiers' section and moved to the centre of the stage.[5]

The next day the soldiers' section endorsed the Revolutionary Military Committee's terms of reference by a large majority: 283 votes to one, with 23 abstentions.

These figures, unexpected even to the Bolsheviks, gave a measure of the pressure of the revolutionary masses [and, it might be added, of the effect of Bolshevik work among the rank and file]. The vote meant that the soldiers' section had openly and officially transferred the administration of the garrison from headquarters to the Military Revolutionary Committee.

On the same day the Executive Committee of the Petrograd Soviet made public the creation under its supervision of a special department of the Red Guard. The matter of arming the workers ... had become one of the most important tasks of the Bolshevik Soviet. The suspicious attitude of the soldiers toward the Red Guard was already far in the past. On the contrary, almost all the resolutions of the regiments contained a demand for the arming of the workers. From now on the Red Guard and the garrison stand side by side. Soon they will be still more closely united by a common submission to the Military Revolutionary Committee.[6]

So by the middle of October there was an interlocking system of Soviet, Revolutionary Military Committee, garrison, Baltic fleet and factory committees, interpenetrated and dominated by the Bolsheviks.

On 16 October Lenin reported to an enlarged meeting of the Central Committee of the party, which endorsed the resolution of 10 October by nineteen votes to two. On the same day the Committee formed the revolutionary military centre to be the core of the Revolutionary Military Committee. It received daily instructions from Lenin.

On 17 October Lenin wrote a long *Letter to Comrades*, published

[5] Trotsky, *op. cit.*, 945–6
[6] *Ibid.*, 948

in three parts in *Rabochiy Put* on 19, 20 and 21 October, in which he criticized the views of those members of the party who thought that the moment for the rising had not yet arrived and were in particular doubtful if the party had the backing of the masses. He followed this up by two more letters, one to party members and the other to the Central Committee, written on 18 and 19 October though not published at the time. In these he vehemently attacked Kamenev and Zinoviev, the two members of the Central Committee who had voted against the resolution for immediate armed uprising and made matters infinitely worse by stating their case in an article published in the non-Party paper *Novaya Zhizn*. Lenin accused them of unpardonable indiscipline in continuing to argue against the rising once the Central Committee had taken its decision, branded them as strike-breakers and traitors and demanded their expulsion from the party. This he did not achieve, but Kamenev was removed from the Central Committee.

By this time the preparations for the rising were almost complete. On the night of the 24th Lenin wrote a final call to arms, *Letter to Central Committee Members*, and secretly took up his position in the Smolny Institute to direct operations. In this letter he wrote:

With all my might I urge comrades to realise that everything now hangs by a thread; that we are confronted by problems which are not to be solved by conferences or congresses (even congresses of Soviets), but exclusively by peoples, by the masses, by the struggle of the armed people ...

We must at all costs, this very evening, this very night, arrest the government, having first disarmed the officer cadets (defeating them, if they resist), and so on.

We must not wait! We may lose everything!

The value of the immediate seizure of power will be the defence of the *people* ... from the Kornilovite government, which has driven out Verkhovsky [the minister of war who had resigned after the Pre-Parliament had rejected his proposals for demobilizing a considerable part of the army] and has hatched a second Kornilov plot.

Who must take power?

This is not important at present. Let the Revolutionary Military Committee do it, or 'some other institution' which will declare that it will relinquish power only to the true representatives of the interests of the people, the interests of the army (the immediate proposal of peace), the interests of the peasants (the land to be taken immediately and private property abolished), the interests of the starving.

All districts, all regiments, all forces must be mobilized at once and must immediately send their delegations to the Revolutionary Military Committee and to the Central Committee of the Bolsheviks with the insistent demand that under no circumstances should power be left in the hands of Kerensky and Co. until the 25th—not under any circumstances; the matter must be decided without fail this very evening, or this very night.

History will not forgive revolutionaries for procrastinating when they could be victorious today (and they certainly will be victorious today), while they risk losing much tomorrow, in fact, they risk losing everything ...

It would be a disaster, or a sheer formality, to await the wavering vote of October 25 [the day set for the opening of the second All-Russian Congress of Soviets]. The people have the right and are in duty bound to decide such questions not by vote, but by force; in critical moments of revolution, the people have the right and are in duty bound to give directions to their representatives, even their best representatives, and not to wait for them.

This is proved by the history of all revolutions; and it would be an infinite crime on the part of the revolutionaries were they to let the chance slip, knowing that the *salvation of the revolution*, the offer of peace, the salvation of Petrograd, salvation from famine, the transfer of the land to the peasants depend upon them.

The government is tottering. It must be *given the death-blow* at all costs.

To delay action is fatal.[7]

The plans went like clockwork. Troops occupied the crucial points without bloodshed. By the morning of 25 October St Petersburg was in Bolshevik hands and the Provisional Government had vanished. At 10 a.m. Lenin issued a proclamation: *To The Citizens of Russia!*

The Provisional Government has been deposed. State power has passed into the hands of the organ of the Petrograd Soviet of Workers' and Soldiers' Deputies—the Revolutionary Military Committee, which heads the Petrograd proletariat and the garrison.

The cause for which the people have fought, namely, the immediate offer of a democratic peace, the abolition of landed proprietorship, workers' control over production, and the establishment of Soviet power—this cause has been secured.

Long live the revolution of workers, soldiers and peasants![8]

Thus the April Theses became the first slogans of the Soviet government.

[7] *Collected Works*, Vol. 26, 234–5
[8] *Ibid.*, 236

## 12  Peace and land

On 25 October/7 November the 2nd All-Russian Congress of Soviets met and elected its presidium, the small group of members of the congress, who made up 'the platform' and controlled its proceedings. This consisted of 14 Bolsheviks, 7 Left SRs and four members of the Right, who immediately refused to serve. The congress also approved the list of ministers of the new government in which the Left SRs refused to serve for the time being, as they thought they could better promote a broad socialist coalition from outside the government. The members of the government at once symbolized the break with the bourgeois past by calling themselves not ministers but people's commissars, and by renaming the cabinet the Council of People's Commissars, often known from the initial syllables of the Russian words as *Sovnarkom*. All the members of *Sovnarkom* were therefore Bolsheviks, as were the leading members of the presidium, many of them the same men. All were tried and experienced revolutionaries, but 'as statesmen entrusted with the fate of the revolution and of the country, they must be acknowledged to be rather unconvincing'.[1] Those already well known in socialist circles were Lenin, Trotsky and Zinoviev.

Zinoviev was so undeviating a supporter of Lenin that he was looked on as little more than his henchman, but he was also an extremely powerful orator with 'a massive and unusually resonant tenor voice [that] could dominate an audience of thousands',[2] capable of making a speech in German that elicited the comment from the German press: 'This man possesses a demonic power of eloquence.'[3] He was also a fluent writer, a hard worker and, as it proved, a chairman of considerable ability. With Kamenev he had argued and voted against Lenin's resolution for the immediate seizure of power and been violently denounced by Lenin for this.

[1] Sukhanov, *The Russian Revolution 1917*, 655
[2] Lunacharsky, *Revolutionary Silhouettes* (1967), 76
[3] *Ibid.*, 80

Perhaps partly on this account he did not become a commissar,
but the editor of the government newspaper *Izvestia*.

Trotsky too was an orator; 'probably the greatest orator of our
age'[4] thought Lunacharsky, only the French socialist Jaurès
being in the same class. He was a theorist of some importance and
a born writer. More valuable for the revolution, he was the only
member of the movement who had played a vital practical part
in the events of 1905–6. His qualities as a leader made Lenin put
him forward as his first choice for chairman of *Sovnarkom*. Lenin
himself planned not to be a member but to devote all his energies
to the party. When the party decided that Lenin himself must be
chairman, he then proposed Trotsky as commissar for home
affairs. Trotsky himself turned this down, partly it seems on the
ground that a Jew in this post might encourage anti-semitism and
thereby endanger the revolution, so on Sverdlov's proposal he
became commissar for foreign affairs.

Trotsky seemed to Lunacharsky a more orthodox Marxist than
Lenin, 'always ... guided by the precise rules of revolutionary
Marxism', whereas Lenin was creative in political thought and in
formulating new lines of policy. Furthermore, despite his never
having been a Menshevik or a Bolshevik but having sought a
middle way, Trotsky was fundamentally less of an opportunist
than Lenin, in the sense that Lenin 'had that sense of reality
which leads one now and then to alter one's tactics, to that
tremendous sensitivity to the demands of the time which prompts
[him] at one moment to sharpen both edges of the sword, at
another to place it in its sheath'. Where Lenin's path to revolution was a zig-zag, Trotsky's was a straight line.

It is usual to say of Trotsky that he is ambitious. This, of course,
is utter nonsense. I remember Trotsky making a very significant
remark in connection with Chernov's acceptance of a ministerial
portfolio (see p. 124): 'What despicable ambition—to abandon one's
place in history in exchange for the untimely offer of a ministerial
post.' In that, I think, lay all of Trotsky. There is not a drop of vanity
in him, he is totally indifferent to any title or to the trappings of
power; he is, however, boundlessly jealous of his own role in history
and in that sense he is ambitious. Here he is I think as sincere as he is
in his natural love of power.

Lenin is not in the least ambitious either. I do not believe that
Lenin ever steps back and looks at himself, never even thinks what

[4] *Ibid.*, 65

posterity will say about him—he simply gets on with the job. He does it through the exercise of power, not because he finds power sweet but because he is convinced of the rightness of what he is doing and cannot bear that anyone should harm his cause. His ambitiousness stems from his colossal certainty of the rectitude of his principles and too, perhaps, from an inability (a very useful trait in a politician) to see things from his opponent's view. Lenin never regards an argument as a mere discussion; for him an argument is always a clash between different classes or different groups, as it were a clash between different species of humanity. An argument for him is always a struggle, which under certain circumstances may develop into a fight. Lenin always welcomes the transition from a struggle to a fight.

In contrast to Lenin, Trotsky is undoubtedly often prone to step back and watch himself. Trotsky treasures his historical role and would probably be ready to make any personal sacrifice, not excluding the greatest sacrifice of all—that of his life—in order to go down in human memory surrounded by the aureole of a genuine revolutionary leader. His ambition has the same characteristic as that of Lenin, with the difference that he is more often liable to make mistakes, lacking as he does Lenin's almost infallible instinct, and being a man of choleric temperament he is liable, although only temporarily, to be blinded by passion, whilst Lenin, always on an even keel and always in command of himself, is virtually incapable of being distracted by irritation.[5]

Trotsky was not, however, inferior in every way to Lenin. He was 'more brilliant ... clearer ... more active'. While Lenin was uniquely fitted to be chairman of *Sovnarkom* and to guide the revolution,

he could never have coped with the titanic mission [to create the Red Army and win the civil war] which Trotsky took upon his own shoulders, with those lightning moves from place to place, those astounding speeches, those fanfares of on-the-spot orders, that role of being the unceasing electrifier of a weakening army, now at one spot, now at another. There is not a man on earth who could have replaced Trotsky in that respect.

Whenever a truly great revolution occurs, a great people will always find the right actor to play every part and one of the signs of greatness in our revolution is the fact that the Communist Party has produced from its own ranks or has borrowed from other parties and incorporated into its own organism sufficient outstanding personalities who were suited as no others to fulfil whatever political function was called for.

And two of the strongest of the strong, totally identified with their roles, are Lenin and Trotsky.[5]

[5] Lunacharsky, *op. cit.*, 66–9

The government wasted no time in declaring its policy. On 25 October/7 November it occupied the State Bank. On 26 October/8 November it issued Decrees on Peace and on Land, both drafted by Lenin, who at the same time drafted Regulations on Workers' Control which were embodied in a decree on 14/27 November. These decrees were not decrees in the sense of government orders to the citizens, but declarations of policy and appeals for support in carrying it out.

The Decree on Peace appealed for peace to the government and peoples of all the belligerent countries and especially to the 'class-conscious workers of the three most advanced nations of mankind ... Great Britain, France and Germany'.[6] It begins by proposing to the belligerent governments and their peoples immediate negotiations for a just and democratic peace. All the workers are longing for such a peace, without annexations or indemnities, and Russia is ready to conclude it at once. It defines annexation as the forcible incorporation of a small or weak nationality, whenever and wherever this has been carried out, and whatever the degree of development of the nationality. Forcible retention of such a nationality against the expressed will of the people is equivalent to annexation. By this definition it deliberately points not only to the annexations since 1914 but also to those before, and not only to Europe but to the whole world. So for example Poland, Alsace and the African colonies would come up for consideration. The continuation of the imperialist war is the greatest crime against humanity. Russia will abolish secret diplomacy and will now conduct all negotiations openly. Russia absolutely denounces all the secret treaties and will begin to publish them right away. Russia proposes an immediate armistice of not *less* than three months, a period long enough to complete the peace negotiations.

As Carr points out,[7] this is Wilsonian rather than Marxist in content and language, and is calculated to appeal to the radical opposition in all countries as well as to the proletariat. On the other hand, the notion that three months is the length of time needed to complete the peace negotiations strongly suggests that Lenin expected the decree to promote immediate revolution. The class-conscious workers freed from their shackles would

[6] *Collected Works*, Vol. 26, 251
[7] E. H. Carr, *The Bolshevik Revolution* (1950)

ant to free the oppressed everywhere and would have no
ifficulty in identifying oppressors and oppressed.

In fact the decree produced no response from governments or
eoples. It therefore became a matter of urgency to end the war
vith Germany, and on 8/21 November the government ordered the
ommander-in-chief to seek an armistice. But desperate as the
osition was, it was not prepared to surrender unconditionally and
argained hard. Trotsky, who as commissar for foreign affairs
vas directly responsible for the negotiations, insisted on the
Germans agreeing not to transfer troops from the eastern to the
vestern front, and, a revolutionary demand, on allowing frater-
ization between the German and Russian troops so that they
ould instil revolutionary ideas. The German commander-in-
hief, General Hoffmann, at first resisted both demands, but
ventually gave way. Whether either demand would be fulfilled
vould depend on German power and German convenience, but
Trotsky had scored a point for the Bolsheviks by getting their
iew written into the armistice terms: that the war was not just a
var between Germany and Russia but international, and that the
rmistice was not just the cessation of hostilities on the Russo-
German front but the prelude to a revolutionary peace.

The armistice took effect at the beginning of December and the
eace negotiations began at Brest-Litovsk on 9/22 December.
Bolshevik tactics were to spin them out to gain time to consolidate
heir power in Russia and for the German workers to come out in
evolution. The Bolsheviks were helped in this by the somewhat
ifferent approach to the negotiations of the German army,
epresented by Hoffmann, and of the foreign office, represented
by Kühlmann. Hoffmann simply wanted to use German military
trength to force a quick peace, so as to be able to get his hands on
he wheat and coal of the Ukraine and the oil of the Caucasus, and
o release troops for the western front. Kühlmann on the other
and was anxious that the peace should appear to be the result
f genuine negotiation and Germany to be the protector and ally
f the minorities oppressed by the Russian government: Poles,
Lithuanians, Latvians, Estonians, White Russians and Ukrainians.
But in the last resort it was the army that held the whip hand,
nd after a month Hoffmann lost patience. On 5/18 January 1918
e produced a map showing the territory the German army was
oing to occupy until the Russian army was completely demobil-

ized: this was almost all the Polish, Lithuanian and Whi
Russian territory and half of the Latvian. In the south the fronti
was not marked and was to be the subject of 'negotiation' with tl
Ukrainian Rada, the anti-Bolshevik government of the Ukrain
Trotsky did not feel himself empowered to accept this on his ov
authority, and managed to have the negotiations suspended f
ten days to enable him to return to St Petersburg to consult h
government.

Lenin reacted quickly and definitely to the news. On 7/2
January he cleared his mind by writing the *Theses on the Questi*
*of the Immediate Conclusion of a Separate and Annexationist Peace.* F
argued that the paramount need was to save the socialist revol\
tion in Russia.

> Nearly all the workers and the vast majority of the peasan
> undoubtedly side with Soviet power ... To that extent the sociali
> revolution in Russia is assured. ... The victory of Soviet power in th
> war is assured, but some time must inevitably elapse, no litt
> exertion of effort will inevitably be required, a certain period
> acute economic dislocation and chaos ... is inevitable before victo\
> is achieved.[8]

So the Soviet required a little time, several months at least', \
win the civil war and safeguard the socialist revolution. As the\
was no sign of revolution breaking out immediately in German
Lenin argued that the Soviet must buy this time by signir
a peace treaty. This treaty would be a separate and annexa
tionist treaty, and would lay the Soviet open to the charg
of being agents of German imperialism. This was not in fa\
a damaging charge, for workers beaten in a strike are n\
regarded as the agents of their capitalist employers when they g
back to work. But even if it had been, it had to be faced. It w\
better to make peace immediately, however distasteful the term
for later they would only be worse. Sooner or later the Sovi\
would have to make peace, as the peasant majority in the arm
was undoubtedly now in favour of peace; a revolutionary war w\
therefore at this moment out of the question. It was indeed th
truth that the peasant soldiers were not only in favour of peace b\
had already deserted in shoals: Trotsky on his way to Bres\
Litovsk had been amazed and distressed to find the Russia
trenches largely empty. Lenin too knew this, and drew th
consequences in the *Theses.*

[8] *Collected Works,* Vol. 26, 442–3

But only a minority of leading Bolsheviks agreed with him. At a meeting held on 8/21 January only fifteen out of 63 Bolsheviks present backed his plea for an immediate peace. A further 32 still believed hopefully in going on fighting, while sixteen were in favour of Trotsky's policy of no war, no peace: the Soviet should stop fighting and so end the war but refuse to sign a formal peace. This would throw the onus of decision on the German high command, and would have the advantage that the Soviet good name would not be tarnished by signing a shameful peace. The Central Committee three days later endorsed Trotsky's policy, but at the same time instructed him to return to Brest-Litovsk and to delay the final breach as long as possible.

During this debate there had been a wave of strikes in Vienna and Budapest, and while Trotsky was on his way back to Brest-Litovsk there were mass strikes and open demonstrations against the war in Berlin which spread to other German towns. Hope that the world revolution had begun flared up, and Lenin in an additional note to the *Theses*, recorded that the strikes were evidence of the beginning of revolution in Germany. But the hope was false. By the end of the month the strikes and demonstrations had fizzled out. On 26 January/8 February the Central Powers signed a treaty with the Ukrainian Rada. Two days later Trotsky put an end to the conference by delivering a tirade against German policy, designed to appeal over the heads of the delegates and their governments to the European proletariat, and declaring that the Soviet government would sign no annexationist peace but regarded the war as at an end. Thereupon the Soviet delegation departed.

It was not long before Russia learned the consequences of this. On 17 February Hoffmann gave notice that he would resume the advance the next day. Lenin, supported by Stalin and three other members of the Central Committee of the Party, was in favour of sending an immediate message offering to resume negotiations, but Trotsky and five other members were for waiting to see what happened. German troops began to advance unopposed on the 18th: their problem was one of communications, not warfare.

The Central Committee met twice on the 18th, in the morning and in the evening. In the morning it again rejected, by one vote, Lenin's proposal for immediate peace. But before the evening session news had arrived that the Germans had captured Dvinsk and were still advancing. This seems to have altered Trotsky's opinion, for after speaking three times against an immediate peace he surprised his colleagues by voting for Lenin's proposal. This gave Lenin a majority and decided the day. A message was sent on the 19th suing for peace.

But this was far from the end of the debate. No answer came from the Germans for four days and when it did, on 23 February, it was so harsh that it roused the anti-peace group to the most violent opposition. It demanded that Russia should cede the remaining Latvian territory and the Esthonian, evacuate Finland and the Ukraine, and demobilize completely. It set time limits of 48 hours for an answer and three days for signature of the terms. Trotsky continued to argue against signing a peace treaty but he was prepared to bow to this necessity if it was the majority decision. He was not, however, willing to sign personally and insisted on resigning as commissar for foreign affairs and therefore as head of the Russian delegation. Bukharin and three others stubbornly opposed signing the treaty and wanted to wage a revolutionary war. In this there was something of what Lenin called 'the human yearning for the beautiful, dramatic and striking', but it was also based on realistic grounds. Lenin and Bukharin agreed that it was essential to save the socialist revolution in Russia. But they disagreed on two closely related questions: would peace give Russia a breathing space? would the peasants fight? Lenin argued that they must have peace with the Germans to allow the government to defeat its civil enemies and so ensure the success of the revolution and give the peasants time to recover their strength and their morale; meantime they had shown in the most unequivocal way that they would not fight, by abandoning the trenches and trekking home. Bukharin did not think peace would necessarily achieve this. Even after the conclusion of peace the Germans would remain implacably hostile to the Soviet and would help its enemies; they would not hesitate to interfere in Russian territory if they thought it advantageous. The breathing space might therefore be illusory. To continue to force the Germans to fight would on the other hand have the advantage of putting more strain on the army and the German people, both of whom were already strained near to breaking point. It was true that the peasants had no more stomach for the war and had been deserting in their thousands, but they would sense at once the difference between an imperialist war and a revolutionary one. In their present mood it was impossible to draw them into the army again in peacetime. They would only fight and recover their spirit in a revolutionary war against invaders who they could see were destroyers, looters and oppressors. A revolutionary war was more likely to save the revolution than peace. It is impossible to be sure that this argument was wrong. It is now known that the Germans were critically short of officers and NCOs, and of petrol, oil and grease, and it was only five months to the collapse of the final German offensive in the west. Furthermore it is true that Trotsky created the Red Army in the course of the desperate civil war. On the other hand an uncoordinated assortment of enemies, White, Green, Czech, British, French and Japanese, was not the same as the German army. On the whole it seems likely that Lenin's intuition was right: for the time being the peasants had had enough. To talk of war was vain beating of the air. What settled the argument was his threat to resign if the government did not accept the German terms. He carried the day in *Sovnarkom* by seven votes to four with four abstentions. On the same evening the proposal was put to the Central Committee of the party, and in the early morning of 24 February it was carried by 116 votes to 84.

Lenin defending the proposal said:

> ... reality has shown us that after three years of war our army is altogether unable and unwilling to fight. That is the basic cause, simple, obvious, and in the highest degree bitter and painful, but absolutely clear, why, living side by side with an imperialist plunderer, we are compelled to sign peace terms when he puts his knee on our chest. That is why I say, fully conscious of the responsibility I bear, and repeat that no single member of the Soviet government has the right to evade this responsibility. Of course, it is pleasant and easy to tell the workers, peasants and soldiers, as it has been pleasant and easy to observe, how the revolution has gone forward after the October uprising, but when we have to acknowledge the bitter, painful, undeniable truth—the impossibility of a revolutionary war—it is impermissible now to evade this responsibility and we must shoulder it frankly.[9]

This hard-hearted realism and this readiness to shoulder responsibility are typical of Lenin, as is his choice of words: 'bitter', 'painful', 'undeniable'; and above all, 'impermissible';

[9] *Collected Works*, Vol. 27, 44

not weak or vain or cowardly, but 'impermissible'. It is not permitted by Marxism nor by the logic of history nor by conscience. He went on to argue that this was only a temporary defeat, for the causes of the class war in Germany were still there and would inevitably produce their effect sooner or later. The masses understood this.

> If you go to the class of real toilers, to the workers and peasants, you will hear only one answer, that we are quite unable to wage war, we lack the physical strength, we are choked in blood, as one of the soldiers put it. These masses will understand us and approve of our concluding this forced and unprecedently onerous peace.[10]

Lenin repeated this argument at greater length and in vivid language to the seventh congress of the Bolshevik party on 6 March. He emphasized the reality and bitterness of the defeat but urged his listeners to make use of the respite the peace had given them:

> We cannot hide the incredibly bitter, deplorable reality from ourselves with empty phrases; we must say: God grant that we retreat in what is half-way good order. We cannot retreat in good order, but God grant that our retreat is half-way good order, that we gain a little time in which the sick part of our organism can be absorbed at least to some extent. On the whole, the organism is sound, it will overcome its sickness. But you cannot expect it to overcome it all at once, instantaneously; you cannot stop an army in flight![11]

The cure for this sickness was self-discipline: 'to create an army capable, not of running away, but of bearing untold suffering'.[12] This was inevitable because the German revolution had not begun and could not be guaranteed to begin to-morrow. But it would come.

> Yes, we shall see the world revolution, but for the time being it is a very good fairy-tale, a very beautiful fairy-tale—I quite understand children liking beautiful fairy-tales. But I ask, is it proper for a serious revolutionary to believe in fairy-tales? There is an element of reality in every fairy-tale. If you told children fairy-tales in which the cock and the cat did not converse in human language they would not be interested.[13]

The reality was that the revolution would come. But to tell the

10 *Ibid.*, 45–6
11 *Ibid.*, 101
12 *Ibid.*, 104
13 *Ibid.*, 102

people that it would come now or tomorrow would be to deceive them. To base policy on it would be to gamble impermissibly.

> Then the masses will say to you, you acted like gamblers—you staked everything on a fortunate turn of events that did not take place, you proved unfitted for the situation that actually arose instead of the world revolution, which will inevitably come, but which has not yet reached maturity.[14]

Lenin wound up with a characteristic exhortation to practical work.

> We should have but one slogan—to learn the art of war properly and put the railways in order. To wage a socialist revolutionary war without railways would be rank treachery. We must produce order and we must produce all the energy and all the strength that will produce the best that is in the revolution.[15]

*The Decree on Land* declared that all private property in land was abolished forthwith without compensation, and that all land belonging to the crown, the church or private individuals, together with its equipment and livestock, was at the disposal of the local land committees and soviets pending the meeting of the Constituent Assembly. In the meantime the local soviets were to ensure the orderly transfer of land and to draw up inventories. For their guidance there was attached to the decree a model set of regulations based on local peasant proposals which outlined 'the most equitable settlement of the land question'. By these all land was 'to become the property of the whole people, and pass into the use of all those who cultivate it' and tenure was to be on the basis of equality. But 'Lands on which *high-level scientific* farming is practised—orchards, plantations, seed plots, nurseries, hothouses etc.—shall not be divided up, but shall be converted into model farms' to the exclusive use of the state; so too mineral wealth, forests and 'waters of state importance'.[16]

But Lenin in presenting the decree to the Congress of Soviets laid stress on local initiative.

> We must be guided by experience; we must allow complete freedom to the creative faculties of the masses ... The peasants have learned something during the eight months of our revolution, they

---

[14] *Ibid.*, 102
[15] *Ibid.*, 108
[16] *Collected Works*, Vol. 26, 258–9

want to settle all land problems themselves. We are therefore opposed
to all amendments to this draft law. We want no details in it, for we
are writing a decree, not a programme of action. Russia is vast, and
local conditions vary. We trust that the peasants themselves will be
able to solve the problem correctly, properly, better than we could
do it. Whether they do it in our spirit or in the spirit of the Socialist-
Revolutionary programme is not the point. The point is that the
peasants should be firmly assured that there are no more landowners
in the countryside, that they themselves must decide all questions,
and that they themselves must arrange their own lives. (Loud
applause).[17]

In practice the peasants seized the land in an orderly or disorderly fashion: most orderly in the areas that were the most
advanced agriculturally and nearest to the government, most
disorderly in the backward and remote.

The government regularized the situation formally by issuing
the law *On the Socialization of the Land* on 19 February 1918, the
57th anniversary of the emancipation of the serfs. This gave the
full sanction of the law to the distribution of land by the local
soviets, and laid down a formula for 'equal distribution' which
took account of the hands that would do the work and the mouths
that would eat the bread. It also, for the time being, glossed over
the question of which lands were to be reserved for the state, and
contented itself with an article defining socialist agricultural
policy in terms of the need for development and for larger units.

Like the decree, this law was largely neglected in practice. But
by the end of the process of seizure and distribution 86 per cent of
the land is said to have gone to the peasants, 11 per cent to the
state and 3 per cent to agricultural collectives. The holdings
within a village were generally more or less equal, but distribution
between one village and another in a wider area tended to be
unequal. Sometimes all the land was pooled, sometimes only
landlords' land was divided and added to the existing peasant
holdings. But the crucial thing was that the peasants got the land;
they had at last recovered what they believed was rightfully theirs.

Parallel to this in the towns was workers' control of factories.
*The Regulations on Workers' Control* laid down that workers' control
should be introduced into all businesses employing more than
five workers or having an annual turnover of more than 10,000
roubles. In small concerns the workers were to exercise control

[17] *Ibid.*, 261

directly, in larger ones through elected representatives; their decisions were binding on owners and could only be annulled by the trade unions. But just as in agriculture there were estates reserved to the use of the state, so in industry there were 'enterprises of state importance' in which the owners and workers were responsible to the state for discipline and for the protection of property: these were defined as enterprises working for defence or manufacturing 'articles necessary for the existence of the masses of the population'.[18] Detailed regulations to apply the policy to the provinces and to individual factories and offices were to be drawn up by local soviets and by committees of office employees.

These decrees and regulations clearly embody Lenin's conviction that the Russians wanted peace, land and, as far as possible, freedom; and that government bureaucracy was as unpopular as it was unnecessary. Running the ordinary affairs of life was not difficult. It was the business of the government to lay down with the utmost clarity the broad socialist principles and then to let the ordinary man and woman get on with things on the basis of these principles. This, Lenin hoped and believed, would content them and release their creative energies. They would support the revolution emotionally and practically. They would turn Bolshevik and produce the food needed to save Russia from starvation and the goods needed to pay the peasants for their produce and, when the war was over, the foreigner for his exports.

[18] *Ibid*, 265

## 13   The state and revolution

An equally urgent problem, and one of more immediate consequence, was how to handle the bourgeoisie and its institutions. There was not much guidance on this in Social-Democratic literature. In the *Communist Manifesto* Marx had written:

> the first step in the revolution by the working class is to raise the proletariat to the position of ruling class, to win the battle of democracy.
>
> The proletariat will use its political supremacy to wrest, by degrees, all capital from the bourgeoisie to centralize all instruments of production in the hands of the State, i.e. of the proletariat organized as the ruling class ...'

Marx listed various measures to achieve this, ranging from a heavy progressive income tax to nationalization of banks and transport. When this process had been completed, he concluded that public power would lose its political character.

> Political power, properly so called, is merely the organized power of one class for oppressing another. If the proletariat during its contest with the bourgeoisie is compelled, by the force of circumstances, to organize itself as a class; if, by means of a revolution, it makes itself the ruling class, and, as such sweeps away by force the old conditions of production, then it will, along with these conditions, have swept away the conditions for the existence of class antagonisms and for classes generally, and will thereby have abolished its own supremacy as a class.

While he was in Finland Lenin had devoted much time and thought to the problem of the state and had produced one of his most important writings, *The State and Revolution*.

This sets out the Marxist doctrine of the state in relation to revolution, slightly amplifies it and proceeds to illustrate it from the events of 1848–51 and 1870–1. Lenin meant to add a chapter on 1905 and 1917, but events overtook him and he never wrote it. He starts from the orthodox Marxist proposition that the state is the product of the irreconcilable class conflicts and the means by which the ruling class enforces its rule over the population, or 'an instrument for the exploitation of the oppressed class'.[1] It embodies its power in 'special bodies of armed men, prisons, etc.'[2] As the class war gets sharper state power gets greater. Finally the class war reaches its climax and explodes in revolution. The revolution ends the war, liquidates the old ruling class and establishes the administration of society by the whole population. The state 'withers away'.

Lenin makes the passage from Engels' *Anti-Dühring* on the withering away of the state the core of his argument:

> *The proletariat seizes state power and turns the means of production into state property to begin with.* But thereby it abolishes itself as the proletariat, abolishes all class distinctions and class antagonisms, and abolishes also the state as state. Society thus far, operating amid class antagonisms, needed the state, that is, an organisation of the particular exploiting class, for the maintenance of its external conditions of production, and, therefore, especially, for the purpose of forcibly keeping the exploited class in the conditions of oppression determined by the given mode of production (slavery, serfdom or bondage, wage-labour). The state was the official representative of society as a whole, its concentration in a visible corporation. But it was this only insofar as it was the state of that class which itself represented, for its own time, society as a whole: in ancient times, the state of slave-owning citizens; in the Middle Ages, of the feudal nobility; in our own time, of the bourgeoisie. When at last it becomes the real representative of the whole of society, it renders itself unnecessary. As soon as there is no longer any social class to be held in subjection, as soon as class rule, and the individual struggle for existence based upon the present anarchy in production, with the collisions and excesses arising from this struggle, are removed, nothing more remains to be held in subjection—nothing necessitating a special coercive force, a state. The first act by which the state really comes forward as the representative of the whole of society—the taking possession of the means of production in the name of society— is also its last independent act as a state. State interference in social relations becomes, in one domain after another, superfluous, and then dies down of itself. The government of persons is replaced by the administration of things, and by the conduct of processes of production. The state is not 'abolished'. *It withers away.* This gives the measure of the value ... of the so-called anarchists' demand that the state be abolished overnight.[3]

Lenin underlines the contrast between the proletariat's aboli-

---

[1] *Collected Works*, Vol. 25, 391
[2] *Ibid.*, 388
[3] Engels, *Anti-Dühring*, quoted by Lenin in *Collected Works*, Vol. 25, 395–6

tion of the *bourgeois* state and the withering away or dying down of the *proletarian* state *after* the revolution. The bourgeois state does *not* wither away or die down. On the contrary the bourgeoisie will defend its state to the last, and a revolution is necessary to overthrow it: the idea cherished by reformist Social-Democrats that the bourgeois state can be gradually transformed by democratic means into the socialist state is an illusion, and a most pernicious one. The proletarian state, on the other hand, really does wither away. It is not abolished. To abolish it overnight, as the anarchists demand, is pointless and illogical. As society after the revolution consists only of the proletariat there can be no further class struggle, and the state has no further function. The proletariat has seized control of the means of production and the task is simply to organize production (and distribution) as efficiently as possible. Modern technology has made this quite simple.

> Capitalist culture has *created* large-scale production, factories, railways, the postal service, telephones, etc., and *on this basis* the great majority of the functions of the old 'state power' have become so simplified and can be reduced to such exceedingly simple operations of registration, filing and checking that they can easily be performed by every literate person, can quite easily be performed for ordinary 'workmen's wages', and that these functions can (and must) be stripped of every shadow of privilege, of every semblance of 'official grandeur' ...
>
> Capitalism simplifies the functions of 'state' administration; it makes it possible to cast 'bossing' aside and to confine the whole matter to the organisation of the proletarians ... which will hire 'workers, foremen and accountants' in the name of the whole of society.
>
> We are not utopians, we do not 'dream' of dispensing *at once* with all administration, with all subordination. These anarchist dreams ... are totally alien to Marxism ... No, we want the socialist revolution with people as they are now, with people who cannot dispense with subordination, control and 'foremen and accountants'.
>
> The subordination, however, must be to the armed vanguard of all the exploited and working people, i.e. to the proletariat. A beginning can and must be made at once, overnight, to replace the specific 'bossing' of state officials by the simple functions of 'foremen and accountants', functions which are ... fully within the ability of the average town dweller and can well be performed for 'workmens' wages'.[4]

[4] Engels, *op. cit.*, quoted by Lenin in *Collected Works*, Vol. 25, 420–1, 425–6

It is quite clear from this that Lenin took seriously Engels's epigram: 'The government of persons is replaced by the administration of things'. He believed that 'bossing' was bound up with the class nature of capitalism and the bourgeois state, and not with the process of production itself. It would wither away with the state. A foreman is not a boss; he is a worker who controls a part of the productive process. In case he may be tempted to regard himself as a boss he is to get ordinary workmen's wages; he is not a privileged person but an ordinary workman performing one of the functions arising out of the process of production. It is not clear whether Lenin thought the process was self-explanatory, that the workmen would automatically see the sense of it and accept it and that there would therefore be no question of disobedience to a foreman; or whether he thought that once the proletariat had seized the means of production the workers would by definition be working for themselves and would therefore work without worrying about wages or the organization of the work or the factory. But it does seem clear that he expected that work could be organized without fuss and without specialist qualifications: ordinary, simple people could perform ordinary, simple functions.

Lenin also drew out another of the consequences of the withering away of the state: the disappearance of democracy.

> In speaking of the state 'withering away', and the even more graphic and colourful 'dying down of itself', Engels refers quite clearly and definitely to the period *after* 'the state has taken possession of the means of production in the name of the whole of society', that is *after* the socialist revolution. We all know that the political form of the 'state' at that time is the most complete democracy. But it never enters the head of any of the opportunists, who shamelessly distort Marxism, that Engels is consequently speaking here of *democracy* 'dying down of itself', or 'withering away'. This seems very strange at first sight. But it is 'incomprehensible' only to those who have not thought about democracy *also* being a state and, consequently, also disappearing when the state disappears. Revolution alone can 'abolish' the bourgeois state. The state in general, i.e. the most complete democracy, can only 'wither away'.[5]

The point Lenin is making here is that all over Europe parliamentary democracy is the form of government, the form of the state, appropriate to bourgeois capitalism. This is true even in

[5] *Collected Works*, Vol. 25, 397

Russia. In 1905 the tsar had been compelled to allow the summoning of a Duma, and, despite the restrictions on the franchise and on its powers, the Duma had continued to exist from then until 1917. After the February revolution Lenin himself said that Russia had the most completely democratic regime in Europe. A democratic government continues to be appropriate so long as the bourgeois revolution is in progress. But as soon as it has been overtaken by the socialist revolution it ceases to be appropriate; bourgeois capitalism and parliamentary democracy disappear together.

'What transformation will the state undergo in communist society?' asked Marx, and answered, 'This question can only be answered scientifically ...'. History and the theory of historical development, i.e. science, show that there must always be a period of transition from one form of society to another. This holds good for the transformation of capitalist into communist society. 'Between capitalist and communist society', Marx went on, 'lies the period of the revolutionary transformation of the one into the other. Corresponding to this is also a political transition period in which the state can be nothing but *the revolutionary dictatorship of the proletariat.*'[6] Neither Marx nor Lenin defines the form that the dictatorship of the proletariat will take, beyond noting that the means of production will belong to the whole of society and that each worker will be issued with a certificate of work done, which he will then exchange for goods at a public store. But during this period there will be, says Lenin, the '*strictest* control by society *and by the state* over the measure of labour and the measure of consumption ...'[7]

How humanity gets to the higher stage of communist society 'we do not and cannot know'.[8] We do however have an inkling of when it will be reached and what it will be like:

> In a higher phase of communist society, after the enslaving subordination of the individual to the division of labour and with it also the antithesis between mental and physical labour has vanished, after labour has become not only a livelihood but life's prime want, after the productive forces have increased with the all-round development of the individual and all the springs of co-operative wealth

[6] Marx, *Critique of the Gotha Programme*, quoted by Lenin in *Collected Works*, Vol. 25. 459
[7] *Ibid.*, 470
[8] *Ibid.*, 472

flow more abundantly—only then can the narrow horizon of bourgeois right be crossed in its entirety and society inscribe on its banners: From each according to his ability, to each according to his needs![9]

The core of the idea is that capitalism by its nature and its motive force, the profit motive, automatically restricts production in order to maximize profits. It follows that once capitalism is abolished production will automatically expand. The problem during the transition period is simply to organize the expansion of production and to distribute the product equally. Here Lenin reverts to the notion of control and accounting by the workers themselves and again emphasizes the simplicity of these operations. He winds up his argument in these words.

> For when *all* have learned to administer and actually do independently administer social production, independently keep accounts and exercise control over the parasites, the sons of the wealthy, the swindlers and other 'guardians of capitalist traditions', the escape from this popular accounting and control will inevitably become so incredibly difficult, such a rare exception, and will probably be accompanied by such swift and severe punishment (for the armed workers are practical men and not sentimental intellectuals, and they will scarcely allow anyone to trifle with them), that the *necessity* of observing the simple, fundamental rules of the community will very soon become a *habit.*
> Then the door will be thrown wide open for the transition from the first phase of communist society to its higher phase, and with it the complete withering away of the state.[10]

There seems to be a hint here of the inevitable influence of forms of production on society and social behaviour. Capitalism, based on the profit motive, is thought to be inevitably competitive and inevitably to produce competitiveness, aggressiveness, hostility to one's fellow men and unscrupulousness in one's dealings; it produces parasites and swindlers. Socialism, based on production to meet society's needs and wants, is inherently co-operative and will gradually form habits of co-operation and equality. Once these habits are formed, the basis of socialist society will be firm, the state will have withered away, social relations will be regulated by what might perhaps be called good manners, and

[9] Marx, *op. cit.*, quoted by Lenin, *op. cit.*, 468
[10] Lenin, *op. cit.*, 474

the way will be open for men to give free rein to their aspirations and talents in the communist society.

It now remained to be seen how Lenin would apply these ideas to the situation that confronted him. For the time being the Bolsheviks had dealt with the economic problem by the decrees on land, on workers' control and on the nationalization of the banks, but the political problem stared them in the face: how to reconcile the soviets with inherited ideas of democratic institutions. The Duma was a dead duck killed by the restrictions on the franchise introduced in 1907 and legally dissolved by the tsar's decree of February 1917. But Lenin and other Bolsheviks had consistently advocated a constituent assembly elected on the most democratic franchise as one of the steps necessary to lead Russia from the tsarist autocracy to the democratic socialist society. Then the 1905 revolution had thrown up the soviet, 'a form of democracy without parallel in any other country'[11] and 'the only form capable of securing the most painless transition to socialism'.[12] In the April Theses Lenin had put forward the slogan 'All Power to the Soviets', and it was through the soviets that the Bolsheviks had made the October Revolution. The soviets were clearly there to stay, and the government and Lenin himself were giving the people the greatest encouragement to back them.

> Remember that *you yourselves* are at the helm of state ... *Your* Soviets are from now on the organs of state authority ... Rally now around your Soviets. Strengthen them. Get on with the job yourselves; begin right at the bottom, do not wait for anyone. Establish the strictest revolutionary law and order, mercilessly suppress any attempts to create anarchy by drunkards, hooligans, counter-revolutionary officer cadets, Kornilovites and their like.[13]

How was the Constituent Assembly to be fitted into this new structure? Could it assist the transition to the socialist society by drawing up a constitution incorporating the soviets? Was there any point in drawing up a constitution at this stage when great numbers of soviets were already in existence and only at the very beginning of their evolution? (The precedent of the Constituent Assembly of the French Revolution was not very encouraging, and

[11] *Collected Works*, Vol. 26, 437
[12] *Ibid.*, 379
[13] *Ibid.*, 297

Lenin was an exceptionally well-informed student of the revolution.) Lenin in fact favoured postponing the elections already fixed by the provisional government for November 1917, and would in all probability have postponed them indefinitely. But it was agreed that this would be too great an affront to public feeling and that they must take place as arranged.

Intimately connected with the elections were two other questions: freedom of the press and freedom of electioneering for the bourgeois parties. Already in September Lenin had written an article headed: *How to Guarantee the Success of the Constituent Assembly: On Freedom of the Press.* In this he argued that the abolition of the censorship of the press so much praised by the liberals was not in fact 'freedom of the press, but freedom for the rich, for the bourgeoisie to deceive the oppressed and exploited mass of the people'.[14] The remedy for this state of affairs was state control of the printing presses, newsprint and advertising, and the equitable distribution of newspaper space to all political parties and groups of citizens in accordance with their size. Then 'we could really help the peasants [by getting to] *every* village half a dozen pamphlets (or newspaper issues, or special supplements) in *millions* of copies from *every* big party'.[15] The implication of the argument is clearly that under these conditions the Bolsheviks would win the elections.

The government closely followed this policy. On 26 October it stopped publication of the bourgeois papers through the Revolutionary Military Committee. On 4/17 November Lenin drafted a resolution *On Freedom of the Press* modelled on his article of 15/28 September and the Central Executive Committee passed a resolution confirming government policy, though only by 34 votes to 24.

But this did not stop the Cadet party campaigning in the elections nor from winning seventeen seats. This was a tiny fraction of the total number and of no importance, but the resistance to the revolution in Moscow and the attempt of Kerensky and the Cossack General Kaledin to mount a military counterattack had already somewhat soured Bolshevik enthusiasm. On 28 November/11 December *Sovnarkom* issued a *Decree on the Arrest of the Leaders of the Civil War against the Revolution.* The title is significant

[14] *Collected Works*, Vol. 25, 375
[15] *Ibid.*, 378

of Lenin's trait of identifying all opposition to his policy with treason, and now that it was treason to the state as well as to the party the consequences were ominous. The decree stated:

> Members of leading bodies of the Cadet Party, as a party of enemies of the people, are liable to arrest and trial by revolutionary tribunal.
>
> Local Soviets are ordered to exercise special surveillance over the Cadet Party in view of its connection with the Kornilov-Kaledin civil war against the revolution.[16]

The revolutionary tribunals had already been set up on 24 November/7 December with jurisdiction over all who organized or took part in risings against the government, over saboteurs and all who hindered production and over all who violated the decrees of the government 'if the violation ... calls for a trial by the Revolutionary Tribunal'.[17] They were empowered to fix penalties to fit the crime, short of the death penalty. Two weeks later, on 6/19 December, *Sovnarkom* set up the Extraordinary Commission of the Council of Peoples' Commissars for the Struggle with Counter-Revolution and Sabotage and Speculation (*Cheka*), with powers to investigate all signs of counter-revolution, to punish by confiscating property and ration cards and to hand over offenders for trial by the revolutionary tribunals. The decree was drafted by Dzerzhinsky, a member of *Sovnarkom* and the designated head of the *Cheka*, but approved by *Sovnarkom* as a whole. Almost at once both the tribunals and the *Cheka* exceeded their powers and carried out summary executions.

The elections held at the end of November and completed by mid-December had totally failed to produce a Bolshevik majority. In a heavy and largely free poll the result was: 370 SR, 175 Bolshevik, 40 Left SR, 17 Cadet and 16 Menshevik. The Bolsheviks got just under a quarter of the votes. Here was a dilemma: to accept the result and resign or to ignore it and govern.

But the dilemma was more apparent than real. All Marxists accepted the dictatorship of the proletariat for the transition period. The only question was: who was to exercise it? The logical answer as the result of the elections was the SR party. But the SRs were the party of Kerensky and Chernov and of the coalition governments which had so lamentably failed to govern. What

---

[16] *Collected Works*, Vol. 26, 351
[17] Bunyan & Fisher, *The Bolshevik Revolution* (1934), 293

chance was there that a purely SR government would be able to govern any better?

Furthermore the SRs represented the peasants. The proletariat was by definition the town workers; and the Bolsheviks had a majority in the industrial centres. They had a clear majority in St Petersburg and Moscow and dominated the soviets there. They also polled about half the votes in the army: the soldiers were mostly peasants in uniform, but they had from the beginning been associated with the workers in the soviets, so they were as much worker as peasant. From a practical point of view control of the big cities and of the army was decisive: it is doubtful whether even a far less dogmatic party than the Bolsheviks would or could have thrown it away.

For the situation was both menacing and hopeful. There was an armistice with the Germans while peace negotiations were going on. But if these broke down there was nothing to stop the German army resuming its advance (exactly what did happen in February 1918). If this should happen there was at least an even chance that it would put paid to the revolution: there would be either German army rule or anarchy. On the other hand, if the revolution in Russia could hold out there was, Lenin believed, every chance that it would soon be only a part of the greater European revolution. Germany could not last much longer, for it was only a matter of time before American troops arrived in such large numbers as to make German defeat certain. Defeat, he believed, would bring utter disillusion with the imperial government, and revolution. Russo-German socialist solidarity would ensure the triumph of revolution all over Europe. Lenin overestimated the revolutionary spirit and capability of the Germans and of the German Social-Democratic party, but the events of 1918–19 prove that his estimate was not so far from the truth. In these circumstances, what government could voluntarily lay down its power without a guilty feeling that it was abandoning its duty and its trust, and without at least the shadow of a thought that it was exposing the revolution to defeat and the workers to an incalculable period of further oppression and exploitation? Certainly not a government headed by Lenin and Trotsky. Their temperaments, their beliefs and their ambitions, as defined by Lunacharsky, all urged them to defy formalism and to govern. As Lenin said in a speech to the 2nd All-Russian Congress of Peasants'

Deputies: 'The sabbath was made for man, and not man for the sabbath.'[18]

The Bolshevik government did not resign. The Constituent Assembly met on 5/18 January 1918. It rejected a Bolshevik declaration of rights incorporating approval of the decrees of the 2nd All-Russian Congress of Soviets by 237 votes to 138. In the early hours of the morning of 6/19 January the Bolshevik deputies withdrew 'in view of the counter-revolutionary majority'. They were followed an hour later by the Left SRs. Shortly afterwards the sailor in charge of the guard, Zheleznyakov, informed the president he had instructions to close the assembly 'because the guard is tired'. It never met again.

Lenin summed up his attitude to it in a speech to the Executive Committee on 9/22 January:

> The people have not yet fully understood the October Revolution. This revolution has shown in practice how the people must take into their own hands, the hands of the workers' and peasants' state, the land, the natural resources, and the means of transport and production. Our cry was, All Power to the Soviets; it is for this we are fighting. The people wanted the Constituent Assembly summoned, and we summoned it. But they sensed immediately what this famous assembly really was. And now we have carried out the will of the people, which is—All power to the Soviets. As for the saboteurs, we shall crush them. When I came from Smolny, that fount of life and vigour, to the Taurida Palace, I felt as though I were in the company of corpses and lifeless mummies. They drew on all their available resources in order to fight socialism, they resorted to violence and sabotage, they even turned knowledge—the great pride of humanity —into a means of exploiting the working people. But although they managed to hinder somewhat the advance towards the socialist revolution, they could not stop it and will never be able to. Indeed the Soviets that have begun to smash the old, outworn foundations of the bourgeois system, not in gentlemanly, but in a blunt proletarian and peasant fashion, are much too strong.[19]

The sailor Zheleznyakov was a fitting exponent of this blunt proletarian and peasant fashion. And as Schapiro remarks in his history of the Communist Party, 'Lenin's instincts had not failed him. The dispersal of the assembly caused little stir either inside the party or in the country at large.'[20]

---

[18] *Collected Works*, Vol. 26, 358
[19] *Ibid*, 440
[20] Leonard Schapiro, *The Communist Party of the Soviet Union* (1963), 181

It did however face the Bolsheviks with the problem of the constitution. Lenin had already stated the general principles on which it should be based, in the Declaration of the Rights of the Toiling and Exploited Peoples to be put before the Constituent Assembly. After its dispersal the declaration was adopted by the 3rd Congress of Soviets. It declared that Russia was a Soviet republic 'on the basis of a free union of free nations, a federation of National Soviet Republics'.

An empiricist like Lenin might well have been content to leave it at that and let relations between the centre and the local soviets and between the state and the party work themselves out in practice. But the examples of the American and French revolutions were unconsciously powerful, and the Bolsheviks were after all a party of Marxist theory, so it was natural enough that they should think it proper to draft a formal constitution. The Central Committee of the Soviet set up a drafting commission on 1 April with Sverdlov as chairman. This worked with considerable speed in the circumstances and produced its draft on 8 July. It was endorsed by the 5th Congress of Soviets on 10 July and published on 19 July when it came into force.

Its first four chapters recited textually the Declaration of the Rights of the Toiling and Exploited Peoples. Chapter 5 set out the general principles on which the state was based. The state was federal in character. State and church were separate, as were church and school. There was freedom of opinion, speech and assembly for the workers, guaranteed by giving them the technical means to produce books and the premises for meetings. There was an obligation to work and to perform military service. Every worker on Russian soil had a right to citizenship, and all discrimination on grounds of race or nationality was abolished. There was a right of asylum for foreigners persecuted for their religion or politics.

Chapters 6 to 8 dealt with the organization of the central government. The supreme power in Russia would reside in the all-Russian Congress of Soviets, consisting of one representative for each 25,000 voters in cities and one representative for each 125,000 voters in the provinces. The Congress was to elect a Central Executive Committee of not more than 200 members to function between meetings of the Congress. The Committee would appoint *Sovnarkom*. *Sovnarkom*'s function was to be 'the general administration of the affairs of the RSFSR' and it may issue 'decrees, orders and instructions'. Chapter 9 concerned the functions of the Congress of Soviets and of the Executive Committee, Chapters 10 to 12 the organization of the local soviets.

Chapter 13 confined the franchise to those who 'earn their living by production or socially useful labour', soldiers and disabled persons, and specifically excluded employers of hired labour, *rentiers*, private traders, monks and priests, officials and agents of the former police.

There is a fundamental contradiction in the Bolshevik doctrine of the state to which Lenin's writing (see pp. 146–51) and practice bear witness. On the one hand is the dogma inherited from Engels of 'the withering away of the state', on the other 'the dictatorship of the proletariat' however this might be interpreted. At this date Lenin certainly held both ideas with equal tenacity and seems scarcely to have been aware of how contradictory they were. This was possible for a number of reasons. The period after the Bolshevik seizure of power was very obviously a period of turmoil and confusion, of intellectual, moral and social ferment, of the end of the war and the beginning of peace, a period, in a word, of transition: pre-eminently a period in which 'the dictatorship of the proletariat' was natural, without prejudice to what would emerge in the course of the transition. Lenin still believed that administration was a very simple matter and that ordinary men and women could easily run their affairs in village and factory: there was no need for a complicated apparatus of government to direct them. The tsarist apparatus had been not only evil but unnecessary, and could and must be dismantled. Lenin's mind was concentrated above all on the immediate problems of national and party survival, and he did not bother about the theoretical problem of the state.

Added to this fundamental problem were important theoretical and practical problems connected with the relation between the centre and the local soviets, and between government and party. Lenin's slogans for revolutionary government had been 'All power to the Soviet!' and 'Democratic centralism'. These were admirable slogans concentrating attention on the essential, but they concealed as much as they illuminated, and of course did nothing to solve the real problems involved. One aspect concealed was the Bolshevik break with the western tradition of the separation of powers, legislative, executive and judicial, which had been a main plank of the programme of the American and French constitution makers. The Bolsheviks thought this a bourgeois idea floated by capitalist means of production and bourgeois society, and doomed inevitably to sink with them into the waters of the past. In its place they set what might be called 'democratic interpenetration'. *Sovnarkom*, as the ultimate representative of the whole proletariat, might issue 'decrees, orders and instructions' and these were to be obeyed; but they would be based on a great body of evidence produced by the local soviets, and they might be issued either direct to the citizens or in the form of decrees of the All-Russian Congress of Soviets, if it was in session, or alternatively of the Executive Committee, or as instructions to the local soviets: however conveyed, they had equal validity and force.

Equally, something drafted, debated, passed and promulgated by the Congress was not labelled a law or Act of Congress, while a decision of *Sovnarkom* was labelled an Order or Decree or Ukase. Each was equally a decree, order or instruction, and had equal legislative and executive force. Neither was subject to scrutiny in the courts to test its constitutional validity.

The local soviet was in the same position. It was a jack of all trades: it made by-laws, issued orders, heard complaints, prescribed penalties and gingered up the local peasants and workers. Its status was unique: it was a legislative, executive and judicial body: It was what It was.

The relations between the centre and the local soviets were governed in principle by the notion of 'authority from below, discipline from above'. The government derived its authority from the governed, from all the citizens: at the very bottom the local soviet in the village, factory or regiment, and on up through the district, county and province to the region, and at the top the All-Russian Congress of Soviets. But representation was not equal: one member for every 25,000 voters in the cities and one for every 125,000 voters in the provinces. This had a theoretical and practical justification. The true proletarians were the factory workers alone; in the country there were only peasants, many of them petty bourgeois in character, and relatively few landless labourers, who might qualify as honorary proletarians. Furthermore the recent elections had shown that the Bolsheviks were strong only in the big towns, and that the peasants were, if anything, SRs. Nor was authority merely a matter of voting. The local soviet had a job to do and got on with it. And there was an expectation that the ordinary citizen would be concerned with his affairs and would take part in them. This expectation was naturally more fully realized in some places than others, but on the whole it seems fair to say that the soviet was the nearest practical embodiment of Rousseau's self-governing community that the world had so far seen.

But authority was exercised under the discipline of the centre. This determined the basis of life: the defence of Russia, its religious and political complexion, the production of food and goods. It made policy and plans. It issued orders in accordance with these.

What was 'the centre'? The All-Russian Congress of Soviets, its Executive Committee and *Sovnarkom*. Whatever the theory of the constitution, in practice power might fall into the hands of any one of these. The traditions of the Russian government and of the Bolshevik Party were strongly in favour of the concentration of power into the hands of a small body, some would say of one man. There was little experience of the widespread exercise of power and responsibility to counter these traditions. The post-war situation and still more, after July 1918, the civil war strongly encouraged this tendency, and indeed made it imperative for *Sovnarkom* to take and execute decisions on its own responsibility, without reference to any other body. (Against this the White occupation of parts of Russia and the utter turmoil of civil war cut off large parts of Russia from control by the centre and forced the local soviets to exercise absolute responsibility.) But Lenin, despite his personal prestige, his temperament, his zest for responsibility and his tenaciously held theory of the party, was concerned to prevent *Sovnarkom* drawing all power to itself. While he was alive, the Congress met annually and was by no means a body of yes-men—witness, for example, the crucial debates on trade unions and workers' control at the 10th All-Russian Congress of Soviets in 1921.

At the height of the civil war in March 1919 the 8th Party Congress set up a political board (*Politburo*) of five men to make decisions not admitting of delay and to report fortnightly to the Central Committee of the party; an organizing board (*Orgburo*) to meet three times a week to organize the work of the party and control the activities of its members; and a Secretariat consisting of a full-time Secretary and five technical assistants. To eliminate clashes between the three bodies and to smooth the work of the party machine as a whole, the Secretary was to be a member of the *Orgburo*, as was one member of the *Politburo*.

By this action the Congress created a party structure strictly parallel to the structure of the state: on the one hand the All-Russian Congress of Soviets, the Central Executive Committee of the Congress, *Sovnarkom;* on the other the All-Russian Party Congress, the Central Committee of the Party, the *Politburo* and *Orgburo*. The Bolsheviks, and Lenin in particular, had always stressed the need for a hard nucleus of party leaders to control and direct the party; and the civil war reinforced their view with the discipline of experience.

Equally, it was the role of the party to lead the masses against the autocracy and to control and direct the revolution; and once they were victorious to guide them through the period of transition to the socialist society. Now they were in this period of transition how was the party to exercise its guidance?

Once again it was by a process of interpenetration. At every level members of the party were members of the appropriate government body. The members of *Sovnarkom* were all members of the party. The leading Bolsheviks were for the most part members of the government and of the highest organs of the party: Lenin, Trotsky, Stalin and Kamenev were members of *Sovnarkom* and of the *Politburo*, and Stalin was a member of the *Orgburo* as well. Dzerzhinsky, head of the *Cheka*, was a member of *Sovnarkom* and of the Central Committee of the party, and after 1920 of the *Orgburo*. In the regions and below the same thing occurred: the leading members of the party took the lead in the soviet, right down to the bottom where the chairman of the village soviet was a Communist. On the eve of the revolution there were 23,600 members of the party; and by the beginning of 1919 only 313,000 out of a total Russian population of about 175 million. But each member counted for ten and did the work of ten. They were everywhere and in everything. Many were careerists, many were less than trained Marxists, many were arbitrary and brutal, some were sadists. But as a whole they fulfilled their function: to act as leaven to the lump of the proletariat and peasantry. Here lies one of the causes of the ultimate Bolshevik victory.

## 14 Famine and civil war

In the spring of 1918 famine in the towns and a complete break-down of the economy threatened Russia. The 1917 harvest had been poor. It was vital that the 1918 harvest should be good and that the grain should reach the towns. By contrast it was vital that industrial production should increase and that the goods should reach the countryside.

Since November 1917 the process of taking over and dividing the land had been going on, sometimes in an orderly fashion, sometimes not. In some areas the local land committee con-trolled the process, in some the soviet; in some there was more or less no control and the peasants seized what land they could; in some there were fights between the richer and poorer peasants. The peasants of Lebyadka, a village near Moscow, refused to share their land with the peasants of the next village, themselves ex-serfs of the same estate and generally poorer than the Lebyadka villagers, arguing that the land had belonged originally to land-lords working it exclusively with Lebyadka serfs and that there-fore the land belonged to them and no one else; the fact that the other villagers had less land had nothing to do with it. This these villagers accepted without argument or fuss. By the summer of 1918 the great bulk of the land of Russia was in the hands of the peasants, formally owned by the state but occupied by millions of individual peasant families.

This created a vast class of contented farmers with a vested interest in the permanence of the revolution, entrenched supporters of any government that could guarantee this. But it also created political and economic difficulties of the gravest kind. Politically the peasants were satisfied and conservative. They could be counted on to give passive support to any government guarantee-ing their possession of the land, but at the same time they could be counted on to offer passive resistance to any form of govern-ment interference and to any form of socialist land policy: a formidable obstacle for any socialist government.

More immediately alarming was the economic threat. The peasants had recovered what they felt in the marrow of their bones was theirs and their one desire was to work it for themselves: broadly speaking they would sow what was needed to feed their families and no more. If they did sow more and harvested a surplus of grain they would store it against a rainy day, not offer it to their proletarian brothers in comradely fashion. The market remedy for this was rising grain prices. Whether this would have worked in the prevailing psychological atmosphere is more than doubtful. But it was ruled out of court on ideological and practical grounds. It was absolutely impossible for a Bolshevik government immediately to base its policy on the profit motive and to adopt normal capitalist methods of trade. Furthermore there was a grave shortage of money with solid purchasing power, and of goods for the peasants to buy. The only way to get more goods on to the market was to get the factory workers to produce more to make up the loss of production due to the German occupation of Russian territory and to the cutting off of supplies of raw materials. Again the market remedy for this was higher wages. But again it was more than doubtful if this would work in the circumstances: the workers were as much on the crest of a wave as the peasants; but what they wanted was not land or money, but an easy life: to work normal hours, to work at their own pace, and every now and again to drink themselves silly on vodka, and sleep it off undisturbed.

In any case the government had nationalized industry and the banks and confiscated gold and bullion in private hands, crediting the holders' accounts in the State Bank with the equivalent in notes. But there had been continuous monetary inflation during the war and since the revolution, and the rouble was rapidly losing more and more of its value. On top of this there was a yawning gap between government expenditure and revenue: expenditure for the first six months of the Bolshevik regime estimated at somewhere between twenty and fifty milliard roubles and revenue at five milliard. Taxes were almost impossible to collect, and the government had been compelled against Lenin's will to leave it to local initiative to levy what were politely called 'contributions'.

In this situation Bolshevik policy was a mixture of centralized planning, moral exhortation and legalized plunder.

At the beginning of January 1918 an All-Russian Food Committee was set up to advise the food commissions attached to the local soviets, working in conjunction with the Food Commissar. But it seems rather to have got in his light than to have helped him and at the end of the month it was superseded by an All-Russian Council of Supply which was to organize internal barter. This in turn gave place in February to an Extraordinary Commission on Food and Transport with Trotsky as its head. This issued an immediate order to seize food from the bagmen, so called because they travelled the countryside with sacks collecting grain for sale, and to hand the bagmen themselves over to the courts on charges of extortion; if they drew in self-defence they were to be shot out of hand. Instead of them the Commission was to rely on armed detachments of factory workers sent into the country and the Committees of the Poor set up by decree in June. In an *Open Letter to the St Petersburg Workers On The Famine* in May Lenin wrote:

> We need a ... 'crusade' of advanced workers to every corner of this vast country. We need ten times more *iron detachments* of the proletariat, class-conscious and boundlessly devoted to communism. Then we shall triumph over famine and unemployment. Then we shall make the revolution the real prelude to socialism ...[1]

Lenin was appealing to their need for food and to their revolutionary zeal to conquer the threat of starvation. In the same way he appealed to the poor peasants to extract grain from the *kulaks*: their reward was to be an allocation of the grain seized, either free or at a very cheap rate.

The Bolshevik organization of industry was closely parallel, though there was one important difference of form due to the difference between the takeover of factories and of land, and to the difference in the nature of the productive process itself. An All-Russian Council of National Economy was set up in December 1917 to take over all branches of production and trade, to centralize and direct all the economic organs of the administration and to submit to *Sovnarkom* all draft decrees on economic matters. Under it were regional councils, but these never got off the ground as the local soviets were already functioning and were unwilling to hand over their responsibilities.

---

[1] *Collected Works*, Vol. 27, 398

An essential condition of success was 'absolute centralization and rigorous discipline', but, Lenin asked:

> How is the discipline of the proletariat's revolutionary party maintained? How is it tested? How is it reinforced? First, by the class-consciousness of the proletarian vanguard and by its devotion to the revolution, by its tenacity, self-sacrifice and heroism. Second, by its ability to link up, maintain the closest contact, and—if you wish—merge, in certain measure, with the broadest masses of the working people—primarily with the proletariat, *but also with the non-proletarian* masses of the working people. Third, by the correctness of the political leadership exercised by this vanguard, by the correctness of its political strategy and tactics, provided the broad masses have seen, *from their own experience*, that they are correct.[2]

This is an appeal both to the left-wing Bolsheviks like Bukharin and to the factory workers: to recognize and learn from experience. Experience had shown with appalling clarity that workers' control of industry had produced a catastrophic decline in production and with it a threat to the very existence of the regime from a lack of goods as serious as the threat from lack of food. In the light of this experience it was, in Lenin's view, 'infantile' to preach the direct and immediate passage from capitalism to socialism. In this critical period there must be a transitional form of organization: state capitalism. By this he meant that the state owned the means of production, distribution and exchange, and made the basic plan for the economy; but that it employed individuals of the relevant experience and technical skill as its agents in the field. It must offer inducements to ex-capitalists, factory managers and technicians to serve it, and it must persuade the workers to accept them. In particular Lenin was determined to re-establish one-man control of factories as the only apparent way of getting work going again.

Here the difference in form from land policy reveals itself. The state owned all the land of Russia. But the peasants had occupied it and were working it. Very many of them were *kulaks* who produced more in proportion on their land than the poor peasants. For the time being they had to remain undisturbed. It was only necessary for the poor peasants and the factory workers to seize their surplus production and hand it over to the state. But in industry it was different. The state owned all the factories and

[2] *Collected Works*, Vol. 31, 24–5

plant. The workers had occupied them and driven out the owners and managers—and were not working. To restore production it was necessary to restore the industrial *kulaks:* or put in another way: the slogan of the revolutionary proletariat had been 'expropriate the expropriators', or, without Latin words ... 'steal back the stolen' ...

> but if the slogan ... has shown itself unrestrainedly in the activities of the Soviets, and if it turns out that in a practical and fundamental matter like famine and unemployment we are confronted by enormous difficulties, it is appropriate to say that after the words 'steal back what was stolen' the proletarian revolution makes a distinction, which runs: 'Count up what was stolen and don't let it be filched piecemeal, and if people start filching for themselves directly or indirectly, these infringers of discipline must be shot ...'.[3]

The situation was immeasurably worsened by the German occupation of the Ukraine under the terms of the Treaty of Brest-Litovsk. On the day of the treaty's signature, 3 March 1918, German troops were in Kiev, but it was not until two months later on 8 May that they occupied Rostov-on-Don and set up a puppet of their own as head of a nominally independent Ukrainian government. This meant that Russia had lost its main granary as well as a third of its industry and three-quarters of its coal and iron, (while the loss of Transcaucasia which had proclaimed itself independent in April meant the loss of all its oil). Further a German army in Rostov controlled the railway from Moscow to the Caucasus, cut Bolshevik communications with the Black Sea, and to a lesser extent with the Caspian, and covered the White troops—which had been disintegrating in the early spring—on the Don and the Kuban. These consisted in the main of Cossacks under their own leaders and of some tsarist generals who had escaped to the south, like the former chief-of-staff Alekseyev. They were not in themselves a serious danger to the regime. For the Cossacks, though strong in defence of their homelands, were unwilling to leave them to overthrow the Bolsheviks and restore the old order.

But there now occurred an episode that altered the whole situation and launched a bitter civil war which lasted until 1920.

There was on Russian soil an army of upwards of 30,000 men, consisting of Czech prisoners of war and deserters from the

Austrian army: the Czech Legion. The Legion recognized the
President of the Czecho-Slovak National Council, Masaryk, as
its leader and was anxious to contribute its services to the allied
cause and so to the creation of an independent Czech state as
soon and as effectively as possible. To this end Masaryk had
agreed with the Bolshevik government that the legion should go
by rail to Vladivostok from where it would be shipped to the
western front via the U.S.A. Naturally the Germans did not
approve this agreement and insisted on a clause in the Treaty of
Brest-Litovsk under which the Bolsheviks would disarm the
Czechs. Accordingly the government came to a further agreement
with the Czechs at the end of March that they would travel 'not
as fighting units, but as groups of free citizens who carry with
them a specified number of weapons of defence against counter-
revolutionary attacks'. The first contingent duly left for Vladivostok on 27 March. Unfortunately the offensive that the Germans
opened on the western front on 21 March made the allies desperate
for more troops as quickly as possible. So the Allied Supreme War
Council on 2 May laid down that all Czech units still west of
Omsk should be re-routed via Archangel, and got Trotsky, now
Commissar for War, to agree to this. But it had the effect of
arousing Bolshevik suspicions that the Czechs were not in fact
destined for the western front but were to link up with allied
troops at Archangel to form the nucleus of a counter-revolutionary
front. Moreover there was a certain amount of friction between the
Czechs and the local population, and between them and the local
party officials, due to their efforts to 'agitate' the Czech soldiers
and gain recruits for the party (in which they were remarkably
unsuccessful for they managed to persuade only 218 men to
desert the legion). On 14 May an incident occurred at the railway station of Chelyabinsk when some Czech soldiers lynched a
Hungarian soldier who had thrown a crowbar at one of them.
This incident decided Trotsky to disarm the legion completely:
he made up his mind to this sometime before 18 May, and sent
out orders to the local soviets two days later. Meantime a Czech
congress met at Chelyabinsk from 18 to 25 May: it took decisions
not to let troops go to Archangel because of the danger of being
split up, and to set up a provisional executive committee. There is
no doubt that these decisions reflected the Czechs' determination to
maintain their units intact and to get out of Russia with the

*Lenin*

minimum delay and friction. They ought to have reassured Trotsky and the Bolsheviks and cleared the way for fulfilling the agreement. But Trotsky's orders were despatched before he knew of these decisions. There were clashes on 25 May, and between then and 7 June the Czechs occupied Chelyabinsk and other important points on the railway to Siberia including Omsk and Tomsk. The tragedy had begun.

There is no evidence that Lenin paid any attention to Trotsky's decision or had any inkling of its significance; and by the end of June he was speaking in a matter-of-fact way of 'the Czechoslovak mutiny ... obviously being supported by Anglo-French imperialism in the pursuit of its policies of overthrowing the Soviet government ...'[4]

It is arguable that there would have been civil war anyway. There was much discontent and some violent protest in Russia already. Peasants resented having their crops seized. Workers resented having to work and were suspicious of signs of the party wanting to boss the trade unions too much. Cossacks were demonstrating in arms their hereditary dislike of central control. The Ukrainians had before the German occupation shown signs of wanting more autonomy than it would suit the government to give. The Finns and the Georgians had broken away. There were still White troops in the south, though dwindling in number. The Japanese had landed at Vladivostok in April. The Left SRs had left the government after Brest-Litovsk and were violently hostile to the peace and to the Bolsheviks' industrial policy. The SRs proper had, of course, been in opposition since the dissolution of the Constituent Assembly.

But their opposition had not produced a counter-revolution and did not seem to present a mortal danger to the regime. There was, too, a hint that relief was at hand in the west. The Germans had launched their great offensive on the western front at the end of March. They had gained ground and again reached the Marne, but they had not achieved the breakthrough they had planned and needed; more and more troops were thrown in on both sides, but whereas the German units were tired defeatists from Russia the Allied forces were good troops from Italy and Americans fresh to the battlefield. Lenin showed that he was aware of the position in a speech he made to the trade unions on 27 June, in which he

[4] *Collected Works*, Vol. 27, 466

also drew attention to the difficulties the Germans were experiencing in the Ukraine. The Germans could not win against the Allies' reserves of men and material; further conquests only made their ultimate position worse. It seemed that the climax might be at hand and history about to fulfil Lenin's prophecy that imperialist war would break down into international revolution.

Here was Russia's opportunity to emerge from 'the stormy waves of imperialist reaction ... hurling themselves at the small island of the socialist Soviet republic',[5] a beacon of light to the socialists of the west. Instead she was about to be submerged in the waters of a prolonged and savage conflict.

For in June the Czechs occupied Samara and under their protection an anti-Bolshevik government was formed there, which rapidly gained control of a large area on the Volga and in the Urals. The tsar and his family were evacuated to Ekaterinburg and, when the Czechs approached, shot on the orders of the Ural Soviet, probably, though not certainly, with the sanction of Moscow. Protected and encouraged by the Czech success the White forces gained ground in Siberia and the south, and set up governments under various tsarist officers; their authority was very limited and they never succeeded in winning the co-operation of the bulk of the population, but their existence meant that the Reds had lost control of these large areas of Russia. In August the Allies landed at Archangel in the north and Baku, on the shores of the Caspian Sea, to protect military stores collected there but also, in the minds of at least some of the allied leaders, to intervene in the civil war should occasion offer.

At the same time the Left SRs staged a terrorist demonstration as a protest against Brest-Litovsk and, more vaguely, a means of bringing down the government. Blyumkin, a Left SR member of the *Cheka*, assassinated Mirbach the German Ambassador on 6 July with the connivance of other Left SRs who were part of the guard on the German Embassy. They seized the chief Bolshevik members of the *Cheka* and took over the Moscow central post office, from which they sent off messages to the provinces telling them to disregard orders signed by Lenin. A handful of troops demonstrated in Moscow, St Petersburg and a few provincial towns. A 'rogue elephant' of a Red Army commander, General Muravyov, came out against the Bolsheviks and the Germans and

[5] *Ibid*, 367

moved on Moscow; but he had got no further than Simbirsk when he heard of the collapse of the demonstration in Moscow and committed suicide. There seems to have been no co-ordinated plan for a general rising. But the Bolsheviks were shaken. Lenin took the assassination of Mirbach so seriously that he went in person to the German Embassy to apologize on behalf of the government. The Left SR delegates to the Soviet Congress were all arrested, though some of them were later released. The members of the Left SR Central Committee were arrested and one was shot. (Blyumkin himself managed to escape.) The Left SR press was closed down. On 7 July Lenin sent a telephone message to the Moscow Soviet that they were to 'take all steps to capture and detain those who had the insolence to rise against Soviet Power'.[6]

Although the following week the Central Committee of the Congress of Soviets passed a resolution that those members of the group who 'categorically renounced their solidarity with the assassination and with the revolt which followed it' might retain their membership of the committee and, as a consequence, of the local soviets that had elected them, Lenin himself wrote to a local branch of the party that it was essential to oust the SRs from the soviets and to destroy their influence.

On 30 July another Left SR assassinated General Eichhorn, the German commander-in-chief in the Ukraine. A month later on 30 August an SR student shot dead the head of the St Petersburg *Cheka*, and Dora (Fanny) Kaplan, a freelance ex-Anarchist, shot and wounded Lenin. There was considerable haemorrhage and at first it was feared he had been seriously wounded. But it proved less serious, and Lenin was back at work again in three weeks.

But the Bolsheviks had had a bad fright. Dora Kaplan was shot on 3 September. Next day Petrovsky, the Commissar for the Interior, publicly appealed for 'mass terror' against the bourgeoisie, and demanded that large numbers of hostages should be taken. The *Cheka* shot indiscriminately those who happened to be in prison, for whatever offence: not more than 600 in Moscow according to Dzerzhinsky. Local soviets imitated the *Cheka* and many more died suddenly all over Russia.

This was the beginning of the terror which reigned throughout

[6] *Collected Works*, Vol. 35, 341

the civil war: sporadically in time and place, capriciously, often the result of the cold-heartedness or sadism of an individual member of the party or Red Army commander, but nevertheless a terror that was government policy.

Its instruments were already in existence: the revolutionary tribunals which had been given the right to impose the death penalty in June; the *Cheka*, which had to a great extent become a law unto itself when Moscow had become the capital in March and it had taken over the Lubyanka Palace as its headquarters and prison; and the dedicated party member whose first duty and pride was to safeguard the revolution. Even before the organization of the *Cheka*, on the outlawry of the Cadets, Trotsky had said: 'You protest against the mild terror which we are directing against our class enemies. But you should know that not later than a month from now the terror will assume very violent forms after the example of the great French revolutionaries. The guillotine will be ready for our enemies and not merely the jail.'[7] And in August Dzerzhinsky remarked in a press interview: 'The *Cheka* is not a court. The *Cheka* is *the defence of the revolution* as the Red Army is.'[8]

But in fact the early days of the regime had been clear and mild. The Cadets captured in the Winter Palace were turned loose on promising 'not to take up arms against the people any more'. General Krasnov was released on parole. The members of the Provisional Government were soon freed and only nominally supervised. In the first three months there were no executions by the revolutionary tribunals or the regular courts. But on 22 February 1918 the *Cheka* issued an order to local soviets to seek out and shoot counter-revolutionaries and speculators; and from the time when the government moved to Moscow the *Cheka* seems to have stepped up its activities.

The terror was barbaric and anachronistic. For well over a century there had been a clear and steady public opinion in Europe against the use of arbitrary violence and torture by governments and their agents and the outcry over the 'atrocities' in the Belgian Congo and on the Amazon showed that this was as much concerned for negroes and Indians as for whites. In this matter tsarist Russia was certainly European. It had a developed,

---

[7] Quoted in E. H. Carr, *The Bolshevik Revolution*, Vol. I, 157–8
[8] *Ibid.*, 167

civilized code of law and a body of lawyers with proper professional standards, while the outcry over such things as Stolypin's gallows or the shooting of strikers in the Lena goldfields showed that there was a public opinion to be outraged in Russia too.

The terror was also doubtfully legal. Lenin and the Bolsheviks logically regarded bourgeois law and law courts as yet one more expression of capitalism in concrete form, and wanted them replaced by socialist law and law courts, 'based on the sense of justice possessed by the masses and not on the justice of the oppressors'. In accordance with this attitude the decree of 24 November 1917 swept away the existing courts and replaced them by new local courts for civil and criminal cases and by the revolutionary tribunals. These courts were to administer a yet unformulated revolutionary law. But it is clear it was not the intention of the lawmakers to legalize terror in advance, for it did not confer the power to pass the death penalty on the revolutionary tribunals until June 1918, and not then on the ordinary courts, while the *Cheka* was originally designed to investigate, not to carry out trials and to execute sentences.

Doubtfully legal, the terror was also in an important sense un-Marxist. Marx himself had an inherited and passionate hatred of injustice, and one of the mainsprings of his attack on capitalism had been his sense of its essential injustice. His Social-Democratic successors in Europe had upheld this tradition with continuous protests against arbitrary acts of justice. Severe punishment in accordance with 'the sense of justice possessed by the masses' was correct in Marxist terms—indiscriminate terror was not.

It was, however, very much in the Russian tradition. The secret police, arrest without trial, incarceration in the Peter and Paul Fortress, mass trial, exile to Siberia and shooting of political criminals were all part of the governmental stock-in-trade, nor in the last days of the tsarist regime did the government scruple to support pogroms committed by the Black Hundreds. Against it were arrayed 'progressives' of various kinds whose weapons were the bullet and the bomb: the Bolsheviks differing from the anarchists in being set against individual terror, which they regarded as futile, for a casual assassination or bomb outrage did not bring the end of the regime any nearer but brought instead severe, and perhaps effective, repression on the perpetrators and other left-wing groups. In the country it had not been unknown for landlords to beat their serfs to death, and in agrarian riots and in the 1905 revolution the peasants replied in kind: with arson and lynching. Not far below the surface of Russian life was an undercurrent of explosive violence symbolized by Dostoyevsky's dream of the driver beating his horses to death.

The crisis of 1918 was tense enough to call for extraordinary measures and it was almost inevitable that a Russian government should call on the Russian tradition in devising and executing them. In a crisis, particularly a war crisis in modern times, any government suspends the ordinary law to some extent and introduces special wartime regulations, designed among other things to safeguard the realm from traitors and citizens of doubtful loyalty: witness the Defence of the Realm Acts of the two World Wars, and the internment of Fascists and Jehovah's Witnesses in the second World War—this by a government with as long a tradition of civilized and civilian behaviour as the British. Further in a serious and nerve-wracking crisis this government is capable of behaviour far below what it would tolerate in normal peacetime, e.g. the concentration of Boer civilians into hastily built camps at the end of the Boer War or the thuggish activities of the Black-and-Tans in Ireland in 1920.

These last may be partly accounted for by fright. Fear breeds panic and ferocity. Probably few regimes can show a record absolutely untarnished by this—neither the British nor the French, to take two examples from western Europe: the brutalities committed in India after the mutiny or in Algeria and France during the civil war were the target of strong criticism at the time, and would now be universally regarded as blots on a civilized record. It is perhaps not irrelevant that these brutalities occurred outside the mother country in colonial or semi-colonial countries. For the attitude of the tsarist government to its people was more that of a paternal government to 'the sullen, half-tamed people' than of a democratic government to its citizens, and the Bolsheviks not only inherited the tsarist tradition but added to it Lenin's theory of the party as an élite leading, not to say driving, the proletariat towards the socialist paradise.

But this apart, there was enough in the summer of 1918 to strike fear into the hearts of the Bolsheviks. The Germans were in the Ukraine and the Allies in Archangel and Baku, the Japanese in Vladivostok, the Whites in Siberia and between the Black Sea

and the Caspian, the Czechs in control of the railway east from
the Urals. The bourgeois were by definition hostile and the
people doubtful. Everywhere was the threat of famine and
industrial breakdown, everywhere degenerating railway track
and abandoned locomotives.

Already in the spring Lenin had let the old army run down and
at the same time had begun the process of organizing a new
Workers'-Peasants' Red Army and a new centralized command.
By the autumn this consisted of two bodies: the Revolutionary
Military Council of the Republic, the supreme military-political
organ of the Soviet, with subordinate military councils at each of
the fronts; and the Council of Workers' and Peasants' Defence,
the supreme military-economic organ, set up in November 1918
with Trotsky as chairman. The strategic direction of the war was
firmly in civilian, party hands, with Lenin acting as 'strategic
mediator, manager and co-ordinator'.[9]

As the chief agent of this policy Trotsky, appointed Commissar
for War in March 1918, began to get a grip on his job and to recreate an army. He had to organize supply and transport, to
recruit soldiers, NCOs and officers, to weld them into an army
and inspire it with fighting spirit. His methods were classical:
scrupulous attention to administrative detail, rigid discipline and
appeal to professional pride; on top of these reliance on the
devoted hard work of the political commissars in raising and
sustaining the morale of units at the front.

It was necessary to tackle the problems of the fronts on the
spot; to do this Trotsky went to the spot himself in his famous
train and investigated.

> After making the round of a division and ascertaining its needs on
> the spot I would hold a conference in the staff car or the dining-
> car, inviting as many representatives as possible, including those
> from the lower commanding grades and from the ranks as well as
> from the local Party organization, the Soviet administration and the
> trade unions. In this way I got a picture of the situation that was
> neither false nor highly-coloured. These conferences always had
> practical results. No matter how poor the organs of the local ad-
> ministration might be, they always managed to squeeze a little
> tighter and cut down some of their own needs to contribute some-
> thing to the army.[10]

[9] John Erickson in *Lenin, the Man, the Theorist, the Leader*, ed. Schapiro & Reddaway
(1967), 167
[10] David Footman, *Civil War in Russia* (1961), 149

This technique was sound not only in producing an accurate picture but also in drawing in all parts of the population to a co-operative effort and in allowing full play to Trotsky's remarkable gifts: his quickness of mind and decisiveness, his powers of persuasion and of intimidation—he could charm the birds from a tree but he could make them drop dead from fright too.

The same mixture of organization and discipline raised the numbers of the Red Army. At the time of the Czech seizure of Chelyabinsk it amounted to some 300,000 men; by the end of the year it numbered 800,000. This was achieved by conscription, by setting up machinery to enlist and train the conscripts, and by keeping the pressure on the local soviets to produce their quota of recruits. It was equally important to stop desertion, which was wholesale. Trotsky again revealed his common sense and imagination. A deserter who returned for service was to receive a free pardon and be made to feel a true patriot; a man who deserted a second time was to pay for his action: if necessary by death. Trotsky made the local soviets and committees of poor peasants responsible for rounding up and returning deserters: the local chairmen were to be arrested if deserters were found in their villages.

Many soldiers and party members were quickly promoted to be NCOs and officers and did extremely well. But it was not possible to get enough officers with the necessary training and quality in this way. Trotsky was insistent—and Lenin agreed with him—on recruiting ex-tsarist officers and NCOs. This was naturally most unpopular with members of the party and of the Soviet, but they carried their point. Some officers were inspired to rejoin out of hatred for their national enemies, the Germans and Poles, some out of professional pride, but most out of an urgent need to support themselves and their families, when ration cards were denied the former ruling classes, and because it was difficult and dangerous to avoid call-up. Many of them gave loyal service from patriotism and professional *esprit de corps*, but the great majority seem to have been kept from desertion only by inertia and fear. For Trotsky had made it clear that the families of deserters would be made to pay for their desertion.

Discipline and morale marched hand in hand. Field tribunals with summary powers were set up: 'Comrade Trotsky's harsh methods were most expedient and necessary for that period of undisciplined and irregular warfare. Persuasion counted for nothing and there was no time for it.'[11] Threats were made against officers' families. Political commissars were attached to each unit: to watch the officers, to cheer the men, to appraise the situation from a party point of view, to put backbone into the army. Technical training and training of morale were given prominence.

> We must now devote our whole attention to improving our material and to making it more efficient rather than to fantastic schemes of reorganization. Every army unit must receive its rations regularly, foodstuffs must not be allowed to rot and meals must be properly cooked. We must teach our soldiers personal cleanliness and see that they exterminate vermin. They must learn their drill properly and perform it as much as possible in the open air. They must be taught to make their political speeches short and sensible, to clean their rifles and to grease their boots. They must learn to shoot and must help their officers in strict observance of regulations for keeping in touch with other units in the field, reconnaissance work, reports and sentry duty. They must learn and teach the art of adaptation to local conditions, they must learn to wind their puttees properly so as to prevent sores on their legs, and once again they must learn to grease their boots. This is our programme for next year in general and next spring in particular, and if anyone wishes to take advantage of some solemn occasion to describe this practical programme as 'military doctrine' he is welcome to do so.[12]

The words are Trotsky's but they might as well be Lenin's: the irony, the contempt for ideological hot air and the horse sense are as much the mark of the one man as the other.

The Red Army grew into a coherent, disciplined force that weathered the crisis of the civil war in the autumn of 1919. In the second week in October General Yudenich launched a drive on St Petersburg which reached the suburbs on the 22nd. At the same time General Denikin, whose troops already held Odessa, Kiev and Kharkov, captured Orel, only 200 miles from Moscow. But he got no further. Exhaustion, lack of supplies and the counter-attack of the Red Army forced him back, and by December the Red Army was again in possession of Kiev and Kharkov. At the same time other units were in hot pursuit of the White troops of the Far Eastern army which were retreating in a more and more disorderly fashion.

[11] Footman, *op. cit.*, 146
[12] *Ibid.*, 148

The crisis was past and victory won, though fighting went on until the end of 1920. The Red Army had played a major part in the victory. But there were other factors too. First there was the inherent weakness and disunity of the counter-revolutionaries. They did not command at any time an adequate supply of war material; and after the defeat of Germany none of the Allies was willing to make good this lack. They did not throw up a general to compare with Trotsky nor any political leaders who could hold a candle to him or Lenin. Nor were they united in aim. Some—true reactionaries—wanted a return to imperial Russia, with its frontiers and institutions intact. Some like Milyukov wanted a liberal Russia within the old frontiers. Some like the Ukrainian nationalists wanted an autonomous or even an independent Ukraine. Some like the anarchists, gathered round the elusive and colourful Makhno, wanted to break up Russia and all centralized political authority. Some like the SRs wanted a community of smallholding peasants with a rather weak central government. This disunity is symbolized by the All-Russian Provisional Government based on the defunct Constituent Assembly and set up at Ufa in September 1918. This consisted of socialists of all shades (except the Bolsheviks), of Cadets, and of two right-wing organizations, the *edinstvo* and the League for the Regeneration of Russia. It set up a directory of five, two SRs, two right-wingers and one Cadet. In the end a right-wing coup arrested the SR members and transferred all power to a Supreme Ruler, Admiral Kolchak.

As the war went on power came more and more into the hands of the reactionaries: a fact that almost guaranteed defeat. The ordinary Russian may have had no love for the Bolsheviks but he was determined not to be thrust back into his old state. The peasant was determined to keep his land, the worker the abolition of private ownership, and the non-Russian the freedom, complete or partial, already won. The civil war brought drawn-out, bitter hardship and suffering to the people, particularly where their territory was fought over, again and again, by the contending armies and by bands of partisans and brigands. They endured it as they endured hunger and thirst and natural disasters. But their passive endurance and their inarticulate desires made them passive supporters of the Bolsheviks.

Working on this passive mass was the dedicated will of the

Bolshevik Party: single-minded, clear, bent on victory. And the very core of this will was Lenin's will. Just as Lenin had been ready to take power in the summer of 1917 when everyone else was hesitant and disorientated, so during the civil war he steadfastly exercised power and never seems to have had any doubts of ultimate victory. His faith was founded on a deep intellectual conviction of the correctness of Marx's theory of history and of Bolshevik timing: the experience of riding the crest of the wave was itself proof of having caught it at exactly the right moment. His faith was fortified by his innate trust in the masses and feeling for them. Lenin, who normally worked a seventeen to eighteen hour day at his desk in the Kremlin, was sustained by his robust constitution, his lifelong habit of physical exercises and of hard work, his humour and *joie de vivre*. Many visitors to the Kremlin commented on his shrewd and humorous scrutiny, with one eye screwed up in concentration, and on his invigorating laugh; and he was always. ready to join children in their fun.

Lenin's will was only once seen to falter in these years, at the funeral of Inessa Armand. She had died of typhus in the Caucasus. When her body was brought to Moscow for burial 'and we accompanied her to the cemetery,' said Alexandra Kollontay, 'Lenin was unrecognizable. He walked with closed eyes; at every moment we thought he would collapse.'[13] Angelica Balabanoff, who was quite close to Lenin at the cemetery, says the same thing.

> Not only his face but his whole body expressed so much sorrow that I dared not greet him, not even with the slightest gesture. It was clear he wanted to be alone with his grief. He seemed to have shrunk; his cap almost covered his face, his eyes seemed drowned in tears held back with effort. As our circle moved, following the movement of the people, he too moved, without offering resistance, as if he were grateful for being brought nearer to the dead comrade. This mood did not influence in the least his activity as statesman and strategist of the workers' movement of the world. From the funeral he went straight back to his desk.[14]

No doubt work was an anodyne for his profound grief. But equally it was impermissible for a communist to allow private grief to distract him from the strategy 'of the workers' movement of the world'.

[13] Bertram D. Wolfe in *Encounter*, February 1964
[14] Angelica Balabanoff, *Impressions of Lenin* (University of Michigan, 1964), 15

The strategy of the civil war was the concern of the centralized command as a whole, but Lenin had a unique breadth of vision and grasp of the interlocking military, political and diplomatic problems. This determined his strategic thinking and gave him a predominant influence on strategic decisions. In December 1918 he was insistent on an advance into the Ukraine to forestall the Allies and to gain for the Soviet its own 'deep rear'; and he was troubled and angry at the failure of the advance. In February 1919, after the German defeat in the west but when their intentions on the Russian front were not yet clear, Lenin overruled the commander-in-chief Vatsetis, who recommended offensives in the Ukraine and on the western front, in favour of concentration on the 'internal fronts', southern and eastern, where the peasants and the Cossacks were disaffected. In May 1919 he was insistent on pursuing Kolchak after the capture of Ufa: a policy that hastened the disintegration of Kolchak's forces and removed any threat from the east when Denikin launched his offensive in the summer. In October, when Yudenich was pushing nearer and nearer to St Petersburg, Lenin was equally insistent on not diverting troops from the south and weakening the resistance to Denikin. He was prepared if necessary to evacuate St Petersburg rather than risk Denikin getting through to Moscow. Nor did he want Trotsky to leave the front himself to take charge of the defence of St Petersburg. Lenin was overruled by the defence council and Trotsky came to St Petersburg where he inspired the Red troops to push Yudenich out of the suburbs in savage hand-to-hand fighting. The loss of St Petersburg would have been serious, but nothing like so serious as the loss of Moscow; Lenin's instinct was surely right in fixing on its retention as the strategic essential at that time.

In June 1920, when the Red Army had held the Poles, who wavered and then began to retreat, there was a vigorous debate whether to pursue them or not. Most of the leading Bolsheviks were against this. Stalin was against it. Dzerzhinsky was against it. Most important Radek and Trotsky were against it. Karl Radek himself born in Poland was an acknowledged expert on foreign affairs and had only returned from Germany in 1918. He had been more recently in the west than any of the others and was almost certainly better informed about the situation in Germany and Poland than anyone else. He was clear that neither was ripe for revolution and that the Poles were in general anti-Russian and bent on national independence rather than on world revolution. Trotsky believed that the Red Army and the Russian people were exhausted by the war and had neither the will nor the means to advance into Poland against military resistance of any kind. They were proved right by events. Lenin was misled by his enthusiasm for world revolution and by the feeling that if they missed this opportunity to link up with the revolutionary forces in Poland and Germany they might have to wait a long time for another. Until it came Russia would have to remain in dangerous isolation as the sole socialist country in a capitalist world. For once Lenin's clear sight was blinded by passion. He overbore all opposition, and the Red Army started to advance. At first it carried all before it but the Polish army, helped by the French, stiffened its resistance and the Red Army exhausted its momentum and its supplies. In mid-August the Poles counter-attacked and a week later the Red Army was in full retreat.

In this instance Lenin had over-persuaded his colleagues. They were the victims of his personality. But in general this was an inspiration to them—and not to them alone. Lenin was not an orator in the sense that Trotsky or Churchill was, able to transform an audience and a situation by the sheer power of words. But he was unique in his hold over the ordinary Russian. Paustovsky has described how he was sent as a journalist to cover a meeting of demobilized soldiers at a Moscow barracks in the spring of 1918.

'It was a rainy evening. The air in the enormous barrack-hall was grey with cigarette smoke. The rain beat on the dusty windows. The soldiers, in dirty foot rags and sodden boots, their rifles beside them, sat on the muddy floor.' Their mood was suspicious and cynical: they were not going to be pushed around by anyone.

> Suddenly there were shouts. The soldiers rose to their feet. The clouds of cigarette smoke swayed. Before I could see anything in the dim light and the smoky air, I heard someone say in an unusually calm, high voice, rolling his r's:
> 'Let me through, Comrades.'
> The men at the back shoved to get a better view. Rifles were pointed at them. The commotion threatened to turn into a shooting match.
> 'Comrades!' said Lenin.

The noise stopped as though sliced off with a knife. The only sound was the wheezing breath of the pent-up crowd.

Lenin began his speech. I couldn't hear him properly. I was hemmed in, a rifle-butt digging into my ribs. The man behind me gripped my shoulder and squeezed it painfully from time to time.

Blue trickles of smoke rose straight to the ceiling. The cigarettes, stuck to the soldiers' lips, were burning themselves out, forgotten.

The rain drummed on the walls. But gradually, through the noise, I was beginning to make out the quiet, simple words. Lenin wasn't urging anyone to do anything. He was merely giving these embittered, inarticulate men the answers to their unspoken questions— answers which perhaps they had been given more than once before, but never in the right words. He explained what obscurely troubled them.

Unhurriedly, he explained the meaning of the Treaty of Brest-Litovsk. He spoke about the treachery of the Left SRs, about the need for the workers' and peasants' alliance, and about bread. The way to get it was not by holding rowdy meetings and generally raising hell in Moscow, nor by waiting for someone to do something, without knowing what, but by getting down to ploughing their fields, and by trusting the Government and the Party.

I could only hear the odd word, but I knew the rest from the altered breathing of the crowd, the hats pushed to the back of the heads, the gaping mouths, and the sudden, unexpected sighs, more like a woman's than a man's.

[Lenin stopped.] Sheepskin hats and caps flew into the air. Frenzied cheering exploded near the platform, echoing through the hall and out into the street. I saw Lenin walking quickly towards the door, surrounded by soldiers. One hand over his ear, not to be deafened by the hurrahs, he was laughing and saying something to the little soldier whose cap kept slipping down over his eyes.[15]

[15] Konstantin Paustovsky, *In That Dawn* (1967), 59–60, 62. cf. Trotsky on Lenin's speaking in *Lenin* (1925), 190–200.

## 15   The nationalities

As the civil war drew to an end the question of the nationalities posed itself: what line is the Soviet government to take on national movements? On closer analysis this question resolves itself into a number of more detailed questions: What is the Soviet attitude to national liberation movements in the colonies and in backward countries like China? What instructions is the Communist Party of the Soviet Union to give to the communist parties of these countries? What is the Soviet attitude to the emergent nations in Europe? What is the attitude to the national minorities within the territory of tsarist Russia?

In principle the Bolsheviks were for self-determination. Lenin had stated the principle before the war, and again and again as the war seemed to be coming to an end and the European empires about to break up, (see p. 89 ff). The principle remained but the circumstances were different. The war was over, the empires had broken up, the allies had imposed the Treaty of Versailles; above all the Soviet Union had come into existence and had survived war and civil war. Here was the first socialist state, alone in a feudal and capitalist world. This was the fundamental fact of contemporary history. It existed and it must survive.

Lenin set out the principle and its consequences once again in *Theses on the National and Colonial Questions* which he drafted in June 1920 for the Communist International (Comintern). He began by criticizing the abstract posing of the question of equality, which he regarded as typically bourgeois and ignoring the real difficulties: 'The real meaning of the demand for equality consists in its being a demand for the abolition of classes.'[1] In contradistinction the Communist Party must base its policy on the real, historical conditions, especially the economic conditions. This entailed making a clear distinction between the interests of oppressed classes and exploited peoples on the one hand

[1] *Collected Works*, Vol. 31, 145

.nd the national interest, i.e. the interests of the ruling class, on the
>ther; and further between the interests of oppressed and exploit-
ng nations, e.g. India and Britain or China and Japan. From
his it followed that the Comintern's policy must rest on the
loser union of all proletarians. World political development was
1ow focused on the Soviet Union as the nucleus of the advanced
vorkers in all countries and of all national liberation move-
1ents. So policy must work for the closest union with Soviet
Russia of all these movements. The form of this union was
lependent on the stage of historical development of the colony
>r country concerned.

In view of the different stages of development federation was a
1uitable form. 'Federation is a transitional form to the complete
1nity of the working people of different nations.'[2] The RSFSR,
1e went on, exemplified this in its external and internal relations:
n the past in its relations with the Soviet republics of Hungary,
"inland and Latvia, and now with those of Azerbaidzhan and the
Jkraine; and, internally, in the federal autonomy granted to the
3ashkirs and Tatars.

The task of the Comintern was to further and study this
ederal development, bearing in mind that Soviet republics
:ould not go on existing in a capitalist world without the closest
1nion between them. Close economic union was of special
mportance. For without this it would be impossible to restore the
:conomic forces shattered in the course of the World War and the
:ivil war. Moreover the tendency towards a single world economy
1ad already shown itself under capitalism: to flout this would be to
lout an inevitable law of economic development.

The Comintern must expose the falsity of bourgeois talk of
:quality and show that 'the Soviet system is capable of ensuring
;enuine equality of nations, by uniting first the proletarians and
hen the whole mass of the working population';[3] it must support
lependent and underprivileged peoples like the Irish and the
American negroes. It was most important to be on guard against
nternationalism in word and petty-bourgeois nationalism in
>ractice. This of course was common form in the Second [Socialist]
[.nternational but was not unknown in parties calling themselves
'Communist'. It was imperative to subordinate 'the interests of

[2] *Ibid.*, 146
[3] *Ibid.*, 148

the proletarian struggle in any one country' to 'the interests of that struggle on a world-wide scale'. For this reason a primary task of the proletariat in countries that were already fully capitalist was 'the struggle against opportunist and petty-bourgeois pacifist distortions of ... internationalism.'[4] In other words the Communist Party of a given nation was not to pursue the supposed interests of its own proletariat to the neglect of the interests of the proletariat as a whole and in defiance of the instructions of the Comintern (in which the Soviet Union inevitably has a predominant voice).

In backward, still feudal countries the Comintern must assist national liberation movements and fight against all reactionaries, including religious reactionaries. But each individual Communist Party must keep itself absolutely independent of bourgeois movements and develop a real proletarian consciousness and party. But it must remember also that the more backward the country the stronger its national prejudice. It must be tender to this prejudice so as to overcome it more quickly. For it could only disappear with the disappearance of capitalism and imperialism.

In the summer of 1920 the Soviet was not in fact called upon to do much in the colonial sphere or in the Far East. It could without fear of complications put forth its anti-colonial propaganda, it could receive Asian delegates to the second meeting of the Comintern in July or the Baku congress in August at which there were Turkish, Armenian and Persian delegates, and a handful of Arabs, Kurds and Chinese. It could even offer mild support to King Ammanullah of Afghanistan against the British and interfere on the Persian frontier to disrupt the Anglo-Persian alliance. That was about the sum of its activities. But nearer home it was very different.

On the western and southern borders of Russia there were lands, which had been incorporated in tsarist Russia, inhabited by non-Russian or quasi-Russian people. The western lands were of great strategic importance, the Ukraine in the south of crucial economic importance and Transcaucasia of some importance because of the oil from Baku on the Caspian Sea. These lands were at very different stages of development. In each case the frontier was finally fixed by force but the details of the settlement varied a good deal, and it is worth looking at four of them and at

[4] *Ibid.*, 149

Lenin's attitude to each of them: Finland, Poland, the Ukraine and Georgia.

The Finns are a non-Slav people and their language is related only to Magyar among the languages of Europe. They had only been incorporated in Russia in 1815 and they had stoutly resisted Russification in the years before the revolution. When the revolution broke out the Finnish parliament took over authority and proclaimed independence. Under pressure from Germany they sought recognition of this independence from the Bolsheviks after they had seized power. In his writings on the national question Lenin had consistently referred to Finland as an example of a nation with a right to self-determination, and the government promptly granted the Finnish request. But there was a cleavage in Finland between the bourgeois and socialist parties and at the moment of independence there were about 40,000 Russian troops on Finnish soil. The hastily formed Finnish army attacked the Russian troops and, simultaneously, the Social-Democrats, under strong pressure from their left wing organized as 'Red Guards', started a revolt in Helsinki. A war and a civil war had begun and merged into one another. At Brest-Litovsk the Russians had to agree to withdraw their troops, and soon after the signature of the treaty the Germans landed in the Gulf of Finland to hasten their withdrawal. The German army was in control of the whole of western Russia, and the Bolsheviks could give no more than moral support to the Finnish socialists. The Finnish army successfully put down the revolt and the capture of Helsinki was followed by a White Terror. After the German defeat in November 1918 the British intervened in northern Russia and Finnish troops took some part in operations within Russian territory in Eastern Karelia, territory partly inhabited by Finns; but the fighting was desultory and by the end of September 1919 the British had evacuated all their troops from Archangel and Murmansk. Unsupported, the Finns could not maintain their troops in Eastern Karelia and had to retreat. Peace was made on 14 October 1920. Russia confirmed its recognition of the Finnish state and accorded it an outlet to the Arctic Sea at Petsamo. Next year there was a rising in Eastern Karelia, but the Finnish government discouraged intervention on behalf of their compatriots and it was put down without much difficulty. Lenin had been consistent in recognizing Finnish independence, but it is clear that

G*

recognition owed more to brute facts than to ideology; or rather that there was bound to be recognition, but that it would have been much more palatable to recognize a Social-Democratic government, which would have joined the Russian Soviet Federation of Socialist Republics. No doubt in that event the area of Eastern Karelia inhabited by Finns would have been incorporated in the territory of the Finnish republic, and the Bolsheviks would not have been open to the charge of forcibly retaining non-Russians, not anxious to be citizens of the RSFSR.

The Polish case was different. Poland had long been an independent kingdom before its disappearance at the end of the eighteenth century and the Poles had never been reconciled to the loss of their independence. They were Roman Catholics to a man and the church was a mainspring of national sentiment. The Poles had suffered perhaps more than any other people from Russification and had resisted it more stubbornly. From the very beginning of the war in 1914 they looked forward to independence and worked for it. Protected by the German advance in 1917 they achieved it and set up their government. Poland was mainly an agricultural country, but there were towns of some antiquity like Warsaw and Cracow and the beginnings of industry. But landlord or peasant, employer or worker, townee or hayseed, the Pole wanted independence, and, most emphatically, no truck with the Russians. When the Red Army advanced to Warsaw in 1920 it was not welcomed with flags and cheers by Polish socialists, nor did Polish recruits flock to join it. Radek was right and Lenin was wrong. As already recorded (p. 179f) the tide of war turned and the Poles counter-attacked and drove the Red Army helter-skelter back. Peace was signed in October 1920 and the frontier was fixed far to the east of the line put forward by the allies at Versailles (the Curzon Line), so as to include large numbers of White Russians and Ukrainians in Poland. Here again the frontier had been fixed by force. By this settlement there were no Poles in the RSFSR, but many Russians in Poland: the seed of future trouble.

More vexed was the question of the Ukraine. This was in a state of anarchy in which guerrilla bands exercised some sort of control over parts of the area and clashed with one another and with the Red Army. Between spring 1917 and spring 1920 it had been continuously fought over and occupied in whole or in part by a Ukrainian nationalist government, by the German army, by a puppet government set up by the Germans under Skoropadsky, by the Poles, by a second nationalist government under Petlura, by the Red Army, by the White army under Denikin and by the troops of the anarchist Makhno. The land and people were exhausted. If the peasants all over Russia longed only for the end of the war and for the chance to cultivate their land unmolested, so even more did the Ukrainian peasants. They were in any case less passive than the peasants of central and north Russia: the spirit of the frontier (*Ukraine* means 'on the border') and the spirit of the Cossack was still powerful. Left to themselves they would probably have preferred a local anarchist non-government to any other. What is quite clear is that they violently resisted Denikin who would have restored the landlords, and were indifferent to the Ukrainian nationalists whose emotions and ideology were meaningless to them. The factory workers were on the whole pro-Soviet. The Jews, who were numerous and had suffered appallingly at the hands of all parties, but worst at the hands of the Petlurists, were whole-heartedly in favour of the Red Army. For this was the only force that had committed no official pogroms and in which men guilty of acts of cruelty to Jews suffered the death penalty. A large part of the middle class was imbued to some degree with Ukrainian nationalist sentiment.

But is it possible to speak of the existence then of a Ukrainian nation? With the exception of the Polish landlords in the west and the Jews the people were racially homogeneous: the differences between them dependent on how long they had been settled in the area and on their social status. The landlords for example bore 'Great Russian' or 'Little Russian' names, but were otherwise identical in their habits, their style of living, their tastes and their allegiance. But there was this difference in speech. The Eastern branch of Slavonic falls into three divisions: Great Russian, Little Russian or Ukrainian, and White Russian. White Russian at the time was no more than a spoken dialect, but Little Russian was already written so that the differences from Great Russian were down in print and perpetuated; it could claim to be a language and not a dialect. But it is important to remember that practically the whole population was illiterate and that the spoken language differed very much from one part of the Ukraine to another.

In fact the question is largely one of history. Before the emancipation of the serfs and the beginnings of popular education in Russia there could be no talk of a Ukrainian language or nation. Fifty years after the revolution, given a Ukrainian bourgeois government, universal education in Ukrainian and no migration of Russians into the area, there might well have been a Ukrainian nation.

A comparison with Poland may bring out the difference. Geographically Poland adheres as much to the great Russian steppes as does the Ukraine, and strategically is perhaps even more crucial for any state with its capital at St Petersburg or Moscow. Racially the origins of the Poles, the Russians and the Ukrainians are indistinguishable. The Polish language belongs to the western rather than to the eastern branch of Slavonic, but the differences between it and Russian are not original but the result of history, and are not absolutely clear-cut; White Russian forms a transition from one to the other, just as White Russia does on the map. The Poles were Roman Catholic, the Russians Orthodox. Until the partitions of Poland at the end of the eighteenth century there had been an independent kingdom of Poland, whose king had been elected by the nobility. From the reign of Tsar Nicholas I the Russian government had steadily whittled away Polish autonomy and done its best to Russify the people, among other ways by persecuting the Roman Catholic church. The result was seen in 1920. The ordinary Pole felt far more solidarity with Pilsudski and his regime than with his Russian comrade; he was first and foremost a Pole, not a peasant or a proletarian.

Lenin had failed to see this and had pressed the invasion of Poland with the result already noted. How accurately had he read the situation in the Ukraine?

During 1919 Lenin had urged the Red Army to the reconquest of the Ukraine. This was in part to block Denikin's route to Moscow and to force him back into the Crimea and the Kuban, but still more to free the best grain land in Russia in time for the autumn sowing. In a speech to the Moscow Soviet in April 1919 he said, 'I must say that guerrilla warfare has been going on there all the time. In the South it is still going on ... We have moved our regular troops in, but that is not enough. We must greatly intensify our efforts, and that is why I insist that at every meeting of workers the question of food supplies and the question of transport must definitely be raised.'[5] And several sections of the Decree *On the Union of the Soviet Republics of Russia, the Ukraine, Latvia, Lithuania and Byelo-Russia for the Struggle against World Imperialism* of 1 June 1919 were devoted to the question of the land and the peasants. Because of the food shortage, it stated, it was vital to win over the middle peasant, to requisition grain for the Ukrainian poor and the Red Army only, and to counter propaganda that grain was being carted off to Russia. For the same reason and in line with the policy adopted towards the peasant in Russia generally, private property in land was to be abolished, and with the exception of a strictly limited number of state farms the peasants were to organize themselves. But the peasants were also to be disarmed and their weapons handed over to the Red Army—a clear sign of the anarchy and of the peasant distrust of all authority.

This was to be carried out within a federal framework. The decree recognized 'the independence, freedom and self-determination of the working people of the Ukraine', and the Communist Party of Russia would work for relations between the RSFSR and the Ukrainian Soviet Socialist Republic on the basis of the decree. But this independence was to be within the framework of a close amalgamation on military organization and army command, on economic questions including finance and labour, and on the railways. Single bodies were to manage these matters and there is no doubt that the predominant voice in these bodies was to be Russian. But the Russian Communist Party would support Ukrainian culture and language and was to see that in all soviets there were enough Ukrainian speakers and that in future all employers could speak Ukrainian.

The essential was to preserve and strengthen the Soviet Union. This overrode all other purposes. But a genuine sympathy between Russian and Ukrainian comrades would decisively contribute to this purpose. As Lenin puts it: 'We want a *voluntary* union of nations ... We must ... strive persistently for the unity of nations ... We must be adamant and uncompromising towards everything that affects the fundamental interests of labour in its fight for emancipation from the yoke of capital. [But by recognizing their independence] we are slowly but steadily

[5] *Collected Works*, Vol. 29, 260

winning the confidence of the labouring masses ...'[9] This process is however much slower than is implied by the use of the present tense: *we are slowly but steadily winning,* as Lenin himself recognizes when he warns Russian Communists that they can very easily seem to advocate unity out of Great Russian imperialism, and Ukrainian communists that they can very easily be thought to advocate 'unconditional state independence' not in the interests of the workers but out of petty-bourgeois national prejudice. The best way to overcome mutual distrust is to work together to overcome capitalism.

The Ukrainian Soviet Socialist Republic was proclaimed on 18 December 1918, and joined the RSFSR in federal union in February 1919. A declaration of 30 December 1922 affirmed that the U.S.S.R. was a 'free and voluntary union of free and equal Socialist Republics', and representatives of the nationalities sat in a second chamber of 114 members. Formally this was satisfactory. What of the practice on the ground? The party pressed on with Ukrainization and made every effort to enlist the support of separatists—with some success, as Hrushevsky, one of the original organizers of the Ukrainian Conference in 1917, and Holubovich, prime minister of the nationalist government set up in March 1918, both came over. Any separatist political activity was naturally taboo, but there was vigorous cultural activity: schools, libraries and newspapers were founded, all of which promoted the use of Ukrainian in speech and writing. But all this made little impression on the bulk of the population; when Kaganovich went into things on his appointment as local party secretary in 1925 he was disappointed at the rate of progress. On the other hand there was no serious trouble until Stalin began to collectivize agriculture in 1929.

Quite different was the situation in Georgia. This had been an independent kingdom until the beginning of the nineteenth century and the Georgians, a Caucasian people speaking a Caucasian language not related to Slavonic, had retained their independence of spirit, their language and their culture. In the course of the century there had been a considerable development of the oil industry at Baku, and by 1917 there was a rudimentary proletariat and a strong Social-Democratic party dominated by the Mensheviks. The Georgians welcomed the revolution and

[6] *Collected Works,* Vol. 30, 293–4

joined with their neighbours to form a Transcaucasian government. But relations with Turkey and German intervention led to the break-up of this union and Georgia proclaimed itself an independent republic. Elections for a constituent assembly took place in February 1919 and resulted in an overwhelming victory for the Mensheviks. The Menshevik government put into practice a policy scarcely distinguishable from that of the Bolsheviks in Russia: radical land reform and nationalization of natural and industrial resources. It confiscated estates belonging to the crown, the church and the big landlords and meant to run these as collective farms, but under pressure sold them in smallish lots to the peasants. It nationalized hydro-electric power, mineral springs, coal, manganese, railways and docks; and would no doubt have nationalized oil had it been in possession of Baku. But on the German defeat this was occupied first by the British and on their departure by the Red Army.

The Georgian government was effectively the government in fact and in law. It made peace with Turkey. It had high hopes of the recognition of Georgian independence by President Wilson and the peace conference. It refused to co-operate with the Bolsheviks against Denikin. But its position was being undermined. The peace conference had more important matters to deal with and was alienated by the continuing squabble between the Georgians and the Armenians. The British withdrew from the Caucasus. The Red Army defeated the Whites and drove their remnants into the Crimea; in April 1920 it occupied Baku. A few days later the Reds made an unsuccessful attempt to seize the military academy at Tbilisi, the Georgian Capital. On 7 May the Soviet-Georgian Treaty was signed: the Soviet Union recognized the Georgian Republic *de jure* and the Georgian government undertook to disarm anti-Soviet forces and to permit unrestricted Bolshevik activity within its borders. The treaty was largely a blind. The Central Committee of the party had already set up a special committee for Georgia whose chairman was the Georgian Ordzhonikidze and deputy chairman Kirov, who was nominated first ambassador to Georgia and arrived in Tbilisi with a staff of no less than 70. Even more important, the Commissar for Nationalities Stalin, himself a Georgian, was in charge of the Red Army operations in the area and was determined on strategic, party and personal grounds to incorporate Georgia in the Soviet Union. Bolshevik propaganda was unrelenting. The Red Army advanced into Transcaucasia. Soviet Socialist Republics came into being in Azerbaidzhan and Armenia. Ossete rebels in North Georgia fled from the Georgian army into Russia to the number of 20,000. The commander of the Eleventh Red Army submitted a plan in December 1920 for the conquest of Georgia. In February disorders broke out in Tbilisi and on the Armenian border. The Eleventh Red Army crossed the frontier and nine days later occupied Tbilisi. Lenin and the *Politburo* sanctioned the invasion only in the belief that there had been a genuine, large-scale rising against the Menshevik government. In this they had been misled by Stalin and were horrified when they heard how heavy the fighting and the casualties had been. They insisted on a truce with mild terms for the Georgian nationalists, and Lenin wrote to Ordzhonikidze to make special concessions to the intelligentsia and the small merchants and 'to devise an acceptable compromise for a bloc with Jordania or similar Georgian Mensheviks, who before the uprising had not been absolutely opposed to the idea of Soviet power in Georgia on certain terms'.[7] Nevertheless, like Maria Theresa they wept but took. It is impossible not to believe that they were less than honest with themselves. They were not properly informed and they were blinded by their own wishes. Lenin had for so long denounced Mensheviks as opportunists and traitors that he could not see straight where they were concerned. It was impossible for him to believe either that they could form a reputable government or that they could command genuine popular backing. The dealings of the Georgian government with the Germans and then the British only confirmed him in his opinion. When Stalin reported a rising he reported what Lenin wanted to hear and what he believed all along that he would hear.

[7] *Collected Works*, Vol. 32, 160

## 16 Economic and political problems

In 1920 and 1921 the essential was to produce more food and more goods. There must be more food for the Red Army and the industrial workers, to enable them to defend the Soviet Union and extract the fuel needed to restore industry and produce the goods the peasants so urgently needed: clothes, boots, salt, matches, kerosene. The problem was how to do this.

In February 1920 Trotsky proposed a grain tax in kind instead of grain requisitioning. Instead of having the whole of his surplus removed by government agents the peasant would pay a tax in kind fixed in relation to the yield of his land, and would keep all the rest of his grain—to eat or to sell. But he got no support from his colleagues. Neither Lenin nor any other leading party member would contemplate introducing any form of private trading: the thin end of a capitalist wedge. So they stuck to a mixture of compulsion and moral exhortation to achieve their end. The war was indeed over and with it 'war communism'. But there was not much difference between having your stores of grain and fodder and livestock seized by an 'iron detachment' and having your surplus requisitioned by a member of the local executive committee on behalf of the government and the party. In theory it was only a *surplus* that was taken. But the needs of the workers and the very bad harvest of 1920 meant that there was very heavy pressure to enlarge the surplus and cut the peasant's share to the bone.

Now that the war was over it was also decided to make use of the large numbers of idle troops to help overcome the difficulties of the situation. At the beginning of January the Third Red Army in the Urals was converted by decree into the First Revolutionary Army of Labour with the task of repairing the derelict railway system and helping the peasants in their tasks. On 21 January the Ukrainian Soviet Army of Labour was set up; and there followed a general decree on labour conscription and another setting up committees to control the process. 'To achieve [our ends]', wrote

Lenin, 'we must at all costs create labour armies, organise ourselves like an army, reduce, even close down a ... number of institutions so that in the next few months ... we can overcome transport dislocation, and emerge from this desperate situation of cold, famine and impoverishment brought by the end of the winter.'[1]

The situation was desperate but not hopeless. Lenin was characteristically blunt—and optimistic:

> We can solve the main problem—to acquire large quantities of grain and foodstuffs, deliver them to the industrial centres so that industrial development can begin. We must concentrate all our efforts on this task. It is inadmissible to allow ourselves to be diverted from it to any other practical task. It has to be solved by military methods, with absolute ruthlessness and by the absolute suppression of all other interests.[2]

At the same time he appealed to the peasants and workers for their co-operation. He admitted that the government could only pay the peasants for their surplus grain in worthless paper money, but went on: 'We say that this is essential, that the peasants must give their grain as a loan. Is there a single well-fed peasant who would refuse bread to a hungry worker if he knew that this worker, once he had been fed, would repay him in goods? No honest and politically conscious peasant would refuse to give grain as a loan.'[3] The snag about this was that hardly a peasant was well-fed or politically conscious. Six months later in April 1921, speaking at the 1st All-Russian Congress of Mineworkers, Lenin offered them the same medicine. 'It is the speculators we are now fighting,' he said, 'the handful of workers who have been corrupted by the old capitalist system and who say to themselves, "I must have higher pay, and to hell with the rest." "Give me double pay, give me two or three pounds of bread a day," they say, heedless of the fact that they are working for the defence of the workers and peasants ...'[4]

But it was not a few speculators that they were fighting but a large number of exhausted and disgruntled workers and peasants. In the industrial field dissatisfaction was not confined to the workers themselves, but was shared by trade union leaders and

[1] *Collected Works*, Vol. 30, 333
[2] *Ibid.*, 332
[3] *Ibid.*, 399
[4] *Ibid*, 499–500

politicians. Throughout 1920 there was a vigorous controversy which at times, especially when it concerned Trotsky and Zinoviev, became bitter. It reached its climax at the 10th Party Congress in March 1921. The root of the controversy was the same as in agriculture: the method of running the country—compulsion of persuasion. But it was more complicated and involved with personal rivalries, and centred on two topics: the functions or *Tsektran* (the Joint Central Transport Committee consisting mainly of members of the Central Committee of the Railway and Water Workers' Unions) and of trade unions.

*Tsektran* had been set up in August 1920 to co-ordinate transport policy and get transport going again. The unions resented it, even though their members largely composed it, because it was a central government body imposed on them without their consent and superseding their union authority. Nor did its working soothe their resentment. Trotsky was appointed its chairman and at once exercised his talent for administrative action and for rubbing people up the wrong way. He overrode the unions with contempt; he made vigorous use of the labour armies; he insisted on finding the ablest and most efficient workers wherever they were and moving them where he wanted them to tackle the hardest problems. He defended his policy in his usual incisive and maddening style, scattering verbal hostages to his enemies. Foremost among them was Zinoviev, who at this time was demanding more party democracy and gunning for Trotsky. He used *Tsektran* and the wider problem of the political control of industry as major pieces of ammunition in his fight.

The question of *Tsektran* thus merged in the wider question of the function of trade unions in the Soviet state, in transition from capitalism to socialism. There were three main views besides a great variety of shades of opinion and compromise positions: Trotsky's, that of the Workers' Opposition (most fully stated by Alexandra Kollontay in her speeches and in her pamphlet, *The Workers' Opposition*), and Lenin's.

Trotsky was for straightforward military methods: a clear-cut policy, a clear chain of command, efficient NCOs and obedient rank and file. As logical consequences of this he wanted the trade unions to lose their independent existence and authority and fuse with the economic organs of the state; and he wanted what he called 'productive democracy'; by this he meant not that the rank and file should elect representatives to the economic organs, whose task should be to raise productivity, but that there should be a 'flow of fresh creative power from below',[5] i.e. that the government should pick out likely men in factories and mines and give them their heads to raise productivity. This point of view was simple and consistent and might have been effective in the short run, but it suffered from horribly visible defects. It was aristocratic, not democratic in tone. It was too evidently inspired by, and identified with, the period of civil war and war communism. It was bound to provoke the trade unions to the most violent resistance, for it ran counter to their professional activities in the tsarist regime, to their experience, and most fundamental of all, to their instinct of self-preservation.

The point of view of *The Workers' Opposition* was that natural to trade unionists. Just as the railwaymen and water transport workers resented *Tsektran*, so the workers in general and their political allies in the party objected to rigid control of industry by the state. In the factories they strongly objected to one-man management, especially when the manager was a pre-revolution factory owner or manager, rather than a worker or a socialist; what they wanted was to manage the factory themselves through an elected trade union committee. At the centre they wanted a Trade Union Council of Production as the controller of industry and production, to which the existing central economic boards should be made responsible: their task would be to produce data and propound economic theories on the basis of which the Council would act.

Lenin regarded it as utopian to return to collective management; the experience of 1917–18 had convinced him that, at least in the period of transition to socialism, it was necessary to make use of capitalist experience and expertise. Further, he had come to see that his original belief in the simplicity of administration was naive, and now thought the trade unions incompetent for the task of running factories, let alone the economy of the Soviet Union. But unlike Trotsky he did not want the unions to lose their identity altogether. They should continue to exist and they had a role to play, or rather a double role. On the one hand their role was protective and educative. In the present state of transition from capitalism to socialism there was still much bureaucracy

[5] Quoted in Leonard Schapiro, *The Origin of the Communist Autocracy* (1955), 279

and red tape inherited from the past against which the workers needed protection. Guiding the transition was the Communist Party exercising the dictatorship of the proletariat as the vanguard of the proletariat. Within this framework the trade unions 'are a *link* between the vanguard and the masses, and by their daily work bring conviction to the masses ... On the other hand the trade unions are a "reservoir" of state power.'[6] By this he meant that they represented not only their members but the state in relation to the members, rather like prefects in a school; in each case the authority, the headmaster/headmistress in the one case and the party in the other, would select the agents of state power from the whole body of the members of the society.

For, as Lenin realized quite clearly, the problem of the trade unions was at bottom a problem of *political* control. This was revealed in a dramatic flash by the revolt that broke out at Kronstadt on 28 February 1921 just before the opening of the tenth party congress. The sailors of the Baltic fleet were fiery and consistent supporters of the Bolsheviks. They had murdered two members of the Provisional Government in hospital; they had dissolved the Constituent Assembly; they were 'the pride of the revolution'. But they were now disaffected: partly through contact with their relations in the country whom they had at last had the chance to visit on leave; partly through sympathy with the strikers in St Petersburg; partly as a natural reaction to the cold and hunger and hardships they had endured; but more powerfully and deeply from a vague malaise. They were itching for freedom; they were anarchic, bloody-minded.

The crew of the battleship *Petropavlovsk* met and formulated their demands on 28 February and these were adopted next day as those of the fleet as a whole. They decided:

1. In view of the fact that the present Soviets do not represent the will of the workers and peasants, to re-elect the Soviets by secret voting, with free preliminary agitation among all workers and peasants before the elections.
2. Freedom of speech and press for workers, peasants, Anarchists and Left Socialist parties.
3. Freedom of meetings, trade unions and peasant associations.
4. [To convene a non-party conference.]
5. To liberate all political prisoners of Socialist Parties, and also all workers, peasants, soldiers and sailors [in prison].

[6] *Collected Works*, Vol. 32, 20–21

6. [To review prison and concentration camp cases.
7. To abolish Political Departments, i.e. special party propaganda departments subsidized by the state.
8. To abolish the special detachments used to search passengers on trains for food.
9. To equalize food rations for all except workers performing very heavy work.]
10. To abolish all Communist fighting detachments in all military units and ... Communist guards at factories.
11. To grant the peasant full right to do what he sees fit with his land and also to possess cattle, which he must maintain and manage with his own strength, but without employing hired labour.
12. [To ask all troops to back these resolutions.
13. To demand publication of these resolutions in the press].
14. To appoint a travelling bureau for control.
15. To permit free artisan production with individual labour.[7]

On 1 March Kalinin and a colleague hurried to Kronstadt to address the rebels, but got a rough reception and made no impression on them. Next day they set up a provisional revolutionary committee. The government decided to have no further truck with them and put them down by force with much bloodshed.

In the course of one of his speeches at the 10th Party Congress Lenin said of the rebels, 'they do not want the White Guards, and they do not want our power either'—probably a very just summing-up of their attitude. But this was not the party line to which Lenin otherwise faithfully adhered. This was that the rebels were inspired by petty-bourgeois (Menshevik and SR) ideas and were in league with White Guard, i.e. reactionary tsarist, officers. They were 'a motley crowd ... of ill-assorted elements' and the rising was 'the work of SRs and whiteguard émigrés and at the

same time the movement was reduced to a petty-bourgeois counter-revolution and petty-bourgeois anarchism. That is something quite new.'[8] This sort of verbiage disgusted the sailors, who until then had kept their admiration for Lenin and their trust in him.

The Kronstadt mutiny was an alarming episode and it is possible that Lenin, together with the other Communist leaders, believed or half-believed, in panic, what he said. But Lenin was a very clearsighted man: he had already come to the conclusion that the discontent in the country necessitated a relaxation of

[7] W. H. Chamberlain, *The Russian Revolution* (1935), Vol. 2, 495–6
[8] *Collected Works*, Vol. 32, 184

government pressure and was about to announce the New Economic Policy (NEP). So it is hard not to believe that he understood the mainspring of the mutiny—'they do not want our power either'—and deliberately falsified it for political reasons. He could not admit a genuine challenge to party rule nor, just as he was about to launch the NEP, show any sympathy for their demands for freedom.

But at a deeper level Lenin's instinct was surely right. At the Party Congress he consistently identified Kronstadt with petty-bourgeois anarchism and a return to white-guardism, and *The Workers' Opposition* with anarchism. He pointed out that the SR leaders at Samara had gone under to the tsarist reactionaries and inferred that democratic socialism in politics and economic democracy in the factories, released from the control of the Communist Party, would lead not to a freer and purer socialist society but to a restored tsarist one. The only bulwark against this was the dictatorship of the proletariat exercised by the Communist Party. It is impossible not to feel that Lenin was right.

But if it was necessary to preserve the dictatorship it was also necessary to carry out a tactical retreat; the attempt to raise productivity by force had failed. So, in the same speech at the 10th Party Congress in which he attacked the Kronstadt rebels and *The Workers' Opposition*, Lenin announced the key proposal in the New Economic Policy, the grain tax. The crucial point of this proposal was that there should be a fixed tax payable in kind instead of requisitioning, and the peasant would be able to dispose of his surplus as he wished: he could keep it or sell it. An attempt was made at first to confine the sale to local co-operatives, markets and bazaars, but this broke down and the government had to allow full freedom of trade. The tax was progressive and designed to bear hard on the *kulaks* and favour the middle and poor peasants; and there were rebates for the most productive. The principle of collective responsibility for production was abolished and the individual peasant was made responsible for paying the tax. At the same time the government made available a fund to supply consumer goods, not to the poor peasant, but to the peasant who delivered a surplus.

This was a complete and sudden reversal of policy and occasioned the sharpest opposition and controversy. Lenin defended it on the ground of necessity and compared it to a forced but orderly retreat in battle. He admitted it was un-Marxist, because free exchange would lead to a revival of capitalism and to the division of society into owners of capital and owners of labour power, but he claimed: 'If we were able to obtain even a small quantity of goods and hold them in the hand of the state—the proletariat exercising political power—and if we could release these goods into circulation, we, as the state, would add economic power to our political power.'[9]

To obtain these goods the government adopted a series of measures designed to encourage small and medium industrial enterprises. It also negotiated a series of concessions to foreign firms, to speed up the production of vital materials like coal, iron and oil. These too came in for much criticism, and Lenin devoted many passages of his speeches to the party to defending them.

But Lenin was convinced that this was only a temporary retreat and that it gave away nothing vital. He believed the peasants had, on balance, gained from the revolution and would never willingly return to the old regime: even if temporarily disgruntled they were a bulwark against reaction. So too was the power of the state. To his opponents, alarmed at the spread of small-scale industry, Lenin boasted that 'all the commanding heights' were in state hands; and he was right. In a census of 165,000 industrial concerns taken in March 1923 almost 90 per cent were in private hands, but the state concerns employed almost 85 per cent of the labour and were responsible for over 90 per cent of production in terms of value. Furthermore Soviet power was intact. The party was in command of the situation and the way was open for an advance to socialism at a later date.

The key to this was electrification. Lenin's imagination was fired by the idea and prospects of electrification. He quoted with approval from *The Main Tasks of the Electrification of Russia* the dictum: 'The age of steam is the age of the bourgeoisie, the age of electricity is the age of socialism',[10] and said of the first plan produced by the State Electrification Commission, 'this small volume ... in my opinion is the second programme of our party'.[11] (The first was *The ABC of Communism* by Preobrazhensky and Bukharin.) He was also keenly aware that electrification would

[9] *Collected Works*, Vol. 32, 219
[10] *Collected Works*, Vol. 30, 334
[11] *Collected Works*, Vol. 31, 514

place private industry in the grip of the state. There was only one way of undermining small scale production, 'namely, to place the economy of the country, including agriculture, on a new technical basis, that of modern large-scale production. Only electricity provides that basis.

'*Communism is Soviet power plus the electrification of the whole country.*'[12]

Here Lenin looks down from the commanding heights and foresees the whole country, from the Baltic to the Bering Sea and from the Arctic Ocean to the borders of Afghanistan and China, bound together by Soviet power and the electric grid. Nor was his vision merely geographical. In March 1920 he went to a peasant festival and was greeted by the village spokesman with the words, 'We peasants were unenlightened, and now light has appeared among us, an unnatural light, which will light up our peasant darkness.' Talking to the Congress of Soviets Lenin commented on this:

> For my part, these words did not surprise me. Of course, to the non-party peasant masses electric light is an 'unnatural' light; but what we consider unnatural is that the peasants and workers should have lived for hundreds and thousands of years in such backwardness, poverty and oppression under the yoke of the landowners and the capitalists. You cannot emerge from this darkness very rapidly. What we must now try is to convert every electric power station we build into a stronghold of enlightenment ...[13]

[12] *Ibid.*, 516
[13] *Ibid.*, 517

## *17*   *Last years*

Once NEP was launched Lenin was largely preoccupied with the problem of centralization, or how to ensure the free flow of authority and power up and down so that 'Soviet Power' would be both popular and real. The problem presented itself immediately in two forms: Georgia and bureaucracy; and the two forms were interconnected. Firstly on the plane of constitutional theory, the Bolshevik slogan had from the first been 'Democratic centralism'. But the slogan gave no help in deciding the degree of democracy or the degree of centralization. The attempt to impose absolute centralized control of the economy had broken down and NEP had been introduced. But there still remained direction of the economy from the commanding heights and the centralized organization of the Communist Party binding the country together politically. This was its function. But what if it had lost the backing of the country as a whole? This would mean that the authority of the party would no longer be sustained from below and there would be no renewal of life at the top by sap from the grass roots. The flow would be one way only, power without authority, and there would be great danger of hardening of the arteries of political life.

Here the theoretical problem merged with the practical: how to preserve the Soviet Union until the imperialist powers next fell out among themselves and opened the way to further socialization. Part of the answer to this was in diplomacy. It was the duty of the Soviet Union to exploit the bitterness caused by the Treaty of Versailles and the suspicion between the Entente and the central powers. Russian diplomacy under the guidance of the astute and experienced tsarist diplomat Chicherin, performed this duty to admiration and pulled off a coup when, under the noses of the allied negotiators at Genoa, their representatives signed the Treaty of Rapallo with Germany on 16 April 1922. By this both sides renounced all claims arising out of the war, established diplomatic relations and accorded each other most favoured treatment in trade. Lenin was delighted with this. But he was not inclined to overrate its importance, for he was convinced by theory and experience that the conflicting interests of the powers would keep them apart and give the Soviet a breathing space.

More dangerous in his opinion was the internal problem: how to preserve the social order based on the co-operation of the workers and peasants. Lenin had harped on this theme in his speeches and writings since the revolution, but now he was particularly concerned that NEP should not cause a split between the classes. It was the duty of the party to prevent this. But this implied the need to retain the party intact and so the need for strong, centralized discipline to prevent the individual members of the party being absorbed into their local environments or even whole local branches of the party disintegrating under the pressure of local interests.

To meet this need there had been a gradual development of party organization. The interlocking party machine—Central Committee, *Politburo*, *Orgburo* and secretariat—had run itself in since 1919, and routine and pressure of business had steadily increased the power of the secretariat and its General Secretary. By 1921 the secretariat was empowered to take routine decisions that had the authority of decisions of the *Orgburo*, provided there was no objection from any member of the *Orgburo*. Finally in March 1922 the key piece was fitted into position. Stalin, already a member of the Central Committee, of the *Politburo*, and of the *Orgburo*, became General Secretary. Many leading men in the party were members of more than one of these but only one man was a member of all four—Stalin. In addition Stalin was a Georgian and had been responsible for the reconquest of Georgia (see p. 191f).

The Georgian theme emerged first. Lenin wrote a letter of greeting to the local communists on 14 April 1921 in which he expressed the hope that 'their close alliance [would] serve as a model of national peace'[1] but, even more important, would maintain and develop Soviet power, in particular economic power. They could do this by speeding up the extraction of coal, oil, copper and manganese, and by expanding trade with the

[1] *Collected Works*, Vol. 32, 316

West as quickly as possible. At the same time they should make concessions to the petty-bourgeoisie and carry out a 'slower, more cautious and more systematic transition to socialism'.[2] In other words they were to toe the party line and see that NEP was applied in Georgia and the other Transcaucasian republics as it was in Russia.

A little later, in November, when the question of a Trans-Caucasian Federation was under discussion, Lenin wrote a memorandum for Stalin in which he said that federation was the right principle but that the time was not yet ripe for it; but that the communists of Georgia, Armenia and Azerbaidzhan should be told to submit the question for discussion 'in the Party and *by the worker and peasant masses*, [agitate] for federation and secure *decisions* to that effect'.[3]

Early in the next year, on 13 February, Lenin wrote to Ord-zhonikidze about the strengthening of the Georgian army. He considered this was essential, but if the peasants were hostile he should adopt a decision in the most general terms. '*Actually*, however, it is necessary, at all costs, and *immediately* to develop and strengthen the Georgian Red Army.' He ended his letter by declaring that 'you personally, and the entire Georgian Central Committee, will be held responsible to the whole Party for this'.[4] It was vital, he held, that Georgia and the other republics should remain within the Soviet Union; the party must do its utmost to rally local opinion; but at the same time it must hold the whip hand: it must press on with building up a local, Georgian, Red Army capable of enforcing party decisions.

Governing Georgia was however only a small part of the problem of governing the Soviet Union. What worried Lenin here was the inefficiency of the bureaucracy, the state apparatus, due to red tape, sloth, and ignorance, technical and cultural. By this he meant that there were very few men trained in science or management or accountancy and far too few genuinely cultivated people in Russia, and so of necessity even fewer in the administration. Far too many bureaucrats were uncultivated, unimaginative boors, who treated subordinates and ordinary people as dirt; they were not civil servants but uncivil servants. Lenin first aired his concern in a *Letter to Stalin: Tasks of the*

[2] *Ibid.*, 317
[3] *Collected Works*, Vol. 33, 127
[4] *Ibid.*, 200

*Workers' and Peasants' Inspection and How they are to be Understood and Fulfilled* of 27 September 1921. The Commissariat of State Control had been reorganized on Lenin's initiative in February 1920 as the Commissariat of Workers' and Peasants' Inspection with Stalin as commissar. The idea behind the reorganization had been to create a special body to check the activities of the other ministries and combat red tape. But that it had not been altogether successful is suggested by the way in which Lenin defines its task. 'It is more the duty of the Workers' and Peasants' Inspection (*Rabkrin*)' he writes, '*to be able to improve* things than merely "detect" and "expose" (that is the function of the courts with which *Rabkrin* is in close contact but with which it is not to be identified).'[5]

He suggested various ways of improving things. First and foremost there must be accurate knowledge—knowledge of the offices, factories and departments with which they were concerned—and this must be obtained by inspection on the spot and by properly handled statistics. Then there must be up-to-date knowledge of accounting. After all there were some things which were common to all enterprises, agricultural, industrial, commercial or administrative; one of these, and a basic one, was accounts, so that there was every reason why accounting should be properly organized on a good model and that *Rabkrin* should see that accounts were properly kept and audited. Lenin reiterated this point in the last thing he ever wrote:

> In order to renovate our state apparatus we must at all costs set out, first, to learn, secondly, to learn, and thirdly, to learn, and then see to it that learning shall not remain a dead letter ... but shall really become part of our very being ...[6]

He also suggested punishment and personal responsibility: the head of the timber board should be given power to arrest men who did not send in their reports, and the name of the inspector in charge of the affairs of the timber board should be sent to Lenin himself.

Lenin returned to the charge at the end of the year when he demanded that the bureaucrats responsible for the failure to produce enough ploughs be brought to trial and punished: members of factory works committees, trade unions and local party groups were to be severely reprimanded, publicly censured

[5] *Ibid.*, 42
[6] *Ibid.*, 488–9

H

for any negligence or connivance at bureaucracy, and threatened with prison for any future offence.

In a memorandum he wrote in March 1922 for the two deputy chairmen of *Sovnarkom* he tackled the problem from a slightly different angle and made two new suggestions. The memorandum was to define the duties and responsibilities of his deputies and the spheres of action of each of them. He urged that they should spend nine-tenths of their time on economic matters. Their main functions were to exercise executive control over the carrying out of decrees and laws, to reduce staffs and reorganize the bureaucracy, and to cut red tape. To perform these functions they must have an adequate staff, a sound office routine (for both of which Lenin makes suggestions), and they must get to know personally the middle-grade officials by summoning them to their office and by themselves going to the provinces. In addition they must distribute communists to the key posts. Again the emphasis is on knowledge but not in quite the same way. The communist chosen for a key post will no doubt have the technical knowledge needed for it, but over and above this he will be a dedicated party man with the zeal and drive needed to get things done. Further, Lenin seems now to recognize that efficient administration depends not only on seeing that people all along the line are kept up to the mark but, at least as much, on informed, intelligent, clear and co-ordinated direction at the top.

But Lenin was denied the opportunity to put his insight to the test. About this time he began to complain of constant headaches. It was thought they might be due to the bullets still in his head and neck. The doctors thought it too risky to try and remove the one in his head but sensible to remove the other. Lenin did not think it would make any difference but agreed sardonically to have it done to please them and his colleagues. The operation took place on 23 April and was a success. It was also pointless, for on 26 May Lenin had a stroke. It was not too severe, though it affected his speech; but it was a warning.

By July Lenin was able to write and by the end of August he was working again at his country retreat at Gorky outside Moscow. The first thing he wrote was a short note to the directorate of *Rabkrin* regretting that the work had not been properly reorganized and that there was still no proper statistical service. He also made a new suggestion: could they not cut the staff to a quarter of its existing size and pay the members treble and so improve their qualifications? Ten days later he wrote to a comrade in Berlin asking him to collect German and American literature on administration and telling him to inspect some efficient German or Norwegian institution if possible. Towards the end of September he wrote to L. M. Khinchuk, who was producing a book, *Central Union of Consumers' Societies in Conditions of the New Economic Policy,* asking to see the proofs and suggesting certain additions to the statistical tables, including details on staff reductions and on 'normalization', i.e. improved administration.

On 6 October he wrote a memorandum for the *Politburo, On Combating Dominant Nation Chauvinism.*

> I declare war to the death on dominant nation chauvinism. I shall eat it with all my healthy teeth as soon as I get rid of this accursed bad tooth.
>
> It must be *absolutely* insisted that the Union Central Executive Committee should be *presided over* in turn by a Russian, Ukrainian, Georgian, etc. *Absolutely!*[7]

Apart from some formal letters of greeting to various party groups and societies, and a letter to Stalin insisting on the state monopoly of foreign trade, Lenin wrote little. He gave interviews to two English newspaper correspondents and made a short speech to the All-Russian Central Committee. On 13 November he appeared at the fourth congress of the Comintern and made a shortish speech on NEP, apologizing in his opening words on the score of his 'lengthy illness' for not being able to deal with the subject he was down to speak on: *Five Years of the Russian Revolution and the Prospects of the World Revolution.* A week later he made a similar speech to the Moscow Soviet ending with the words:

> We have brought socialism into everyday life and must here see how matters stand. That is the task of our day, the task of our epoch. Permit me to conclude by expressing confidence that difficult as this task may be, new as it may be compared with our previous task, and numerous as the difficulties may be that it entails, we shall all— not in a day, but in a few years—all of us together fulfil it whatever the cost, so that NEP Russia will become socialist Russia.[8]

These were the last words he spoke in public.

[7] *Ibid.*, 372
[8] *Ibid.*, 443

On the agenda for the meeting of the Central Committee to be held on 15 December was the question of the state monopoly of foreign trade and Lenin had planned to attend and speak, but on 13 December he had two more slight strokes. So he dictated a short memorandum in which he argued against Bukharin that tariffs would open the way to foreign goods and traders because the capitalist countries were so much stronger economically than Russia that they would be able to sell their goods inside Russia however high the tariff barrier, and that the only safe policy was to retain the state monopoly of foreign trade and arrange for the sale of foreign goods in Russian markets by mixed companies, i.e. companies composed of Russian and foreign members but under Russian control. On the 15th he dictated a further short note in which he explained that he had arranged with Trotsky to put his views to the forthcoming 10th Congress of Soviets but that he still hoped his doctors might allow him to attend and make a short speech, 'one that will take three-quarters of an hour'. In fact he got worse and the doctors ordered him to the country again.[9]

There, between 23 and 31 December, Lenin dictated a series of notes to his secretaries on the state apparatus and the nationalities' question. None of these was published until after his death, and because of this the first three notes, *Letter to the Congress*, together with a postscript dictated on 4 January 1923, have been called Lenin's 'will' or 'testament'.

In the first note Lenin recommended that the number of members of the Central Committee of the party should increase by up to 100, 'to do a thorough job of improving our administrative machinery'.[10] He considered it possible to find 50 to 100 members from the working class with the right personal and technical qualifications. He also suggested giving legislative authority to the State Planning Commission. In the second note, he went on to say that another reason for enlarging the Central Committee was to prevent a party split which might arise from the rivalry of Stalin and Trotsky.

> Comrade Stalin, having become Secretary-General, has unlimited authority concentrated in his hands, and I am not sure whether he will always be capable of using that authority with sufficient caution. Comrade Trotsky, on the other hand, as his struggle against the

---

[9] For the end of Lenin's life see Moshe Lewin, *Lenin's Last Struggle* (1969)
[10] *Collected Works*, Vol. 36, 593

C[entral] C[ommittee] on the question of the People's Commissariat of Communications has already proved, is distinguished not
only by outstanding ability. He is personally perhaps the most
capable man in the present C[entral] C[ommittee], but he has
displayed excessive self-assurance and shown excessive preoccupation
with the purely administrative side of the work.[11]

In the postscript to this he added: 'Stalin is too rude and this
defect, although quite tolerable in our midst and in dealings
among us Communists, becomes intolerable in a Secretary-
General.' He therefore suggested his replacement by someone
'more tolerant, more loyal, more polite, and more considerate to
the comrades, less capricious, etc.'[12] In the third note he reiterates
his theme that the Central Committee should be enlarged to
train more men and so lessen 'the danger there will be a split
due to some indiscretion',[12] and to improve the administrative
machinery, which is bad because of the evil heritage of tsarism
and because of the civil war. The thought here seems to be that if
either Stalin or Trotsky, or possibly some other member of the
Committee, should try to pack it in support of some unprincipled
action (possibly inspired by personal ambition?) he would be
checked by the large number of straightforward, sensible working-
class members of the Committee. In the seventh note Lenin again
urges the Committee to concentrate on improving the administrative machinery and explains they must use specialists
supplied by *Rabkrin* for the purpose.

In notes four to six Lenin considers Trotsky's proposal that the
State Planning Commission should be given legislative authority.
He had been against this on the ground that it would lead to
confusion in the system, but he had changed his mind now that
affairs had become so much more complicated and so many
more decisions had to be taken on technical grounds. To guard
against the danger of too much decision by experts there must be
an arrangement by which their decisions could be rejected by
some political body, e.g. the Central Committee of the Soviet; and
the chairmen of the Commission should be technically educated
but men of 'broad experience and the ability to enlist the services
of other men'. The existing chairman of the Commission, Krzhizhanovsky, and his deputy, Pyatakov, ought to form a good

[11] *Ibid.*, 594–5
[12] *Ibid.*, 596

combination of executive and administrative ability. In the Commission there would be a need for trained communists to check the bourgeois scientists' zeal and prejudices.

Next day Lenin turned to *The Question of Nationalities or 'Autonomization'* (the idea of uniting the Soviet republics on the basis of autonomy within the Soviet Union). He began by remarking sadly: 'I suppose I have been very remiss with respect to the workers of Russia for not having intervened energetically and decisively enough in the notorious question of autonomisation …'[13] This was because of his illness. He had only had time for a short talk on the question with Dzerzhinsky and for a few words with Zinoviev. Now he was very much disturbed by the evidence of brutality and Great Russian chauvinism in Dzerzhinsky's report. It was said that a 'united apparatus' of state was needed for Georgia and Russia, but it is just this apparatus that is Lenin's concern in these notes. In the circumstances he was afraid that 'freedom to secede from the union … will be a mere scrap of paper, unable to defend the non-Russians from … the Great Russian chauvinist … [They had not created enough safeguards against this chauvinism.] I think that Stalin's haste and his infatuation with pure administration, together with his spite against the notorious "nationalist-socialism", played a fatal role here.'[14] For Stalin and Dzerzhinsky not being Russian meant that they behaved worse than Russians would have in the same circumstances. 'It is common knowledge that people of other nationalities who have become Russified overdo this Russian frame of mind … No provocation or even insult can justify [Ordzhonikidze striking a member of the Georgian Committee]. Dzerzhinsky was inexcusably guilty in adopting a light-hearted attitude towards it.'[15]

What practical measures had to be taken to put matters right?

First, the union of socialist republics must be maintained and strengthened. Secondly, the union of socialist republics must be kept for the sphere of foreign affairs What Lenin had in mind was that Georgia could not be allowed to become independent, but that there should be no interference from Moscow in the Georgians' internal affairs. In this way the Georgians would not be thrust

[13] *Ibid.*, 605
[14] *Ibid.*, 606
[15] *Ibid.*, 606–7

back into capitalist servility, but would be able to develop their culture within the freedom of communist society.

Thirdly, Ordzhonikidze must be punished, though Lenin regretted this as he was his friend. Lenin did not specify any punishment, but presumably he meant Ordzhonikidze to lose his job, and perhaps to be degraded within the party. If necessary, Dzerzhinsky's commission had to be re-constituted to take evidence all over again. The political responsibility for what has happened must be laid on Stalin and Dzerzhinsky.

Fourthly, the national language must be used: a code of behaviour must be drawn up by the Georgians. It might be necessary to take a step backward by restoring 'full independence to individual People's Commissariats', but this could be compensated by the authority of the party.

Lenin wound up his criticism by saying that it was absolutely vital to stop this chauvinism, as the harm done to Russian prestige in the emerging nations far outweighed the risk of giving freedom to the nationalities. For anti-imperialists to lapse into imperialism was unpardonable. 'The morrow of world history will be a day when the awakening peoples oppressed by imperialism are finally aroused and the decisive long and hard struggle for their liberation begins.'[16]

During January Lenin's health fluctuated, but he was frustrated and angered by his inability to work properly and by his suspicion that the Central Committee of the party was withholding documents from him. His mind was still preoccupied with the questions of bureaucracy and the nationalities.

He returned to the first of these questions in two articles in *Pravda: How We Should Reorganize Rabkrin* on 25 January and *Better Fewer, But Better* on 4 March. In the first, which contained his recommendations to the twelfth party congress, he rehearsed the reasons for the inefficiency of the administration and again recommended that the congress should elect, say, 75 to 100 workers, but this time not to the Central Committee of the party, but to the Central Control Commission, a parallel body to *Rabkrin* set up in September 1920 to check corruption, inefficiency and immorality in the party. He then went on to suggest that *Rabkrin* should be reduced to between 300 and 400 members, and that it and the Control Commission should

16 *Ibid.*, 611

amalgamate, (a process usually described as 'fusion'); there should be a joint session of the 'fused' body and the Central Committee of the party every two months. Lenin foresaw two objections to this proposal, from conservatives who objected to any change, and from people who thought it would only lead to chaos. 'The members of the central control commission will wander around all the institutions, not knowing where, why, or to whom to apply, causing disorganization everywhere, and distracting employees from their routine work etc., etc. ... I think that the malicious source of this objection is so obvious that it does not warrant a reply.'[17] It is not clear whether he had a particular person or group in mind or whether the source of the malice was his own true intelligence, for his own words are surely an only too accurate description of what would happen. But Lenin went on to make a different case for fusion. The Central Committee would be in much more direct contact with the masses, i.e. it would replenish its strength at source, and its members would be much better briefed for meetings of the *Politburo*. The Central Committee was 'a strictly centralized and highly authoritative group, but the conditions under which it is working are not commensurate with its authority'. This suggested reform would enable the control commission to function as a compact group 'which should not allow anybody's authority without exception, neither that of the General Secretary nor of any other member of the Central Committee, to prevent them from putting questions, verifying documents, and, in general, keeping themselves fully informed of all things and from exercising the strictest control over the proper conduct of affairs'.[18] Here Lenin is clearly brooding not only on the bureaucracy but on the leadership of the party and the danger that the dictatorship of the proletariat might be replaced by dictatorship pure and simple.

In his very last writing, *Better Fewer, But Better*, Lenin treated fusion from the angle of combining devoted party workers and non-party men of superior education and culture, and again laid great emphasis on the need for up-to-date knowledge of the theory and practice of contemporary administration. He then asked, 'Is it expedient to combine educational activities with official activities? I think it is not only expedient but neces-

---

[17] *Collected Works*, Vol. 33, 483
[18] *Ibid.*, 485

sary.'[19] Why? To overcome conservatism and bureaucracy. And he went on to consider the paradox of revolutionary audacity and bureaucratic timidity. He attributed the existence of this paradox partly to the nature of Russian society with its political and social revolution working in an intensely conservative society barely emerged from feudalism, but also to a deeper cause. It existed 'because really great revolutions grow out of the contradictions between the old, between what is directed towards developing the old, and the very abstract striving for the new, which must be so new as not to contain the tiniest particle of the old'.[20]

Could the revolutionary Soviet Union survive? In the long run, certainly: because the nature of society would be determined by the populations of Russia, China and India. But there was a risk of succumbing to the capitalist states in the short run. To prevent this it was necessary to build a state in which the peasants retained their confidence in the workers, to reduce bureaucracy and to develop large-scale industry.

> In this, and in this alone, lies our hope. Only when we have done this shall we, figuratively speaking, be able to change horses, to change from the peasant, muzhik horse of poverty ... to the horse which the proletariat is seeking and must seek—the horse of large-scale machine industry, of electrification, of the Volkhov Power Station, etc. ... That is how I link up in my mind the general plan of our work, of our policy, of our tactics, of our strategy, with the functions of the reorganized [*Rabkrin*].[21]

Lenin was trying here to come to grips with what he sensed was a baffling, amorphous problem: a true wrestling with Proteus. He saw that the administration was bad. He knew well enough the heritage from tsarism and could see only too clearly how it was bedevilling the situation at every turn. His experience of Western Europe had taught him that the civil service need not be a byzantine bureaucracy and he rightly sensed that Western superiority was connected with its older and more deeply rooted civilization. What eluded him but what is clear to us is that the problem arises, paradoxically, not from antiquity but from modernity. The problem is not at bottom the problem of a state scarcely emerged from feudalism but of a modern state grappling with the problems inherent in complex, industrial society.

[19] *Ibid.*, 496
[20] *Ibid.*, 497
[21] *Ibid.*, 501

Capitalism with its belief in laissez-faire and the regulating mechanism of the market had to a considerable extent sidestepped this problem up to the first World War, and this was especially true of the advanced industrial societies of Britain and the U.S.A. But the dislocation of the market with the consequent unemployment and over-production after the war forced the problem on every state and involved more and more state intervention to achieve the stability and health of its society. This in turn involved a massive growth in the civil service and in the technical, political and psychological problems that flow from that. All this is part of our experience and is painfully clear to us. But it all lay in the future in 1923.

The dictatorship of the proletariat of course made the problem still more intractable. Lenin had moulded the Communist Party to exercise this dictatorship, had seized power with confidence and had set about occupying and holding the commanding heights of the economy. Despite NEP the party and the state still held them, and Lenin could with reason describe the existing Soviet system as 'state capitalism'. But this meant state control. Furthermore, the centralized organization of the party duplicated the centralized organization of the state. The interaction of the two, the interlocking, the fusion where it occurred, made the authority of the centre even greater, the centralization more complete. There was no check, no counterweight, no balance in the mechanism. Lenin called for more flexibility, but what he got was greater rigidity.

Meanwhile during February he formed a private committee, consisting of his assistant secretary at *Sovnarkom* and his two private secretaries, to find out what had really happened in Georgia and what was happening now. His secretary Foteva discovered that compromising documents had disappeared from the files, especially an eyewitness account of the Ordzhonikidze incident. On 3 March the official party commission investigating the situation in Georgia issued its report. (This has not yet come to light; has it too disappeared?) On 5 March Lenin dictated a note to be read to Trotsky over the telephone asking him to stand in for Lenin at the discussion of Georgian affairs in the Central Committee. The same day he began to dictate a note to Stalin about his conduct to Krupskaya, whom Stalin had abused on the telephone for trying to ensure that the Central Committee sent Lenin the documents he wanted. But he was too tired to finish it. Next day, 6 March, he got Trotsky's reply, undoubtedly affirmative. He then finished dictating his note to Stalin: 'I must ask you to consider whether you would be inclined to withdraw what you said and apologize, or whether you would prefer to break off relations between us.'[22]

Trotsky rang up to ask if he should show the memorandum of 30 December about Georgia to Kamenev, who was going to the Caucasus on business, and brief him for an investigation of the Georgian affair on the spot. At first Lenin said no, but later changed his mind and planned to explain the whole position to Kamenev and show him a note he had just dictated to Mdivani and the other ousted Georgian communists: 'I follow your affair with all my heart. I am outraged at the rudeness of Ordzhonikidze and the connivance of Stalin and Dzerzhinsky. I am preparing for you notes and a speech. With esteem, Lenin.'[23]

But Lenin was unable to carry out his plan. On 7 March he had another stroke from which he never recovered. He died on 21 January 1924.

Lenin's body was brought from Gorky to Moscow on the 23rd and lay in state for the next four days. Then it was embalmed and given temporary resting-place in a crypt until the mausoleum was ready to receive it. His brain was removed from his skull, and later dissection revealed exceptionally large cells in the third cell layer of the cerebral cortex. Their existence would tend to confirm the impressions of people who knew Lenin and were struck by the speed and realism of his thinking.[24]

[22] Lenin, *Sochineniya* (5th edn.), Vol. 54, 329–30, quoted in Lewin, *op. cit.*, 101
[23] Lenin, *op. cit.*, 330, quoted in Lewin, *op. cit.*, 102
[24] Oskar Vogt, 'Bericht Über Das Moskauer Hirnforschungsinstitut' in *Journal für Psychologie und Neurologie*, Bd. 40, Heft 3 u. 4, 1929. I am indebted to Professor Marthe Vogt for this reference and an explanation of its technicalities.

# Epilogue

Lenin was a man of simple habits and tastes. He loved the country, and was never happier than when walking, bicycling or bathing. After the Bolshevik seizure of power, when he was working fanatically hard, his greatest relaxation and pleasure was to escape for a while to his country retreat. The pleasure was the greater from his having lived most of his life in cheap lodgings. He was accustomed to spartan life and sparse furnishings, and when he moved into the Kremlin he took his habits with him. He lived with Krupskaya, his sister Maria and a maid in a few rooms, and like everyone else they were short of food and firewood. His study was bare: as Bertrand Russell describes it, 'it contains a big desk, some maps on the walls, two book-cases, and one comfortable chair for visitors in addition to two or three hard chairs'.[1]

His simplicity spoke to simple people, whether Italian fishermen or Russian peasants. 'On one excursion out of Moscow Lenin came upon an old peasant who was picking mushrooms in the woods. Soon the two men were engaged in warm conversation. As they parted, the peasant sighed: "They say a certain Lenin rules Russia these days. If that Lenin were like you things would really start moving".'[2]

Lenin was also entirely without vanity. When he was being sculpted he would not pose for the sculptor, feeling this to be unnatural (and not wanting to waste the time), but told him: 'Work as much as you must, Comrade Altman. I shall not disturb you.'[3] And Stalin's account of his first meeting with Lenin is well known:

> Usually, a great man comes late to a meeting so that his appearance may be awaited with bated breath. Then, just before the great man

---

[1] Bertrand Russell, *The Practice and Theory of Bolshevism* (1949), 33
[2] David Shub, *Lenin* (Pelican edn. 1966), 425
[3] *Ibid.*, 416

enters, the warning goes round: 'Hush ... silence ... he is coming.' The rite did not seem to me superfluous, because it created an impression and inspired respect.

But this was not Lenin's way, and his very ordinary appearance with his short figure, bald head and reddish beard enabled him to pass unnoticed in company:

> How great was my disappointment to see that Lenin had arrived at the conference before the other delegates ... and had settled himself somewhere in a corner and was unassumingly carrying on a conversation, a most ordinary conversation, with the most ordinary delegates.[4]

But though modest, Lenin was not humble. Once he had soaked himself in Marx he was confident that he understood him and that he was better equipped to interpret him than any of his fellow socialists. Confident and pugnacious, Lenin set about those who misunderstood and perverted Marx: nine-tenths of his writing is polemic. In the same way, once he had taken the measure of Plekhanov and his colleagues, Lenin felt in his bones that he was the man who had to make the party and forge it into a weapon with a truly revolutionary, cutting edge. From 1903 he had a clear vision of what the party must be and ruthlessly pursued it. When he arrived in St Petersburg in April 1917 he was impatient to embody his vision in action. *He* was ready for power; his task was to judge the correct moment to seize it and to prepare the Bolsheviks for its seizure.

Lenin's self-confidence was partly temperamental. But it was also based on hard work, knowledge and self-discipline. Even as a boy he had unusual powers of work and concentration. These he had developed by years of systematic study. He had a naturally good memory; study had given him an extensive knowledge of philosophy, history, economics and politics. This knowledge massively buttressed his Marxism: he believed that Marx was right in his claim that Marxism was the only *scientific* socialism, and the more he read the more strongly he believed this.

Above all Lenin disciplined himself. He recommended to party members who were in prison that they should keep themselves fit by regular physical jerks, and he practised them himself. He gave up skating when he found that it seemed to tire him too much and stop his working in the evening. He did not allow

---

[4] Isaac Deutscher, *Stalin* (Pelican 1966), 90

himself the luxury of much music, for he felt that it was enervating, not fortifying. He worked regular hours and consciously narrowed his interests. Theodore Dan remarked of him that he was the only Social-Democrat who was a revolutionary first, last and all the time. But Lenin was not a natural revolutionary. He made himself one by dedication to the revolution and by concentrating his mind and energies to this purpose. When he came to London Lenin's imagination was stirred by the British Museum and its millions of books; he would have liked to read them all. Before this Lenin's mind and imagination had been seized by Hegel. This was due in part to the accident of his birth: European intellectuals in the middle of the nineteenth century were captivated by Hegel. But there is more to it than this. The unity of Hegel's philosophy, and the dialectic, reconciling and integrating opposites, seem to have had an instinctive appeal for Lenin. He writes in one of his *Philosophical Notebooks*

> Philosophical idealism is *only* nonsense from the standpoint of crude, simple, metaphysical materialism. From the standpoint of *dialectical* materialism, on the other hand, philosophical idealism is a *one-sided*, exaggerated ... development (inflation, distention) of one of the features, aspects, facets of knowledge into an absolute, *divorced* from matter, from nature, apotheosised ...
>
> Human knowledge is not (or does not follow) a straight line, but a curve, which endlessly approximates a series of circles, a spiral. Any fragment, segment, section of this curve can be transformed (transformed one-sidedly) into an independent, complete, straight line, which then (if one does not see the wood for the trees) leads into the quagmire, into clerical obscurantism (where it is *anchored* by the class interest of the ruling classes). Rectilinearity and one-sidedness, woodenness and petrification, subjectivism and subjective blindness —voilà the epistemological roots of idealism. And clerical obscurantism (philosophical idealism), of course, has *epistemological* roots, it is not groundless; it is a *sterile flower* undoubtedly, but a sterile flower that grows on the living tree of living, fertile, genuine, powerful, omnipotent, objective, absolute human knowledge.[5]

Lenin might well have said with Whitman:

> Do I contradict myself?
> Very well then, I contradict myself;
> I am large, I contain multitudes.

[5] *Collected Works*, Vol. 38, 363

This was the man who was turned into a myth from the moment of his death.

On January 21 1924, Lenin, our leader and teacher, the creator of the Bolshevik Party, passed away in the village of Gorki, near Moscow. Lenin's death was received by the working class of the whole world as a most cruel loss ... As Lenin was borne to the grave, the working people of the whole world paid homage to him in overwhelming sorrow, as to a father and teacher, their best friend and defender.'[6]

Stalin's *Biographical Chronicle* defines the place of the funeral in the process of Lenin's apotheosis:

21 January: 6.50 a.m. Lenin dies at Gorky; 9.30 a.m. Stalin and other members of the Politburo arrive at Gorky.
22 January: Stalin co-edits a manifesto 'To all toilers of the U.S.S.R.', and sends out messages to the provincial branches of the party, calling them to keep faith with the teachings of the dead leader.
23 January: 9 a.m. Stalin and other leaders carry the coffin with Lenin's body from Lenin's home at Gorky; 1.30 p.m. Stalin and his friends carry the coffin from the Paveletsky Station to the House of the Trade Unions in Moscow, where Lenin lay in state for the next four days; 6.10 p.m. Stalin stands in the guard of honour at the bier.
25 January: Stalin calls upon the party to collect relics of Lenin for the newly founded Lenin Institute.
26 January: 8.24 p.m. At the second congress of the Soviets Stalin reads an oath of allegiance to Lenin.
27 January: 8 a.m. Stalin takes his place in the guard of honour at Lenin's bier; 8.30 a.m. Stalin moves to the head of the bier; 9 a.m. Stalin and others carry the coffin out of the House of the Trade Unions; 4 p.m. end of the funeral procession at the Red Square— Stalin and others carry the coffin into the crypt of the future Mausoleum[7]

where his embalmed body was placed against Krupskaya's wishes.

The oath of allegiance or 'solemn vow in the name of the Party' read:

We Communists are people of a special mould. We are made of a special stuff. We are those who form the army of the great proletarian strategist, the army of Comrade Lenin. There is nothing higher than the honour of belonging to this army. There is nothing higher than the title of member of the Party whose founder and leader is Comrade Lenin.
Departing from us, Comrade Lenin adjured us to hold high and

[6] *History of the Communist Party of the Soviet Union* (1945), 268
[7] Deutscher, *op. cit.*, 270-1

guard the purity of the great title of member of the Party. We vow to you, Comrade Lenin, that we will fulfil your behest with credit!

Departing from us, Comrade Lenin adjured us to guard the unity of our Party as the apple of our eye. We vow to you, Comrade Lenin, that this behest, too, we will fulfil with credit!

Departing from us, Comrade Lenin adjured us to guard and strengthen the dictatorship of the proletariat. We vow to you, Comrade Lenin, that we will spare no effort to fulfil this behest, too, with credit!

Departing from us, Comrade Lenin adjured us to strengthen with all our might the alliance of the workers and the peasants. We vow to you, Comrade Lenin, that this behest, too, we will fulfil with credit!

Comrade Lenin untiringly urged upon us the necessity of maintaining the voluntary union of the nations of our country, the necessity for fraternal co-operation between them within the framework of the Union of Republics. Departing from us, Comrade Lenin adjured us to consolidate and extend the Union of Republics. We vow to you, Comrade Lenin, that this behest, too, we will fulfil with credit!

More than once did Lenin point out to us that the strengthening of the Red Army and the improvement of its condition is one of the most important tasks of our Party ... Let us vow then, comrades, that we will spare no effort to strengthen our Red Army and our Red Navy.

Departing from us, Comrade Lenin adjured us to remain faithful to the principles of the Communist International. We vow to you, Comrade Lenin, that we will not spare our lives to strengthen and extend the union of the toilers of the whole world—the Communist International![8]

Lenin took his place beside Marx in the Communist Pantheon. Marxism became Marxism-Leninism.

The Marxist-Leninist theory must not be regarded as a collection of dogmas, as a catechism, as a symbol of faith, and the Marxists themselves as pedants and dogmatists. The Marxist-Leninist theory is the science of the development of society, the science of the working-class movement, the science of the proletarian revolution, the science of the building of the Communist society. And as a science it does not and cannot stand still, but develops and perfects itself. Clearly, in its development it is bound to become enriched by new experience and new knowledge, and some of its propositions and conclusions are bound to change in the course of time, are bound to be replaced by new conclusions and propositions corresponding to the new historical conditions.[9]

This is well said; and certainly new experience, for example in

---

[8] *History of the Communist Party of the Soviet Union*, 268–9
[9] *Ibid.*, 355

agriculture and foreign affairs, enriched the content of Marxism-Leninism. But in a more fundamental sense the future falsified this statement. For this Lenin himself was in a way responsible: there was a basic ambiguity in his idea of science. On the one hand he was a staunch supporter of the idea of evolution: he accepted Darwin whole-heartedly and laid great stress on the dynamic and dialectical nature of the universe. On the other hand he was passionately convinced that Marx had stood Hegel the right side up and had enunciated the laws of social development: laws not in the sense of working hypotheses that for the time being accounted for all the available facts in a satisfactory manner, but laws that were inherent in nature, immutable, waiting to be discovered. Marx was their Newton. Lenin did not envisage an Einstein appearing in due course.

This gave a fundamentalist tinge to Lenin's thought. Though he was a political realist of a high order and though he made important additions to the body of Marxist thought, he framed them as mere deductions from Marx's premises and continually referred back to Marx as the source of communism and quoted from his writings much in the manner of a Biblical scholar quoting biblical texts. With Stalin this tendency was accentuated. In a lecture on *The Foundations of Leninism* that he gave at Moscow University in April 1924 he defined Leninism as 'the Marxism of the epoch of imperialism and of the proletarian revolution', and proceeded to demonstrate his orthodoxy by embroidering a series of Leninist texts: his lecture is nothing more than a commentary.

The writings of Marx and Lenin were turning into the scriptures. The relics were housed in the Marxist-Leninist Institute. Lenin's body was moved from the crypt to a great mausoleum of red granite and black diorite in the Red Square. It became at once a place of pilgrimage.

> So I came down the steps to Lenin.
> With a herd of peasants before
> And behind me, I saw
> A room stained scarlet, and there
> A small wax man in a small glass case.
>
> Greedy of detail I saw,
> In those two minutes allowed,
> The man was not wax, as they said,

But a corpse, for a thumb nail was black,
The thing was Lenin.

Then a woman beside me cried
With a strange voice, foreign, loud.
And I, who fear not life nor death, and those who have died
Only a little, was inwardly shaken with fear,
For I stood in the presence of God;

The voice I heard was the voice of all generations
Acclaiming new faiths, horrible, beautiful faiths;
I knew that the woman wailed as women wailed long ago
For Christ in the sepulchre laid.
Christ was a wax man too,
When they carried **Him down** to the grave.

(from Dorothy Wellesley, Lenin)

# Select Bibliography

*Note: Unless otherwise indicated, the place of publication is London.*

## THE BACKGROUND

W. H. Bruford, *Chekhov and his Russia* (1947). An illuminating investigation of imperial Russia through the works of Chekhov.
W. O. Henderson, *The Industrial Revolution on the Continent* (1961). A useful textbook placing the Russian industrial revolution in its European context.
A. Leroy-Beaulieu, *L'Empire des Tsars* (3 vols., Paris, 1890–6). A detailed and thorough contemporary study of tsarism and its institutions.
P. I. Lyashchenko: *History of the National Economy of Russia* (N.Y., 1949). A good Soviet textbook.
D. Mackenzie Wallace, *Russia* (2 vols., 1877). Covers the same ground as Leroy-Beaulieu but in a more intimate and informal way. Both are based on widespread, first-hand experience.
John Maynard, *Russia in Flux* (1941); *The Russian Peasant* (1942). Studies based on a deep knowledge of Russian life and literature, and especially valuable because of Maynard's experience as a civil servant in India.
Hugh Seton-Watson, *The Russian Empire* (1967). The best available textbook, with full bibliography.
Warren B. Walsh, *Readings in Russian History* (Syracuse University Press, 1963): Vol. 2, *From the Reign of Paul to Alexander III*. A useful collection of texts.

## LENIN: WORKS AND LIFE

Lenin, *Collected Works* (4th edn., Moscow, 1960–7). (The 5th

Russian Edition Moscow, 1958–66) is not yet translated into English.

Lenin, *Selected Works* (2 vols., Moscow 1947, and other edns.) *Letters of Lenin*, ed. Hill and Mudie (1937). A convenient selection. The complete letters are in Vols. 36 and 37 of the *Collected Works*.

Angelica Balabanoff, *Impressions of Lenin* (University of Michigan, Ann Arbor, 1964). Impressions by the international socialist who was the first secretary of the Communist International.

Louis B. Fischer, *The Life of Lenin* (N.Y. 1964, London 1965). A mine of information by an American journalist who worked for some time in Russia and met Lenin.

Maxim Gorky, *Days with Lenin* (N.Y. 1932). Reminiscences by the Russian novelist who knew Lenin well, but was too much of an artist to accept everything Bolshevik without criticism.

Christopher Hill, *Lenin and the Revolution* (1947). A good 'assessment of the place of Lenin, and of the revolution which was his life's work, in history', written when the author was a member of the Communist Party.

N. K. Krupskaya, *Memories of Lenin* (2nd edn., 1930; 3rd edn., 1959). Memories by Lenin's widow; the most valuable source for Lenin as a person.

*Lenin, A Biography* (Moscow 1965). The official Soviet biography.

*Lenin: The Man, the Theorist, the Leader*, ed. Leonard Schapiro and Peter Reddaway (Hoover Institution Publications, 1967). Very valuable re-appraisal of Lenin in his various roles.

A. V. Lunacharsky, *Revolutionary Silhouettes* (1967). Sketches of Bolshevik leaders including Lenin by the first Soviet Commissar for Education.

David Shub, *Lenin* (Pelican 1966). A detailed biography of Lenin as a man and a politician by a Russian Social-Democrat; especially valuable because of his lifelong involvement in party affairs and knowledge of the leading figures.

Adam B. Ulam, *The Bolsheviks* (N.Y., 1965; English edn., *Lenin and the Bolsheviks*, 1966). A large-scale work based on much research, hostile to Lenin and the Bolsheviks.

Nikolay Valentinov, *Encounters with Lenin* (1968). Very interesting account of Lenin by a Social-Democrat who was taken up as a young man by Lenin and dropped after a violent disagreement on empirio-criticism.

Bertram D. Wolfe, *Three who made a Revolution* (N.Y., 1948; Pelican, 1966). The best biography of Lenin, which unfortunately goes only to 1914.
Clara Zetkin, *Reminiscences of Lenin* (N.Y., 1934). Reminiscences by a warm-hearted but uncritical Social-Democrat, of most value for Lenin's views on women and sex.

## MARXISM-LENINISM

Karl Marx and Friedrich Engels, *The Communist Manifesto*; Karl Marx, *Capital*, Vol. 1 (Everyman edn., 2 vols.; Karl Marx, Vols. 1–3 (Moscow, 1957–62); Karl Marx, *Selected Works* (Moscow, 1950); Karl Marx and Friedrich Engels, *Selected Correspondence* (Marxist-Leninist Library No. 9, 1934); Friedrich Engels, *Selected Works* (Pelican, 1967).
*The Essential Left: Four Classic Texts* (Communist Manifesto; Marx: Value, Price and Profit; Engels: Socialism Utopian and Scientific; Lenin: The State and Revolution) (1960).
*A Handbook of Marxism* (1935). A generous selection from Marx, Engels, Lenin and Stalin.
N. Bukharin and E. Preobrazhensky, *The ABC of Communism* (Pelican Classics, 1969). First published in 1919, this circulated 'widely in many countries as an authoritative exposition of the "aims and tasks" of communism' for ten years and then shared the authors' disgrace.

H. B. Acton, *The Illusion of an Epoch* (1955). A brilliant critique of 'Marxism-Leninism as a Philosophical Creed'.
Isaiah Berlin, *Marx* (Home University Library, 3rd edn., 1965). A very good short biography with short, annotated bibliography.
R. N. Carew Hunt, *The Theory and Practice of Communism* (Pelican, 1963). Admirably succinct study of Marxism, Leninism and Bolshevism in action.
E. H. Carr, *1917: Before and After, I* (1969). A suggestive introductory lecture on the relation of Lenin to Marx.
L. H. Haimson, *The Russian Marxists* (Beacon, 1955). The intellectual background to Bolshevism.
Z. A. Jordan, *The Evolution of Dialectical Materialism* (1967). Stimulating on the relation of Lenin's materialism to that of Marx and Engels.

Alfred G. Meyer, *Leninism* (2nd edn., N.Y., 1962). Splendidly compact 'survey and analysis of those of Lenin's ideas which have played a role in determining and justifying the conduct of the Communist Party's work'.

D. W. Treadgold, *Lenin and his Rivals* (N.Y., 1955). A study of the various groups in opposition to the tsarist autocracy.

Edmund Wilson, *To the Finland Station* (Fontana, 1960). 'A study of the writing and acting of history', and the best study of Lenin's relation to Marx.

Bertram D. Wolfe, 'Leninism' in M. M. Drachkovich, *Marxism in the Modern World* (Stanford University Press 1965; London, 1966).

## INTERNATIONAL SOCIALISM

Jane Degras (ed.), *The Communist International*, Vol. 1 (1956). Admirably edited volume of documents.

Julius Braunthal, *History of the International*, 2 vols. (1966–7). The classic account.

G. D. H. Cole, *A History of Socialist Thought* (1963–7). A thorough and sober survey of socialist thought.

## THE PARTY

*History of the Communist Party of the Soviet Union* (Bolshevik), (Moscow, 1938). Edited and in part written by Stalin to supersede previous 'unreliable' histories, it rewrote history in the light of the contemporary treason trials.

Theodore Dan, *The Origins of Bolshevism*, (1964). A difficult work by a leading Menshevik, who was Martov's brother-in-law, but indispensable for the relationship of Menshevism to Bolshevism.

Merle Fainsod, *Smolensk under Soviet Rule* (1958). A unique study of party rule at local level, based on captured party documents.

I. Getzler, *Martov* (1967). A good biography.

J. L. H. Keep, *The Rise of Social Democracy in Russia* (1963). A solid, well-documented account of the party up to 1906.

Leonard Schapiro, *The History of the Communist Party of the U.S.S.R.*

(University Paperback, 1960). An invaluable account, hostile to Lenin and Communism.

Leonard Schapiro, *The Origins of the Communist Autocracy* (1955). A detailed and fascinating investigation of the first years of Bolshevik government.

L. Trotsky, *My Life* (N.Y., 1960). This covers much more than party history and is continuously interesting.


## THE REVOLUTION

James Bunyan and H. H. Fisher, *The Bolshevik Revolution* (1934). Olga Hess Gankin and H. H. Fisher, *The Bolsheviks and the War* (1960). Ample selections of documents, with commentary, by authors sympathetic to the February Revolution.

Jane Degras (ed.), *Soviet Documents on Foreign Policy*, Vol. 1 (1951).

Warren B. Walsh, *Readings in Russian History* (Syracuse University Press, 1963): Vol. 3, *The Russian Revolution and the Soviet Period*

E. H. Carr, *A History of Soviet Russia*, Vols. 1–3, *The Bolshevik Revolution*; Vol. 4, *The Interregnum* (1950–4), (Pelican, 1966–70). The best account, on an extended scale, in any language, with full bibliography.

W. H. Chamberlain, *The Russian Revolution* (2 vols., 1935). The best narrative of events from 1917 to 1924.

Robert V. Daniels, *Red October* (N.Y., 1967). An excellent narrative of the October Revolution.

I. Deutscher, *Life of Trotsky*: Vol. 1, *The Prophet Armed* (1954). A biography of the power and vividness to match its subject by a fine scholar and a convinced Marxist.

David Footman, *Civil War in Russia* (1961). A lucid narrative of the incredibly confused events of the civil war.

*The Kerensky Memoirs* (1966). The latest of Kerensky's auto-biographical writings defending his part in the revolution.

Lionel Kochan, *Russia in Revolution* (1966). A clear narrative of the years 1890–1918 designed to answer the question: why did 'old Russia mutate, into a proletarian state?'

Bernard Pares, *The Fall of the Russian Monarchy* (1939). A most readable account of the last years of tsarism, based to a considerable extent on personal knowledge and experience.

Roger Pethybridge (ed.), *Eyewitnesses of the Russian Revolution* (1964). A useful collection of extracts from the writings of eyewitnesses.

John Reed, *Ten Days that Shook the World* (Penguin, 1966). Eyewitness account of the October Revolution by an American Communist, which splendidly matches the chaos and exhilaration of those days.

Bertrand Russell, *The Practice and Theory of Bolshevism* (2nd edn., 1949). A description of Bolshevism based on a journey to Russia in 1920.

N. N. Sukhanov, *The Russian Revolution 1917* (1955). Very full selection from the contemporary notebooks of this 'on-the-spot' political journalist.

L. Trotsky, *History of the Russian Revolution* (1965; abridged edn., Anchor, 1959). One of the very small class of works written by a protagonist in the great events described, like Thucydides, *History of the Peloponnesian War*, Clarendon, *History of the Great Rebellion*, and Winston Churchill, *The Second World War*. It is arguably the greatest of them and is in any case a masterpiece.

## THE NATIONALITIES

R. B. Schlesinger, *The Nationalities Problem and Soviet Administration* (1956). Documents with a useful, short introduction.

E. H. Carr, *Nationalism and After* (1945). Interesting lectures on the relation of nationalism to internationalism in the modern world.

Elie Kedourie, *Nationalism* (1960). Excellent short introduction.

Richard Pipes, *The Formation of the Soviet Union* (Harvard, 1954). A detailed analysis of the political aspect of the national question.

J. Stalin, *Marxism and the Nationalities and Colonial Question* (Marxist-Leninist Library No. 12, 1942). Classic statement by Lenin's expert on the nationalities.

Arnold Toynbee, *Nationality and the War* (1915). Consideration of the national problem written early in the first World War; valuable as a witness to the contemporary liberal attitude.

*Three good histories of the nationalities:*

W. E. D. Allen, *The Ukraine* (1940).
D. M. Lang, *A Modern History of Georgia* (1962).
Geoffrey Wheeler, *The Modern History of Soviet Central Asia* (1965).

## THE REVOLUTION IN PERSPECTIVE

I. Deutscher, *The Unfinished Revolution* (1967). Masterly lectures considering the state of the revolution after fifty years.
J. P. Nettl, *The Soviet Achievement* (1967). A brilliant account of the Soviet achievement, highly relevant to the nature of Lenin and Leninism; attractively illustrated.
Boris Pasternak, *Doctor Zhivago* (Fontana, 1969). A book that recreates the revolution through the imagination of a poet and uniquely conveys the whole revolutionary experience.

# Index of Names and Places

# Index of Subjects